This series of three guides to Norfolk churches is
dedicated to those who have assisted me in compiling
and checking my text:
Elizabeth Arkieson, Ann Johnson & Bryan Samain.

part four of the parishfinder series

Published by ASPYE.
aspye@talktalk.net

Front cover: West Harling All Saints, Norfolk.
Back cover: The Norman doorway at Heckingham St Gregory, Norfolk.

A photographic and historical guide to the

Parish Churches

of

Central Norfolk

as defined by the 1914 Deaneries of :

Hingham, Holt, Humbleyard, , Rockland, Sparham,
Thetford and most of Depwade, Ingworth, Redenhall,
Repps, and Taverham and part of Breccles.

Including supplements for identifying
Architectural Styles,
The Saints and their Emblems,
Interesting objects found in churches,
Glossary of Terms, Architectural & Ecclesiastical

compiled and with photographs
by
Adrian S. Pye

Preface

Since the completion of my first book, Parish Churches of East Suffolk, the response I received, even before completing the West Suffolk companion, was extremely encouraging. These Norfolk guides meanwhile have been eagerly awaited.

It was decided to cover Norfolk in three volumes due to the quantity of churches in the county. The parishes in the east of the county are, however, considerably smaller than those in the west. The division for each guide is along a very rough north to south line in an effort to achieve an equal number of churches in each volume. In the case of West Norfolk, the division is almost central to the county, running from Stiffkey to Thetford. The corresponding division for the East Norfolk guide is from Runton near Cromer in the north to Thorpe Abbots near Diss in the south.

Readers will notice that although Lothingland is in the Norfolk Diocese, not all of that particular deanery have been included. I have adhered to the County boundaries as they are at the time of going to press. The Suffolk portion of the Lothingland Deanery can be found in the East Suffolk edition.

In compiling the information contained in the guides, I have found that postcodes in certain instances were, some distance away from the church, especially in scattered communities. Therefore, although the postcode given is that of the nearest inhabited dwelling it may be some distance away, although the church will usually be in sight. I have endeavoured to give the best directions possible in the limited space available.

I would like to make it quite clear that the impressions I give in the text on visiting a church, and the people I meet in so doing, are those experienced at the time, and do not necessarily reflect those of other people associated with the church. The sentiments expressed regarding the contents and conditions I find when entering a church are mine and mine alone, and I accept that sometimes they may differ from the opinions of others.

I have endeavoured to give a truthful impression of what is to be discovered when visiting a church but interests differ and opinions vary on all matters aesthetic and ecclesiastical.

Except where there is no ancient church in the parish, 20th century churches have not been included in the guides as this is a historical guide and the churches concerned have no great historical interest.

Only Anglican churches are featured in the guides. Cathedrals, Roman Catholic, Baptist, Methodist, and Reformist churches or chapels etc. do not come under the designation or description of a Parish church and are therefore not included.

I hope that as a result of my campaigning activities to campaign for churches to be kept open for all, at least during daylight hours, anyone visiting a church will find the door open. Whist I have every sympathy with the dilemma of some Parochial Church Councils in protecting a church and its contents, I feel a better effort could be made, and an answer found, if they were willing to consider the visitors instead of themselves. It is no good leaving a sign on the door proclaiming 'Welcome to St Mary's church' if the door is locked. "There is no salvation outside a church". A locked door is not a very Christian welcome to the traveller. In my travels, I have found not only some churches locked, but also the porch containing information about the keyholders barred. Yet others have a wonderful open door policy, and at some there is a kettle, fresh water, tea, coffee, milk and even biscuits waiting for the visitors to avail themselves of refreshment.

The reader will notice some churches have been awarded four or five stars (i.e.*). These are churches which in my opinion have something extra special to offer, and should interest any visitor.

Out of necessity, I have adhered rigidly to one church, one page. throughout the guides, whether the church is large or small. It is not a reflection on the church or the wealth of the interior, simply a matter of convenient format and ease of reading.

Almost every parish is listed alphabetically under the name on the Ordnance Survey maps; South under S; North under N; Great under G and Little under L, etc.

I hope the reader will get as much enjoyment from reading these guides and visiting the churches as I did in compiling them.

Adrian S. Pye. Lowestoft 2010

Table of Contents

The author gratefully acknowledges the information gleaned from the following sources, not all of which has been verified as being completely up to date.

White's Directory for Norfolk 1864   William White
Norfolk Churches   H. Munro Cautley
The King's England, Norfolk   Arthur Mee
Scores of guide booklets supplied in the individual churches.
Ordnance Survey for the grid references.
Norwich Diocese for the post codes, 21st c. Deaneries & Benefices.

For any errors in this publication, I apologise in advance.
No liability can be accepted for any loss or damage however caused as a result of reading or following directions given in this publication.

Printed by Microress Printers, Halesworth, Suffolk

ISBN 978-0-9558797-3-9

ALBY St Ethelbert 5 m N of Aylsham turn left
No of Bells: 1 off the A140, signposted to
19th c. Deanery: Ingworth Aldborough. The church is
Hundred: South Erpingham about ½ mile along the road,
Union house: Aylsham near the next road junction.
21st c. Deanery: Ingworth O.S. grid ref: TG 202337
Benefice: Scarrowbeck, Erpingham Post Code: NR11 7HF

This is a pleasant and interesting little church which was built in the 15th c. Inside the small south porch a bishop and a king are depicted on the hood-mould and to the right is a stoup built into the corner. The coeval font has shields on each of the eight facets of the bowl and shallow arcading on the shaft. On display to the left of the font is the old clock mechanism. Two windows high in the wall of the nave can only loosely be regarded as a clerestory, above them is a simple arch-braced roof. Poppy-heads decorate the lovely old bench-ends but the 15th c. screen has been stripped and varnished! Just below the rood loft stairs is a Victorian pulpit which has been dark stained, seemingly to give it a Jacobean appearance. Corbels supporting the wall-posts are carved heads. There is a plain piscina and sedilia.

ALDBOROUGH   St Mary

No of Bells: 1
19th c. Deanery: Repps
Hundred: North Erpingham
Union house: West Beckham
21st c. Deanery: Ingworth
Benefice: Scarrowbeck, Erpingham

5 m N of Aylsham turn left off the A140, signposted to Aldborough and continue west 400 yds to Matlaske at the staggered cross-roads.
O.S. grid ref: TG 181359
Post Code:W of NR11 7NT

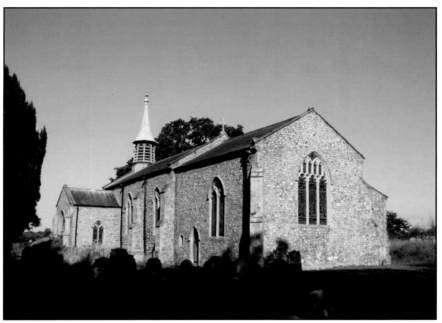

A broached spirelet added in 1906 where the tower should be makes the church easily recognisable, although not obvious from the road. In the nave is an octagonal font with quatrefoil designs around the bowl and tracery on the shaft. The church was virtually rebuilt in 1847 and most of the interesting fittings discarded. However, the brasses have been preserved, the earliest is to Anne Herward dated 1485. It is simply furnished with Victorian benches and a carved linen-fold pulpit. Strange shapes carved from stone appear here and there in the north aisle wall, but their meaning is unclear to me. At the east end of the aisle is the organ. The rood stairs remain in the wall east of the chancel arch, above which Madonna and Child is set into a niche. Beyond this is a simple piscina and dropped-sill sedilia.

ALDERFORD St John the Baptist

No of Bells: 1

19th c. Deanery: Sparham

Hundred: Eynesford

Union house: Horsham St Faiths

21st c. Deanery: Sparham

Benefice: Wensum

9 m NW of Norwich off the A1067 at Attlebridge and keep bearing left for 1½ miles to destination in Hall Road.

O.S. grid ref: TG 128188

Post Code: NR9 5NF

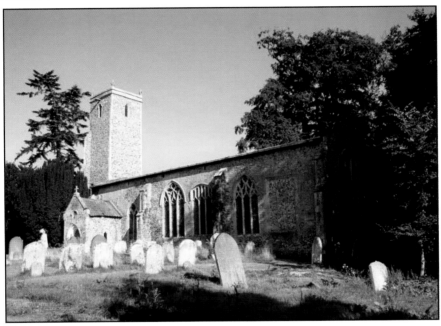

The roof is continuous over both nave and chancel. Above the porch door is a sundial that proclaims 'Redeem the Time'. Inside the porch is a fine old 14th c. mediaeval door (plastered with notices) with the original handle and knocker. On a double pedestal is a crudely carved 16th c. Seven Sacrament font standing incorrectly against the north wall, perhaps unmoved since the north aisle was demolished. The 14th c. piers remain as evidence of a north aisle. Old benches still serve as seating but their quality too is very crude, with poppy-head shapes devoid of any carved decoration. In the chancel is a simple piscina and sedilia under a plain arch. It is a simple church, which I normally like, but this one I'm not too sure about; perhaps because it's always locked without any consideration for visitors.

ASHWELLTHORPE All Saints

No of Bells:	5
19th c. Deanery:	Depwade
Hundred:	Depwade
Union house:	Pulham St Mary
21st c. Deanery:	Humbleyard
Benefice:	Upper Tas Valley

9 m SW of Norwich. Turn off the B1113 to Ashwell Thorpe at the signpost and the church is situated on the right, in 'The Street'.

O.S. grid ref: TM 146977

Post Code: NR16 1EZ

The exterior of the church and tower are worth looking around before entering the church itself. Atop the well buttressed tower is a brick and flint embattled parapet and below is a good example of Early English method of construction from about the late 13th c. In fact the whole building is from around the same period, with a few later additions, such as the 18th c. Dutch gable over the porch and parvise. The 17th c. octagonal armorial font has carved shields with the crests of the Knevett and Burgh families painted in the true colours. The pulpit has a carving of David and Goliath. In the chancel is the alabaster tomb and effigies of Sir Edmund de Thorpe (1446) and his wife. A 17th c. poker-work chest is also unusual. Carefully lift the lid if you can, to see the detail of the interior. Royal Arms of George III.

ASLACTON	St Michael	13 m SSW of Norwich. At
No of Bells:	5	Long Stratton turn west and
19th c. Deanery:	Depwade	follow road 3 miles through
Hundred:	Depwade	Wacton and Great Moulton
Union house:	Pulham St Mary	to Aslacton.
21st c. Deanery:	Depwade	O.S. grid ref: TM 156911
Benefice:	Pilgrim	Post Code: NR15 2JU

The Saxon tower is coeval with the oldest part of the church. The double windows in the belfry stage are pointed with a slab and pillar supporting the arch. Long and short work at the corners confirm this. The embattled parapet and porch are 15th c. additions. Above the entrance to the flush-worked porch is a canopied niche with a winged St Michael ensconced within. The clerestory was added in the 16th c. On the rather mundane pulpit is a Flemish carving depicting David and Goliath. A series of shields decorate the bowl of the 15th c. octagonal font. The rood stairs remain open though redundant, the screen has been completely removed. There is a double piscina under a simple trefoil arch, which is rather unusual. Sympathetic Victorian restorations have left much of the Saxon builders' work to be seen.

ATTLEBOROUGH St Mary

No of Bells:	6
19th c. Deanery:	Rockland
Hundred:	Shropham
Union house:	Rockland All Saints
21st c. Deanery:	Thetford & Rockland
Benefice:	Attleborough

15 m SW of Norwich. Turn off the A11 to Attleborough and follow the B1077 into town centre. Takes you straight to the church.

O.S. grid ref: TM 048953
Post Code: NR17 2AH

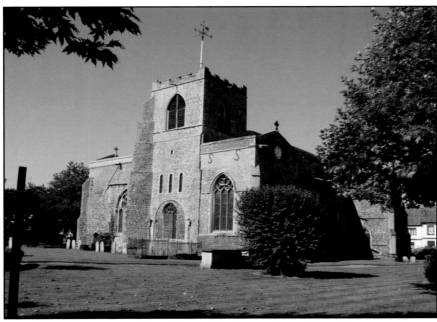

A Norman tower dominates the east end of the church which was originally dedicated to the Assumption of the Blessed Virgin Mary. For a time the dedication was to the Holy Cross. Once this was a cruciform church but the chancel was demolished around the 15th c. when the nave was rebuilt. Entry is gained through the north porch which has a parvise above. On the east wall are mediaeval paintings, but the most remarkable thing is the beautiful rood screen complete with loft which stretches from north to south across the width of the aisles and nave. The groining above the screen is spectacular and above are the Arms of the twenty-four Episcopal Sees of England as crisp as they were in the 16th c. when constructed. The font has quatrefoil decoration and a 16th c. iron-bound poor-box is on view.

ATTLEBRIDGE   St Andrew

No of Bells:	4	
19th c. Deanery:	Taverham	
Hundred:	Taverham	
Union house:	Horsham St Faith	
21st c. Deanery:	Sparham	
Benefice:	Wensum	

8 m NW of Norwich just off the A1067 in Old Fakenham Road on the crossroads in the centre of the village.

O.S. grid ref: TF 897276

Post Code: NR9 5SU

Although the churchyard was overgrown and neglected the church itself is not. Obviously the women of the village are more industrious than the men. The 14th c. tower is without buttresses and has only two crenulations on each face of the parapet. Inside the nave is a late octagonal font with trefoil and quatrefoil decoration and a memorial inscription on the plinth. Beside the south door is a niche containing a carved piece of stone probably salvaged from a sepulchral tomb. Set into the floor is a small brass to John Batram dated 1454. In the chancel which has a modern 'trefoil' arch is a simple piscina and sedilia. Behind the organ almost hidden from view, is a wall plaque to George Cooper Graver (1824). This is a lovely little rural church but unfortunately little of historical interest remains here.

AYLMERTON St John the Baptist

No of Bells:	1	
19th c. Deanery:	Repps	
Hundred:	North Erpingham	
Union house:	West Beckham	
21st c. Deanery:	Repps	
Benefice:	Aylmerton	

3 m SW of Cromer. Leave Cromer on the A148 westbound and turn off left at the crossroads after petrol station to Aylmerton. O.S. grid ref: TG 182401 Post Code: NR11 8PZ

There is a round embattled tower which is probably Norman, although the foundations may be even earlier. It is flanked by two 14th c. windows and a doorway has been added to the south side of the tower, probably at the same time. On the north side of the nave is what is left of the north transept which has been ruinous for centuries. The Victorian octagonal font has quatrefoil designs around the bowl and arcading on the facets of the shaft. In the chancel is a lovely matching piscina and double sedilia which have traceried trefoil arches and crocketted pinnacles. Just inside the north doorway is what appears to be a pillar stoup which has been set into the wall. Unfortunately, the Victorian restorations have removed much of the historical interest but the old wine-glass style pulpit with tracery on the panels is a treat.

AYLSHAM	St Michael	12 m N of Norwich and 9
No of Bells:	10	m S of Cromer. Turn off
19th c. Deanery:	Ingworth	the A140 and head into
Hundred:	South Erpingham	Town Centre where the
Union house:	Aylsham	church is signposted.
21st c. Deanery:	Ingworth	O.S. grid ref: TG 193271
Benefice:	Aylsham	Post Code: NR11 6EH

There are many add-ons to this church. The south aisle has a transept and the porch had a parvise added a century after it was originally built in the 14th c. Although architecturally interesting on the outside there is more to see inside. Probably the most striking thing is the lovely base of the screen which dates from 1507. On the sixteen panels are mediaeval paintings of the saints, some of whom are named. Nearby is the wine-glass style pulpit, delicately perched on the slimmest of stems, complete with spiral stairs, back-board and tester. The lovely octagonal font is carved with the crucifixion and other emblems on the bowl, with more around the shaft. A substantial tomb to William Jermy of Bayfield is in the south aisle. Five simple arches in the chancel decorate the double piscina and sedilia.

BACONSTHORPE St Mary the Virgin   2½ m ESE of Holt. From
No of Bells: 8 tubular + 1 clock bell   the A148 at Holt take the
19th c. Deanery: Ingworth   Hempstead road and
Hundred: South Erpingham   follow the road through
Union house: West Beckham   Baconsthorpe, then right.
21st c. Deanery: Holt   O.S. grid ref: TG 128369
Benefice: Barningham Winter   Post Code: NR25 6LT

Parts of the church date back to the mid 13th c. but most evidence of
that era has now gone. The tower was re-built in 1788 after a collapse
in 1739. There were originally 3 bells but two were sold to pay for
repairs to the nave roof. Apart from arcades and a very rare and lovely
Easter sepulchre from the 14th c., most of the architecture one sees
today is Victorian 'restoration'. Standing on a Maltese cross plinth is
the octagonal Victorian font, behind it is part of the old screen set into
the tower arch. A good sized 16th c. parish chest stands nearby. Three
arches form the double 13th c. corner piscina and adjacent to it is the
dropped-sill sedilia. Faces form the corbels for the modern roof which
has painted armorial shields instead of bosses. There are some brasses
hanging on the wall of the south aisle, and interesting ledger slabs.

BALE	All Saints	5 m WSW of Holt. From
No of Bells:	5	Holt take the A148. Right
19th c. Deanery:	Holt	at the crossroads after
Hundred:	Holt	Sharrington, then bear left
Union house:	Great Snoring	to village centre.
21st c. Deanery:	Holt	O.S. grid ref: TG 011368
Benefice:	Stiffkey & Bale	Post Code: NR21 0QZ

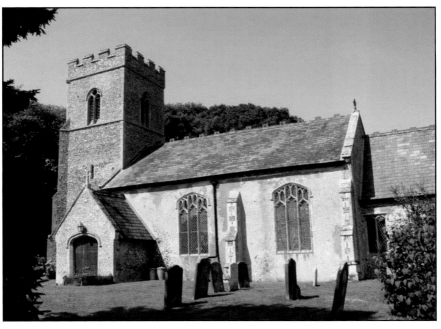

Bale church is tucked away behind trees and well worth visiting. On the west of the 14th c. embattled tower there is a niche once occupied by a saint, similar to the one at Brinton. Cement rendering is flaking from the nave wall, but this is nevertheless an attractive church. Inside the nave, the 15th c. corbelled octagonal font is decorated with roses and shields bearing emblems of the Trinity and Passion. The pulpit and other furnishings are Victorian. Seven consecration crosses adorn the walls in various places. The iron-bound parish chest dates from around 1500. Interestingly the Royal Arms are Charles II (1666) but were re-dated for William and Mary (1698) and amended again for George I with the addition of the Hanoverian Arms in the fourth quarter. Note the 15th c. glass in the south-east window.

BANHAM	St Mary the Virgin	6 m NE of Diss. Leave Diss
No of Bells:	6	on the B1077 and follow
19th c. Deanery:	Rockland	road signs to Banham. Turn
Hundred:	Guiltcross	right once in Banham to the
Union house:	Kenninghall	village green & church.
21st c. Deanery:	Thetford & Rockland	O.S. grid ref: TM 063881
Benefice:	Quidenham	Post Code: NR16 2HN

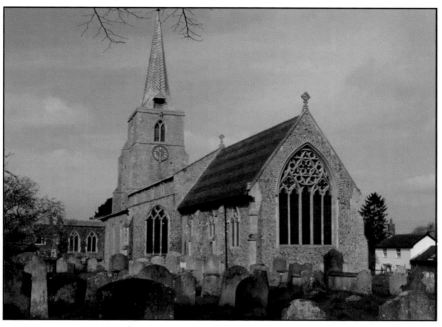

Banham church is easily recognised by its fine 'woven' leaded spire with a Sanctus bell beneath a hood on the east face. The plain octagonal font has a modern cover with columns supporting arches and a crown of foliage, with a crocketted conical spire. In the cambered tie-beam roof above, the date 1622 and the initials TR and IC can be seen. The apex is supported by braced king-posts. Close by, on the floor is the 14th c. iron-bound parish chest. Beyond the benches, which have a variety of poppy-heads, is the Victorian pulpit standing on a Portland stone base. In a pinnacled niche is an effigy of a knight which dates from about 1340, thought at one time to be Sir Hugh Bardolph who died in 1203. In the chancel is a matching piscina and sedilia which have a simple trefoil decoration.

BANNINGHAM St Botolph

No of Bells:	2
19th c. Deanery:	Ingworth
Hundred:	South Erpingham
Union house:	Aylsham
21st c. Deanery:	Waxham & Tunstead
Benefice:	King's Beck

2½ m NE of Aylsham. Easy to find by taking the A140 north out of Aylsham and then right onto the B1145, then first left.
O.S. grid ref: TG 216295
Post Code: NR11 7DY

The 15th c. embattled tower has a simple panelled base course. The clerestoried nave has a lead roof and the chancel is thatched. A stoup within a niche can be seen in the porch. The fine hammerbeam roof of the nave has traceried spandrels with two special carvings at its easternmost end just above the old rood beam which is still in place. Most of the building work is from the 15th c. or thereabouts but many of the fittings are Victorian, the Stuart holy table being a fine exception. Another exception is the round-topped 15th c. parish chest which has seven locks. High on the wall of the nave among some old wall paintings hangs the Royal Arms of George II. The wine-glass style pulpit compliments the beautiful lectern, which is carved from wood in the form of an angel.

BARFORD   St Botolph

No of Bells:	3	
19th c. Deanery:	Hingham	
Hundred:	Forehoe	
Union house:	Wicklewood	
21st c. Deanery:	Dereham & Mitford	
Benefice:	Barnham Broom & Upper Yare	

7 m W of Norwich & 4 m N of Wymondham. Turn north off the B1108 west of the village opposite PH towards Church Road.
O.S. grid ref: TG 107080
Post Code: NR9 4AU

At some time in the past, render has been applied and is now mostly flaked off, marring the general appearance of this fine 14th c. church. The tower and chancel were probably built a century earlier, the former has small quatrefoil windows to the ringing chamber. In the nave is the octagonal font decorated with quatrefoils around the bowl. Built into the north wall are steps which used to lead to the rood loft. Immediately to the right, set into the chancel arch, are three niches, which match another three on the south side. On the wall hangs the Royal Arms of George III. The screen is very short and seriously reduced from its original height, where it used to reach up to the bressummer beam which is still visible as a stump in the wall. The holy table dates from the 17th c. Stuart period.

BARNHAM BROOM Sts Peter & Paul

No of Bells:	5	
19th c. Deanery:	Hingham	
Hundred:	Forehoe	
Union house:	Wicklewood	
21st c. Deanery:	Dereham & Mitford	
Benefice: Barnham Broom & Upper Yare		

9 m W of Norwich. From the B1108 Kimberley to Barford all roads north head into B'ham Broom. Go to Honingham Road. O.S. grid ref: TG 082078 Post Code: NR9 4DB

This is a sad little church, concealed by trees and unable to see the light of day. It seems dingy, even before you enter the dark, lifeless interior. Although the church was originally built in the 13th c. the rebuilding in the 15th c. is what is seen here today. Atop the 15th c. tower are three apostles, a fourth is missing having fallen in a storm. Inside the nave is a west gallery which contains the old 14th c. ark style parish chest beneath the tower. The Royal Arms of George III are from the period before Hanover became a Kingdom and are correctly dated 1808. Of greater interest is the lower portion of the screen upon which 10 depictions of saints appear. Two panels are blank and were probably badly restored by someone with good intent and later scrubbed clean. The font has 12 facets in the form of a cross.

BARNINGHAM NORTHWOOD   St Peter

No of Bells: 0 (1 removed 1874)
19th c. Deanery: Repps
Hundred: North Erpingham
Union house: West Beckham
21st c. Deanery: Holt
The Churches Conservation Trust

5 miles E of Holt. From Holt
take the A148 and turn left
after the A1082 to Sheringham
and follow 2½ miles.
O.S. grid ref: TG 151372
Post Code: NR11 7LB

Otherwise known as North Barningham! The church has been redundant for some time and is cared for by the C.C.T. and is always open. Unfortunately, as with almost all such redundant churches, the fixtures and fittings have been removed and a hollow shell remains for us to use our imaginations as to what it once was. Still there are a bench against the west wall; a small pillar piscina in the north aisle; and in the clerestory, a glorious monument to Sir Austin (1639) and Dame Elizabeth (1633) Palgrave. This is flanked by Margaret Pope (1624) their daughter on one side and John Palgrave (1611) on the other. On the opposite wall are the remains of what once was a beautiful 14th c. piscina and sedilia combination. A few mediaeval benches stand forlornly in the south aisle.

BARNINGHAM WINTER St Mary

No of Bells:	1 in the ruined tower
19th c. Deanery:	Repps
Hundred:	North Erpingham
Union house:	West Beckham
21st c. Deanery:	Holt
Benefice:	Barningham Winter

6 m ESE of Holt. From Barningham Northwood continue for 1 mile and enter the 'Cromer Gate' of Barningham Hall. 500 yds.
O.S. grid ref: TG 146357
Post Code: NR11 7JY

This church was almost lost when the tower collapsed and smashed through the nave roof in the 17th c. Only the 14th c. chancel remained. The ruinous tower remarkably still contains a working bell, and in its base is the font. During the 19th c. a small porch-like extension was erected west of the chancel and a gallery installed above. There are some good memorials here to various members of the Paston and Mott families. A brass which hangs on the wall of the entrance is to a knight by the name of Wynter, from whom the parish inherited its name. The reredos is a War Memorial. A black tablet tells of Lt.Col. Charles Radcliffe who went missing in 1915 and despite his widow's efforts his body was never found. The Royal Arms of Charles I are in glass and form part of the east window.

BAWBURGH St Mary & St Walstan

No of Bells:	1	
19th c. Deanery:	Hingham	
Hundred:	Forehoe	
Union house:	Wicklewood	
21st c. Deanery:	Dereham & Mitford	
Benefice:	Easton	

5 m W of Norwich. Turn off the A47 at the Colney roundabout & briefly onto the B1108 then take the first right and next left.
O.S. grid ref: TG 153086
Post Code: NR9 3NA

This is an ancient church, rededicated in 1016 shortly after the death of St Walstan and partly rebuilt in 1309. The low conical roof was added long ago when the upper section of the tower was removed. Notice the nice crow-stepped gables to the nave. Inside the church, a bulbous round font catches the eye. On the walls are the sad remains of some mediaeval wall paintings and a nice example of the Royal Arms of Charles II. Most of the seating is very plain but a few poppy-head bench ends remain. The roofs have been plastered at sometime in history. In the nave is what is left of St Walstan's chapel. A very different style of poor-box seems to have been adapted from a table leg, but I think purpose made. The holy table dates from the Stuart period as do the altar rails.

BAWDESWELL All Saints

No of Bells:	1
19th c. Deanery:	Sparham
Hundred:	Eynesford
Union house:	Gressenhall
21st c. Deanery:	Sparham
Benefice:	FLEBBS

7 m NE of Dereham. Approached from the B1145 or the A1067, the church stands alongside the main street.

O.S. grid ref: TG 216059

Post Code: NR20 4RT

Looking as if it should belong on a private estate this splendid church stands serenely in the street at Bawdeswell. There have been three churches on this site; the mediaeval church was partially destroyed when the tower collapsed onto the nave in 1739. After a further collapse in 1829, the site was cleared and another church was built in 1843 which was itself destroyed when a plane returning from a bombing raid crashed into it in 1944. The present church, with its broached spirelet and apsidal east end is the loveliest. In the crisp interior of the nave is a cone shaped font and a triple-decker pulpit with a faded pine patina. It is different and very pleasant but historically void of interest. Even the parish chest was made by a parishioner in 1952. The oldest items here are the photographs *(inset)*.

BAYFIELD   St Margaret

No of Bells:	-, (once 2)	
19th c. Deanery:	Holt	
Hundred:	Holt	
Union house:	Gimingham	
21st c. Deanery:	-	
Benefice:	-	

2½ m NW of Holt in the private grounds of Bayfield Hall. There is no public access to view the ruins which may be seen from the road.
O.S. grid ref: TG 050405
Post Code: NR25 7JN

There is not much I can say about the church. By the end of the 18th c. it had reached the end of its usefulness and while the 19th c. owner of Bayfield Hall, Sir Alfred Jodrell, ensured the continued existence of near-by Glandford and Saxlingham it would seem he preferred a ruin rather than a living church in his front garden. The chancel arch was blocked and a door inserted, probably after the nave became ruinous and the tiny chancel utilized for worship. The double bellcote is similar to those seen on mediaeval churches in Spain and Italy. Perhaps the owner of the Hall at the time was well travelled and liked the idea of one for 'his' church. The church is all that remains of the original village of Bayfield before the village was razed to build the Hall and establish the estate. Bayfield is united with Letheringsett.

BEESTON REGIS   All Saints

No of Bells:	1 (4 before 1765)	
19th c. Deanery:	Repps	
Hundred:	North Erpingham	
Union house:	West Beckham	
21st c. Deanery:	Repps	
Benefice:	Aylmerton	

3 m W of Cromer on the A149, Take the road down onto the caravan park just past the railway bridge. Bear left & go under the bridge.
O.S. grid ref: TG 175432
Post Code: NR27 9QZ

Standing overlooking The Wash, the tower is unusual in that it has no quoin stones and is entirely of flint and mortar with a low parapet. This is surprising when one considers the view from the top. Dating from around the mid 13th c., with a 14th c. three window clerestory and north and south aisles, over-restoration has removed much of interest. However, there are still a few points worth noting; a stoup just inside the door for instance and in particular the lovely lower half of the well restored 15th c. screen with twelve saints in good condition and easily identifiable. The upper part of the screen is Victorian as are the pulpit, lectern, benches and other fittings. There are brasses, some beneath the choir stalls, and a 16th c. one to John Daynes in the centre of the chancel, where you will also find the piscina and sedilia.

BESSINGHAM St Mary

No of Bells:	2	
19th c. Deanery:	Repps	
Hundred:	North Erpingham	
Union house:	West Beckham	
21st c. Deanery:	Repps	
Benefice:	Roughton	

5 m SSW of Cromer. Between Matlaske and Gresham. Situated at the north end of Bessingham Street.

O.S. grid ref: TG 168370
Post Code: NR11 7JP

The church, built mainly of carstone, stands on an acclivity above the village to the north. The fine Saxon defensive tower has been crenellated at a later date. Inside the nave a doorway can be seen where the populace would have sheltered in the event of an invasion. The plain octagonal font is badly cracked. A fine trefoil window is above the north door, and above that, the arch-braced design of the roof is matched with that of the chancel. Victorian bench-ends have good interesting carved poppy-heads. Even better are the carvings of fourteen saints at the end of the wall plates in the nave, each easily identifiable by their symbols. There is no longer a piscina or sedilia both were probably removed during Victorian restorations of 1869, although a trefoil niche survives in the north wall of the chancel.

BESTHORPE   All Saints

No of Bells:	5	
19th c. Deanery:	Rockland	
Hundred:	Shropham	
Union house:	Rockland All Saints	
21st c. Deanery:	Thetford & Rockland	
Benefice:	Attleborough	

1½ m NE of Attleborough church, in Bunwell Road. Over the level crossing keep left then left again. Church 300 yds on right.
O.S. grid ref: TM 066956
Post Code: NR17 2NZ

This is an immaculate church. The clean lines of the windows and roof accentuate its importance to the community. The east window of the chancel is particularly pleasing with its beautiful curvilinear tracery. Inside the nave the roofs are modern and so is the round font with four columns around a central shaft. The north transept has glass doors and is a committee room, called 'The Drury Room' after a local family of that name. There is a splendid memorial in the chancel to Sir William Drury (1639) lying recumbent with his wife Mary kneeling at his head, and his surviving daughters at his feet. On the opposite wall are four cinquefoil arches with crocketted ogee pinnacles beneath which are the piscina and sedilia. Most of the furnishings are modern but not at all incompatible with their surroundings.

BILLINGFORD St Leonard

No of Bells:	1
19th c. Deanery:	Redenhall
Hundred:	Earsham
Union house:	Pulham St Mary
21st c. Deanery:	Redenhall
Benefice:	Scole

4 m E of Diss off the A143.
1½ m east of Scole turn left
onto an unmade gravel road
a few yards past the turnoff
to Billingford mill.
O.S. grid ref: TM 168790
Post Code: IP21 4HL

The parish was anciently known as Pyrleston. This is a lovely church,
if somewhat dilapidated in appearance. The tower fell down centuries
ago and was never rebuilt. The porch once had a parvise, the door to
which remains, probably because of the fine tracery on the upper part.
Inside the nave is a 15th c. traditional East Anglian font with lions
around the base. The pulpit complete with back-board and tester is
two centuries later. On the wall is what remains of a mediaeval
painting, hardly recognisable for what it is. Nearby are the Royal
Arms of Queen Anne, although the altered inscription reads George
II. Stairs which once led up to the rood loft ascend from a dropped
window sill. A 13th c. piscina and sedile indicate the early origins of
the church. There are interesting grotesque faces on the poppy-heads!

BILLINGFORD St Peter

No of Bells:	1
19th c. Deanery:	Sparham
Hundred:	Eynesford
Union house:	Gressenhall
21st c. Deanery:	Sparham
Benefice:	Elmham

5 m NNE of Dereham. From the A1067 Fakenham to Norwich road, turn west onto the B1145 near Bawdeswell. Turn right after 2 miles.
O.S. grid ref: TG 013205
Post Code: NR20 4AJ

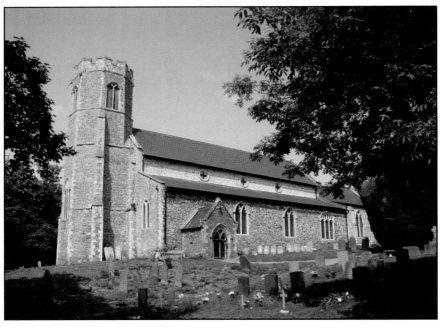

This pleasant little church is set on an acclivity above the road to Bintree. The 14th c. embattled tower is quite unusual in being completely octagonal, as can be found at Buckenham St Nicholas in East Norfolk. A clerestory of three small quatrefoil windows does little to improve the gloom inside. A very good 13th c font with a modern cover and four pillars around a central shaft stands at the west end of the nave. Nearby an old handcart bier has been preserved. A modern wine-glass style pulpit cut from Portland stone doesn't look too out of place against the clustered columns of the 14th c. arcades which line the nave. A simple arch over the early piscina is adjacent to the dropped-sill sedilia. There are plenty of poppy-head bench ends to look at, every one different from the other.

BINTREE	St Swithin	6 m W of Reepham. On
No of Bells:	2	the west side of the A 1067
19th c. Deanery:	Sparham	at the 'T' junction of
Hundred:	Eynesford	Church Road, Church Lane
Union house:	Gressenhall	And Yarrow Road.
21st c. Deanery:	Sparham	O.S. grid ref: TG 017235
Benefice:	Elmham	Post Code: NR20 5NJ

Sometimes spelt as Bintry! This is a lop-sided church with a south aisle and transept, making it impossible to capture all the features in a single photograph. It is an interesting church however, as it began its life in the 12th c. However, much modernisation has taken place in the last nine hundred years, most recently in 1864 when new roofs were put on. Almost everything externally is 15th c. Just inside the door is a niche for a stoup and in its correct place is the 14th c. font, slightly lop-sided. The attractive arch decoration around the octagonal bowl is crisp, but the bowl has been repaired. A superb iron-bound chest dates from the same period. The seating is all modern. In the sanctuary is a very rare pillar piscina. The sedilia, if there ever was one, has been removed. The stone pulpit is akin to a block of cement!

BLAKENEY   St Nicholas ****   4½ m NW of Holt. Just
No of Bells: 3   south of the A149 Coast
19th c. Deanery: Holt   Road on Wiveton Road.
Hundred: Holt   The church is well sign-
Union house: Great Snoring   posted.
21st c. Deanery: Holt   O.S. grid ref: TG 033435
Benefice: Glaven Valley (Blakeney)   Post Code: NR25 7NJ

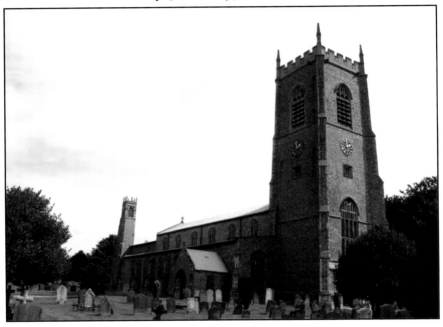

Anciently called Snitterley! A church has stood here for many years
as part of the Carmelite friary but most of the building we see today
was erected in the 15th c. At the eastern end, over the chancel, is
another tower used as an early lighthouse to guide the mariners safely
back to port. Above the narrow nave is a good hammerbeam roof.
There is plenty to see here, twenty-two misericordes as well as the
animal carvings on every bench-end, and a well traceried pulpit on a
matching stone base. Standing on a large plinth is the 15th c.
octagonal font with the Four Latin Doctors and symbols of the
Passion around the bowl. An old bier stands in the south aisle.
Although the Royal Arms are dated 1818 the Arms are actually pre-
1801 in design and were probably originally George I (circa 1720).

BLICKLING   St Andrew
No of Bells: 1
19th c. Deanery: Ingworth
Hundred: South Erpingham
Union house: Aylsham
21st c. Deanery: Ingworth
Benefice: Seven Churches Itteringham

2 m NW of Aylsham. From Aylsham take the Blickling Road and follow the NT signs. The church is 100 yards before Blickling Hall. O.S. grid ref: TG 179285 Post Code: NR11 6NF

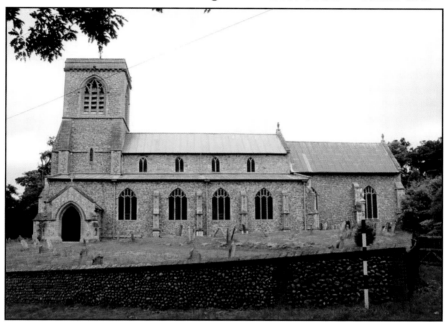

If you visit Blickling Hall don't forget to also visit the church. Although it has been restored on a fairly regular basis by the owners of the Hall it still retains much of interest. The 13th c. doorway for instance, has an engaged column either side. On entering the nave your eye will be drawn to the flamboyant marble tomb of the Marquis of Lothian (1870). The 15th c. octagonal font is traditional style, but lacking in religious emblems which saved it from the Puritan axe. It has been re-coloured by some well-meaning person at some time, probably when the ogee cover with a pelican at the apex was added. A Jacobean wine-glass style pulpit with a simple backboard is a treat. An enormous safe-like totally iron-bound chest, with five locks, must weigh a ton. Opulence or simplicity, you will find both at Blickling.

BLO NORTON   St Andrew

No of Bells:	6	
19th c. Deanery:	Rockland	
Hundred:	Guiltcross	
Union house:	Kenninghall	
21st c. Deanery:	Thetford & Rockland	
Benefice:	Guiltcross	

5 m S of East Harling.
From the A1066 turn off
south at South Lopham and
follow the road for exactly
2 miles to the church.
O.S. grid ref: TM 012797
Post Code: IP22 2JE

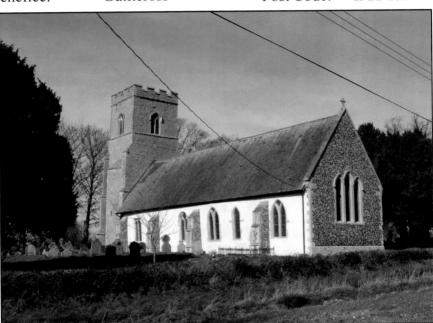

On the south side of the 14th c. embattled tower is the square
staircase which rises to the roof height of the nave (this was thatched
until the restorations in the 19th c.). The entrance to the church is
through the 500-year-old timber framed north porch. Within the nave
is the 14th c. font with quatrefoil and Y tracery designs around the
bowl. Over the doorway are the unmistakable Royal Arms of James I
with his motto (J R has been over-painted W R et M R for William
and Mary). There is no chancel arch or screen, but the stairs to the
rood loft are still open and a line in the wall determines where the
screen once was. Set into the sill of the chancel window is the piscina
adjacent to the sedile. It would appear that the window has been
enlarged and the niche totally removed. A pleasant little church.

BODHAM   All Saints
No of Bells: 1
19th c. Deanery: Holt
Hundred: Holt
Union house: Gimingham
21st c. Deanery: Holt
Benefice: Weybourne

3 m E of Holt. From the A148 turn south in Bodham at the x-roads into The Street, then Hart Lane for ¾ mile to Church Road.
O.S. grid ref: TG 126402
Post Code: NR25 6PT

The clean lines of this 14th c. church are very pleasing. Modern roofs now replace the thatch which once protected it for centuries. Heavy restoration by the Victorians removed much of the charm and character of the church, but enough remains to make it interesting. The plain octagonal font is coeval with the building of the church. Square head-moulds over the 17th c. perpendicular windows of the nave contrast with the low round hood-moulds of the chancel and between the latter are the signs of a blocked priest's door. Wood salvaged from the old box pews now form the ceiling of the vestry. The Victorian pulpit is rather ornate with barley-twist balustrades from the gates of the altar rails. The Royal Arms of Queen Anne, (post-1707) and a lovely old bier are two additional points of interest.

BOOTON St Michael ***** 6 m SW of Aylsham off the
No of Bells: 1 in each tower B1145. From Reepham take
19th c. Deanery: Ingworth the Booton road east for 1½
Hundred: South Erpingham miles, or from Cawston
Union house: Horsham St Faiths head south for 1½ miles.
21st c. Deanery: - O.S. grid ref: TG 122224
The Churches Conservation Trust Post Code: NR10 4NZ

The twin towers make this church unmistakable and quite unique as a parish church. Built around the nave of the old 14th c. church they were the brainchild of the Rev. Whitwell Elwin. Building began in 1876 with elements of Glastonbury Abbey and Lichfield cathedral included in the design. The interior is no less impressive, even the porch roof is spectacularly carved. The hammerbeam roof of both nave and chancel have an angel on every hammer and the spandrels are full of tracery. The crocketted theme of the pinnacles outside are reflected in the furnishings and fittings of the interior. This is Victorian architecture at its most extravagant in a rural setting. Although my taste is for the mediaeval I could not help but be overwhelmed by this most remarkable of Norfolk's churches.

BOWTHORPE   St Michael

No of Bells: -
19th c. Deanery: Hingham
Hundred: Forehoe
Union house: Wicklewood
21st c. Deanery: -
Benefice: -

3 m w of Norwich. South
of the A1074 Dereham
Road. Situated next to the
Worship Centre in
Bowthorpe Hall Road.
O.S. grid ref: TG 175190
Post Code: NR5 9AA

This church was un-roofed in 1792, when the parish had just twenty-one inhabitants, and for the past 200 years it has remained a ruin. The parish was consolidated with Earlham. It was never a great church; in fact it was built on a simple 12th c. foundation which served the small parish until the congregation fell to unsustainable levels. It has been made structurally sound but unfortunately all its real character has been lost in the process. It is now just a garden feature around the village community centre, but I am not critical of what has been achieved here. Children can come and learn about architecture and the structure of a church, albeit a skeleton of its former self. It is far better than a ruin with a fence and notices proclaiming 'Dangerous Structure - Keep Out.' You can't get a feel for something you cannot touch!

BRACON ASH	St Nicholas	6 m SW of Norwich. From
No of Bells:	1	the B1113 turn right just
19th c. Deanery:	Humbleyard	before the village towards
Hundred:	Humbleyard	Hethel. Church within 400
Union house:	Swainsthorpe	yards on the left, set back.
21st c. Deanery:	Humbleyard	O.S. grid ref: TG 179001
Benefice:	Mulbarton	Post Code: NR14 8HJ

This is one of the grade 1 listed buildings that dates from the early 14th c. probably because it has an 18th c. mausoleum of the Berney family leading off from the chancel, which can be clearly seen from the outside. There has never been a tower, and since the bellcote fell a single bell has hung in a frame near the south doorway. A fairly simple but unusual 14th c. font stands at the west end of the nave. Behind the Victorian pulpit are the winding stairs which once led to the rood loft. In the chancel is a piscina with an ogee arch but no sedilia. On the opposite wall is a classical façade and entrance into the mausoleum containing a hatchment; more of which are scattered willy-nilly around the church. Above the chancel arch is the Royal Arms of George III. The holy table is early 17th c. Different!

BRAMPTON   St Peter

No of Bells:	1
19th c. Deanery:	Ingworth
Hundred:	South Erpingham
Union house:	Aylsham
21st c. Deanery:	Ingworth
Benefice:	Bure Valley

2½ m SE of Aylsham. From the A140 take the Buxton Road, then take the sixth exit on the left and left again after crossing the railway.

O.S. grid ref: TG 219247
Post Code: NR10 5HW

The base of the stratified Norman tower has a nice slit window. A 15th c. octagonal belfry stage is built from brick with stone dressings, as is much of the nave and chancel. A few disseminated parts of the 13th c walls remain. This is a church that has been added to and altered many times over the centuries, much to its detriment. The chancel is completely out of line with the nave and the altar out of sight of most of the congregation. Just inside the traceried south door is a niche for a stoup. A 14th c. octagonal font with shields in quatrefoils around the bowl stands at the west end of the nave and a modern pulpit at the east. The roofs are relatively modern probably coeval with the benches and other furnishings. There is very little of interest inside; probably the reason why it is permanently locked.

BRANDISTON   St Nicholas

No of Bells:	1	
19th c. Deanery:	Sparham	
Hundred:	Eynesford	
Union house:	Horsham St Faiths	
21st c. Deanery:	-	

The Churches Conservation Trust

3 m ESE of Reepham. West off the B1149 south of the Aylsham roundabout towards Eastgate. Left at crossroads, then next right.
O.S. grid ref: TG 141214
Post Code: NR10 4PJ

Almost concealed from the road, it shares a driveway with Church Farm and is easily missed. Anciently, the parish church of Guton (a long dilapidated parish) stood in the same churchyard. Originally a Norman church stood here but it was rebuilt in 1400 leaving most of what is seen today, apart from the east wall rebuilt in the 18th c. The nave was extended southwards, leaving the 14th c. arcade. The truncated tower is a result of a fall centuries ago and was only rebuilt with an octagonal top in 1890. Immediately inside the south door is an ancient stoup. Standing on an oblong plinth is a late 19th c. off-the-shelf font supported on five columns. Most of the furnishings are Victorian. A few 19th c. memorials to the Rev. Atthill and members of his family adorn the walls.

BRANDON PARVA All Saints

No of Bells:	1
19th c. Deanery:	Hingham
Hundred:	Forehoe
Union house:	Wicklewood
21st c. Deanery:	Dereham & Mitford

Benefice: Barnham Broom & Upper Yare

5½ m NNW of Norwich. From Barnham Broom x-roads head west & right at the T junction then left through Manor Farm.

O.S. grid ref: TG 070081

Post Code: NR9 4DQ

Very easily missed! Look for the Log Cabins factory and go though the yard and up the lane for 200 yards. This parish has no relationship with Brandon near Thetford. The early 14th c. tower has recently undergone repairs and consolidation work. The tower arch has a hood-mould with a carved trail and head stops. Leading to the belfry is the original 14th c. studded door. 15th or 16th c. re-building is evident, but the east window is a 19th c. botched job. The octagonal font is 14th c. and probably coeval with the original building of the church. The roof of the nave is Victorian as are most of the fixtures and fittings. The keen eye will find a significant number of grotesques and faces scattered throughout the building. This is an interesting little church and worth including in a crawl of local churches.

BRECCLES	St Margaret	5 m SSE of Watton. Turn
No of Bells:	1	off the A1075 3½ miles
19th c. Deanery:	Breccles	south of Watton onto the
Hundred:	Wayland	B1111 for just over 1 mile.
Union house:	Rockland All Saints	Easily found on the left.
21st c. Deanery:	Breckland	O.S. grid ref: TL 958946
Benefice:	Wayland	Post Code: NR17 12EW

The unusual 15th c. octagonal top of the very late Saxon tower distinguishes this church from most. Traces exist of Saxon work here too. Inside is the most impressive of Norman fonts, with carving on the top as well as on each of the four facets and corners: four figures beneath arches on the east face, interlaced arches on the north, two demonic faces on the west, fleurs de lys on the south. The 15th c. Screen, too, is carved although somewhat primitively, still retaining the original doors with their crocketted tops. In the north wall the stairs to the rood loft are still wholly intact with the opening above. On the south wall, where the pulpit used to stand, is the old hour-glass holder complete with replacement glass. Note the memorial to Ursula Hewyt 'Stat ut vixit erecta' it reads, meaning she was buried upright.

BRESSINGHAM   St John the Baptist   *****

No of Bells:	5	2 m W of Diss in Low
19th c. Deanery:	Redenhall	Road, off the A1066, just
Hundred:	Diss	west of and on the same
Union house:	Kenninghall	side as the garden centre.
21st c. Deanery:	Redenhall	O.S. grid ref: TM 076807
Benefice:	Upper Waveney	Post Code: IP22 2AA

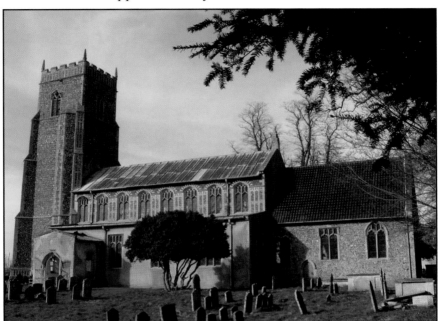

This is a nice-looking church with a fine clerestory and an attractive 15th c. tower which has good flushwork around the base. If you can manage to get into the church there is a treat awaiting you, if you are like me, into the 'traditional'.   Here we have probably the finest collection of 16th c. bench-ends in the county. Depictions of saints, animals and grotesques are beautifully executed. A few have suffered the wrath of Puritanism but that is part of their history. Above, there is a lovely single hammerbeam roof. A 14th c. font, Jacobean pulpit complete with canopy, the Royal Arms of Charles II hung high on the tower arch, a 14th c. ark chest as well as the remains of the village stocks are all here to see. A fine canopied bier is also on display. A 14th c. sedilia and a piscina are in the weeping chancel. Impressive!

BRETTENHAM St Andrew

No of Bells:	5	
19th c. Deanery:	Rockland	
Hundred:	Shropham	
Union house:	Thetford St Mary	
21st c. Deanery:	Thetford & Rockland	
Benefice:	East Harling	

4 m E of Thetford. Coming from Thetford on the A1066 turn first left at 3½ miles and follow the road another ½ mile.

O.S. grid ref: TL 931833
Post Code: IP24 2RP

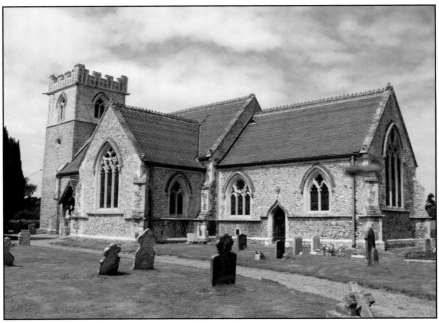

From the outside this is a lovely church, but at the time of writing the interior is dreadful. The plaster is falling off the walls and the whole place smells of damp and fungus. In 1693 the church was burnt down and rebuilt shortly after. In 1853 it was restored and all that is to be seen is of that date or later. The octagonal font has a simple quatrefoil design. The base of the elaborately carved screen is marble and the reredos is a fine example of Victorian craftsmanship, as are the choir benches. Stencilled designs adorn the chancel roof to great effect, set off with fine gilding. Screens that span the transepts are totally out of place however, and ought to be removed as they are metallic and painted in drab grey. I hope when I return the damp and decay has been corrected and the church kept open for visitors.

BRIDGHAM   St Mary the Virgin

No of Bells:	1	
19th c. Deanery:	Rockland	
Hundred:	Shropham	
Union house:	Kenninghall	
21st c. Deanery:	Thetford & Rockland	
Benefice:	Harling United	

5 m E x N of Thetford. From the A11 4 miles east of Thetford turn south to Bridgham. In 2 miles bear left, then turn left.
O.S. grid ref: TL 957858
Post Code: NR16 2RY

An unusual church, to say the least. St Mary's lost its round tower centuries ago and a louvered bellcote rises above the nave roof, as does the chancel roof. Most of the church can be dated to about the 13th c. or a little later. It is worth a look around the outside as one or two unusual features reveal themselves to the watchful eye. In the nave is the 15th c. octagonal font, on one facet depicting The Assumption, one of only two in Norfolk. Near the pulpit are a much older Norman font and a bell which were at Roudham church; in the wall is a piscina still with its credence shelf. Opposite, the rood stairs are still open to the top. A lovely double piscina and matching sedilia can be seen in the chancel. At the west end of the nave are the Decalogue boards from which Moses and Aaron are missing.

BRININGHAM St Maurice

No of Bells:	1
19th c. Deanery:	Holt
Hundred:	Holt
Union house:	Great Snoring
21st c. Deanery:	Holt
Benefice:	Brinton

4 m SW of Holt. Leave Holt on the B1110 and once in Briningham turn right & right again. Turn left by Church Cottage. O.S. grid ref: TG 039344 Post Code: NR24 2QB

Tucked away down a quiet little lane the church is a pleasure to find. The 14th c. south-west tower serves also as a porch to enter the cosy nave. There is no grandeur, no fancy screen or wall paintings and the octagonal font is new and undecorated, yet it is everything a church should be; humble and serving the community. Pammant-tiled throughout it has rush matting in the chancel. It has modern roofs and in the apex of the arch-bracing are kingposts with some tracery. A date on the pulpit tells us it is early 20th c. Each side of the east window is a large niche; on the left, a knight (St Maurice) is ensconced and on the right, Mary holding the Child. A pleasing ogee hooded trefoil piscina and dropped-sill sedilia embellished with carved peonies on the south wall. Opposite is a wafer oven. I love it!

BRINTON	St Andrew	4 m SW of Holt. From Holt
No of Bells:	1	take the B1110 through
19th c. Deanery:	Holt	Thornage then first right for
Hundred:	Holt	¾ of a mile to destination at
Union house:	Local poor support	first 'T' junction.
21st c. Deanery:	Holt	O.S. grid ref: TG 038357
Benefice:	Brinton	Post Code: NR24 2QH

If this church looks different it's because the chancel has been demolished and the east end of the nave now serves as such. This is likely to have taken place in the 15th c. as the course of Religion changed. The rood stairs are concealed behind a door next to the altar. On the jamb of the south door is a scratch dial (pre-porch) and immediately inside there is a 13th c. stoup, evidence of the age of the building. Another relic from the same era is the rare pillar piscina in the chancel. An undecorated 14th c. font stands beneath the tower arch. Above the 15th c. arcade is the 15th c. arch-braced roof from which hangs a rowel pulley. Some of the older benches have mutilated carved figures on the ends and bear a date of 1544. An old parish chest stands almost neglected beneath the tower.

BRISTON	All Saints	4½ m S of Holt. Leave Holt
No of Bells:	1	on the B1149 towards
19th c. Deanery:	Holt	Saxthorpe but bear right
Hundred:	Holt	after ½ mile to Hunworth
Union house:	Great Snoring	and follow into the village.
21st c. Deanery:	Holt	O.S. grid ref: TG 060328
Benefice:	Briston	Post Code: NR24 2LF

The tower was totally demolished in 1724, due to its collapse leaving it in a dangerous condition. The single brick bell turret was erected at a later date. At one time there was also a north aisle but that too has been demolished, along with the south porch, and the door bricked up. Were it not for the windows and the bell turret it could be a barn. The only entrance to the nave is through the west door. Inside the nave is the 14th c. octagonal font decorated on each facet with quatrefoils and billeting around the rim. The square-headed screen has simple but fine tracery. Most of the furnishings and fittings are Victorian as is the scissor-frame roof of the nave and arch-braced roof of the chancel where there is an attractive piscina and sedilia. In a cabinet on the south wall is a cello manufactured in steel by the local blacksmith.

BUNWELL St Michael & All Angels

No of Bells:	6	
19th c. Deanery:	Depwade	
Hundred:	Depwade	
Union house:	Pulham St Mary	
21st c. Deanery:	Depwade	
Benefice:	Pilgrim	

3 m NE of N Buckenham, in Church Road, Bunwell. On the B1113 from Norwich turn right just after the crossroads.

O.S. grid ref: TM 125927
Post Code: NR16 1SN

Most of the exterior is cement-rendered but has been executed quite well. The slender 15th c. tower is surmounted by an oversize double crenulated parapet. Good flushwork can be seen on the south porch. In the nave the 14th c. font has shields in multi-foil designs. Two styles are incorporated in the make-up of the roof, a conventional arch-braced roof supplemented by arch-braced tie-beams. In the locked vestry is a large parish chest. Most of the furnishings are modern including the linen-fold wine-glass pulpit. The Stuart holy table is an exception. In the chancel is the simple piscina niche, but with no drain, and a plain dropped-sill sedilia. A large set of Queen Anne Royal Arms hangs over the north door. There are nice carved angels on the front benches, and poppyheads galore!

BURGH (next-Aylsham) St Mary*****
No of Bells: 1
19th c. Deanery: Ingworth
Hundred: South Erpingham
Union house: Aylsham
21st c. Deanery: Ingworth
Benefice: Bure Valley

2 m SE of Aylsham. At Aylsham on the A140 turn off to Burgh & Swanton Abbot for 1½ m. Turn right into Church Lane.
O.S. grid ref: TG 218251
Post Code: NR11 6TR

For well over a millennium a church has stood on this site. The thatched chancel is the oldest structure we can see today. Built in the early 13th c. it has two steps down into it, a feature rarely encountered and continuous restored arcade around the walls with seats between the columns. A nice columned arch leads into the chancel chapel. At the east end are three deeply recessed windows with a rose window centrally above. It is very elegant and looks part of a cathedral. Pevsner describes it as 'The finest Early English chancel in East Anglia.' I must agree! A 15th c. Seven Sacrament font is another treasure the church has to offer, although somewhat damaged. The Royal Arms, in white plaster, are those of George I. They were probably purchased by Matthew Burr, whose name appears below.

BURGH PARVA St Mary (old church)

No of Bells:	-	
19th c. Deanery:	Holt	
Hundred:	Holt	
Union house:	Great Snoring	
21st c. Deanery:	-	
Benefice:	-	

4 m SSW of Holt. On a minor road off the B1110 to Melton Constable. Or take first left in M. C. Or west from B1354 first left. O.S. grid ref: TG 043335
Post Code: NR24 2PU

Here is what remains of a once fine church. Many centuries have passed since it was deserted and the parish was united with Melton Constable. In reality it was part of the Hall Estate and a little too remote in what was, and still is, a very small parish. The tower is almost intact and has 'Y' tracery windows which indicate a date sometime in the late 13th c. The arch is lined with Roman bricks. Very little history of the ruin remains but it would seem it only lasted for about four centuries. The dimensions of the church are easily recognised by what walls remain. Part of the chancel north wall and east wall are still in evidence and the south wall with the doorway reveal the complete footprint. Never a large church, it is kept free of overgrowth and is always open, unlike its neighbour.

BURGH PARVA St Mary (new)

No of Bells:	1	
19th c. Deanery:	Holt	
Hundred:	Holt	
Union house:	Great Snoring	
21st c. Deanery:	Holt	
Benefice:	Briston	

4 m SSW of Holt. On a minor road off the B1110 to Melton Constable. Or take first left in M. C. Or west from B1354 first left O.S. grid ref: TG 043335 Post Code: NR24 2PU

Standing in the graveyard, south of the old church (see opposite page) is this corrugated iron church, erected in 1903 as a temporary measure before a replacement church was built. Plans for the new church are displayed on the walls inside. Obviously it never happened and the Melton community are very happy with their tin church. It served them (Melton), as well as Burgh and is known as Melton church. The Norman church in the Park is commonly called 'the Park church'; and is regarded as somewhat superior. The nave is lined with chairs, as you might expect in a 'temporary' building. The reredos was salvaged from St Philip's in Norwich after it was bombed in WWII. Despite its 'village hut' appearance it is worth a visit and although locked, a keyholder is not far away.

BURSTON   St Mary

No of Bells: 1
19th c. Deanery: Redenhall
Hundred: Diss
Union house: Kenninghall
21st c. Deanery: Redenhall
Benefice: Winfarthing

3 m NE of Diss. From the A140 towards Norwich turn left to Shimpling and follow the road for 3 miles. The church is in village centre.
O.S. grid ref: TM 137832
Post Code: IP22 5TP

Burston church lost its tower in 1753 when it collapsed and it was never rebuilt. A small bellcote was erected to house a single bell. Really there is little of interest here but what there is, I suppose, is worth a visit. The church dates from the 14th c. and the interesting plain octagonal font is coeval with the church. Around the base are the figures of eight saints. For some reason the chancel is barred to visitors by a large pair of iron gates which are well padlocked. Above the south porch are the wonderfully preserved Royal Arms of James I. The nave has been stripped of all the benches and individual chairs and tables scattered throughout. I fear that the church is turning into a village hall and although it is a sign of the times it, and the offensive iron gates, somehow unsettles me about this church. Good and bad.

BUXTON   St Andrew   8 m N of Norwich. From
No of Bells: 5   the A140, Norwich to
19th c. Deanery: Ingworth   Aylsham road, turn right to
Hundred: South Erpingham   Stratton Strawless and
Union house: Aylsham   follow 3 miles to Buxton.
21st c. Deanery: Ingworth   O.S. grid ref: TG 234227
Benefice: Bure Valley   Post Code: NR10 5JE

Situated slightly to the north of the village it serves, this well maintained church was built in the 14th c., probably on the site of an earlier church. The porch has been built at an angle to face the churchyard gate. Despite the three useless quatrefoil windows, the interior is bright. The chancel may be the oldest part of the church, having a 13th c. piscina and sedilia beneath four arches. Two columns forming the centre sedile are detached. I believe the undecorated octagonal font is of the same period. The tower arch has been glazed to good effect. A combination hand and horse-drawn bier stands, minus one shaft, at the west end of the nave. Traces of colour remain on the 16th c. screen, and although unattributed to Queen Victoria by name, the Royal Arms are hers by virtue of the shape of the crown.

BYLAUGH	St Mary the Virgin	6 m NE of Dereham. From
No of Bells:	1	the B1147, north of
19th c. Deanery:	Sparham	Swanton Morley, take the
Hundred:	Eynesford	1st right after crossing the
Union house:	Gressenhall	Wensum, continue 1 mile.
21st c. Deanery:	Sparham	O.S. grid ref: TG 035183
Benefice:	FLEBBS	Post Code: NR20 4QE

The only truly original part of the church is the tower base, which is round and probably 12th c. The embattled octagonal top was added two hundred years later. We cannot blame the Victorians for the restoration, for it was virtually rebuilt in the Norman style during 1809/10. King George III's Royal Arms, new at the time, confirm the date of reconstruction. An octagonal font on a matching shaft has tracery and shields on each facet. Both north and south transepts have fireplaces, and outside the chimney stacks are disguised as turrets. A panelled three-decker pulpit complete with tester is regarded by some as one of the finest in the county. My interest was held by the early iron-bound parish chest and the brasses set into the floor beneath the carpet, in remembrance of Sir John Cursun (1471) and his wife.

CALTHORPE Our Lady & St Margaret   3½ N of Aylsham.

No of Bells: 1
19th c. Deanery: Ingworth
Hundred: South Erpingham
Union house: Aylsham
21st c. Deanery: Inworth
Benefice: Scarrowbeck, Erpingham

From the A140 turn west to
Erpingham and continue
straight for almost 2 miles
through Calthorpe.
O.S. grid ref: TG 181318
Post Code: NR11 7QR

This is not an attractive church by any stretch of the imagination but it does have its charms. Built in the 15th c. it has suffered from poor maintenance and is now a patchwork of flint, brick and cement rendering. It was entirely re-faced in flint cobbles in the early 19th c. The square tower has a plain parapet and wallflowers growing from the stonework. Inside the church is musty and suffering from dampness, especially in the proximity the lovely 15th c. font which has four lions around the base. The lofty font cover is, although quite spectacular is a recent acquisition. A simple arch-braced roof has covered the nave for two centuries. At the west end of the nave a small Sanctus bell window can be seen high in the tower wall. Of special interest is the lovely 'wine-glass' style Jacobean pulpit.

CARBROOKE Sts Peter & Paul ****

No of Bells:	6
19th c. Deanery:	Breckles
Hundred:	Wayland
Union house:	Rockland All Saints
21st c. Deanery:	Breckland
Benefice:	Watton & District

2 m ENE of Watton. From the B1108 turn north on to minor road to Carbrooke 2 miles east of the centre of Watton.

O.S. grid ref: TF 950022

Post Code: IP25 6SW

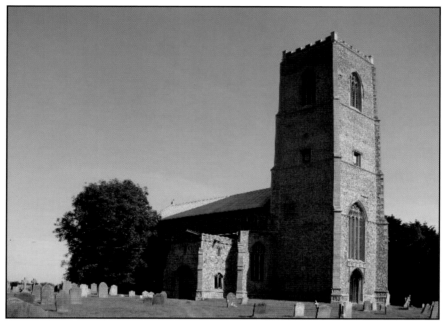

This is a grand 15th c. church: the north porch has a parvise and a south porch as well as a west doorway beneath the lofty tower which is worthy of close examination. A flushwork base course runs all the way around the building. A 14th c. ogee south doorway is also unusual to find. A five window clerestory casts plenty of light onto the arch-braced false hammerbeam nave roof with its angels and carved flowers at each intersection. The 14th c. octagonal font has geometric decoration. The benches all have charming animal carvings on their ends, some of which are renewed. The only piscina is in the chapel of the south aisle and the sedilia in the chancel seats only two. On the altar is a mediaeval stone mensa. Hanoverian Arms and an ancient parish chest are on display and more. All very interesting.

CARLETON FOREHOE St Mary
No of Bells: 1
19th c. Deanery: Hingham
Hundred: Forehoe
Union house: Wicklewood
21st c. Deanery: Dereham & Mitford
Benefice: Barnham Broom Upper Yare

3 m N x W of Wymondham.
Midway between Kimberley
& Barford turn south to
Wymondham. The church is
200 yds set back in a field.
O.S. grid ref: TG 089059
Post Code: NR9 4AL

The tower was built in 1713 in the reign of Queen Anne, with brick dressing on the corners and around the windows. It is surmounted by four large crocketted pinnacles. The Victorians had a field-day here and have left little of the original 15th c. church to see. All the roofs and fittings are mid-to-late 19th c. Over the porch doorway is a sundial which rarely sees the sun. There is absolutely nothing inside to get excited about, which makes me wonder why it is always locked. There is nothing to nick except the visitors book, which is used about once a fortnight. Perhaps if the door were left open a few more visitors might decide it is worthwhile entering, instead of not bothering to go the half-mile to get the key. But an Elizabethan holy table and piscina in the sanctuary do not make it worth the effort.

CARLETON RODE   All Saints

No of Bells: 6
19th c. Deanery: Depwade
Hundred: Depwade
Union house: Pulham
21st c. Deanery: Depwade
Benefice: Pilgrim

2 m ENE of New
Buckenham in Church
Road. From the B1113 take
3rd left. The church is in ¾
of a mile on the right.
O.S. grid ref: TM 114925
Post Code: NR16 1RN

Easily recognisable by the crenellated squat tower and clerestoried nave. The 14th c tower, which partially collapsed after three hundred years, is coeval with the church onto which it fell. There are two mass dials on the south aspect. It is inside however where the interest lies. Ignore the plain font, and make your way past the 14th c. arcades to the screen. Twelve Apostles are represented and the guide book helpfully names each one. They have been well restored (Puritans had scored out the faces). They are probably by the same hand as those at Ranworth. Beyond, in the chancel which is the oldest part of the church, is a fine 14th c. double piscina with a central column beneath trefoil arches set into a larger single arch. In the north aisle is a smaller piscina which still retains its credence shelf.

CASTON	Holy Cross	3 m SE of Watton. Leave
No of Bells:	6	Watton heading east on the
19th c. Deanery:	Breckles	B1108. Then take to B1077
Hundred:	Wayland	and 2nd right into Caston
Union house:	Rockland all Saints	and 4oo yds to the church.
21st c. Deanery:	Breckland	O.S. grid ref: TL 959975
Benefice:	Wayland	Post Code: NR17 1DB

The steep roof indicates that the church was thatched and unlike most has retained its pitch. Over the north porch, now serving as a vestry is a small chamber. Enter the church beneath the fine west window by the door set into the 14th c. tower and you are greeted by a wagon headed roof which still shows traces of its mediaeval colour. The plain 15th c. octagonal font is uninteresting compared with the large bench-end carvings of birds and animals, and two good misericordes with faces below the seat and return stalls, all of the same period. A new base supports the Stuart pulpit and the Royal Arms are also Stuart. In the south wall is a small piscina set into a sedilia. In the chancel is a plain piscina and sedilia and a Stuart holy table. Much glass has been broken, but some remains alongside modern glass.

CAWSTON   St Agnes   *****   4 m WSW of Aylsham. Set
No of Bells: 8 now unstable   just to the south of the
19th c. Deanery: Ingworth   B1145 in the centre of the
Hundred: South Erpingham   village just off Reepham
Union house: Aylsham   Road.
21st c. Deanery: Ingworth   O.S. grid ref: TG 134238
Benefice: Cawston   Post Code: NR10 4AJ

There is much to admire about this lovely church. The tower is early
15th c. and has a fine west window, beneath which is an equally fine
doorway with a wodewose and dragon in the spandrels, above is a
frieze of armorial shields. The wodewose and dragon are repeated on
the piscina. Canopied niches flank the doorway. The double base-
course is exceptionally rare and finely carved. In the porch is a
groined ceiling and there is a parvise above, accessed by turret stairs.
Below the tall crocketted font cover is the 15th c. font and behind that
a western gallery within the base of the tower. Above the clerestoried
nave is a superb hammerbeam roof with many angels peering down.
A quite beautiful screen with sixteen saintly figures and fine carvings
define the chancel. A 15th c. pulpit, an iron-bound chest, and more!

CLEY-next-the Sea   St Margaret *****   7 m W of Sheringham.

No of Bells: 1

19th c. Deanery: Holt

Hundred: Holt

Union house: Erpingham

21st c. Deanery: Holt

Benefice: Glaven Valley (Blakeney)

From the A149, coast road, turn south into Cley. The church is easily found on the left, behind The Green.

O.S. grid ref: TG 048432

Post Code: NR25 7TT

Pronounced Kly! The early 15th c. tower stands NW of the nave, allowing for a huge west window. The splendid coeval south porch has canopied niches and a large parvise and a pierced tracery parapet. Attached to the tower is a restored Galilee porch with a multi-cusped arch over the doorway. The spacious nave has 14th c. arcades with octagonal pillars. Cinquefoil and arch windows alternate in the lovely clerestory. The pulpit is Stuart as are the remains of the Royal Arms. In the chancel six misericordes and dropped sill sedilia for the congregation. Good brasses are under carpets, a particularly nice one to John Symondes (1511) and Agnes his wife and eight children. So much to see here and everything is interesting and well worth seeing. The ruinous south transept has glorious tracery in the east window.

COLBY St Giles

No of Bells: 1

19th c. Deanery: Ingworth

Hundred: South Erpingham

Union house: Aylsham

21st c. Deanery: Waxham & Tunstead

Benefice: King's Beck

3 m NNE of Aylsham.
From the A140 turn right
for 1 mile at the crossroads
with Erpingham on the left.
Take the 1st right, 2nd left.
O.S. grid ref: TG 220312
Post Code: NR11 7EE

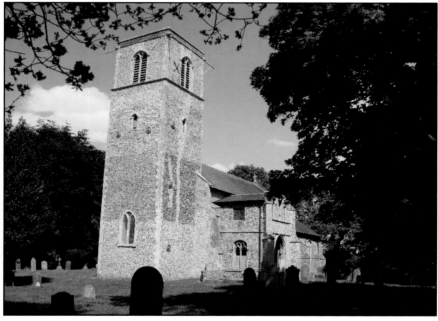

Almost hidden from the road, this church has suffered at some time from neglect, thankfully no longer. The plain topped tower is 13th c. and has been recently repaired. The porch is 15th c. and coeval with the building of the church. Above the doorway each side are the parvise windows; centrally is a stooled and canopied niche devoid of an occupant. Inside the nave at the west end is the octagonal 15th c. font bearing Evangelistic emblems and other carved decorations; beneath the bowl is a carved corona and buttressed shaft. In the chancel is the piscina paired with a sedile beneath ogee arches. Two further double dropped-sill sedilia are adjacent. Behind the altar is the 17th c. reredos flanked by Moses and Aaron, originally, it is understood, from Gunton. Memorials to Ashwood, Walsh and Sadler.

COLNEY	St Andrew	3 m W of Norwich In Old
No of Bells:	2	Watton Road, Colney. From
19th c. Deanery:	Humbleyard	the B1108 opposite the N & N
Hundred:	Humbleyard	Hospital entrance, 200 yds
Union house:	Swainsthorpe	towards Norwich then turn left.
21st c. Deanery:	Humbleyard	O.S. grid ref: TG 181080
Benefice:	Cringleford	Post Code: NR4 7TX

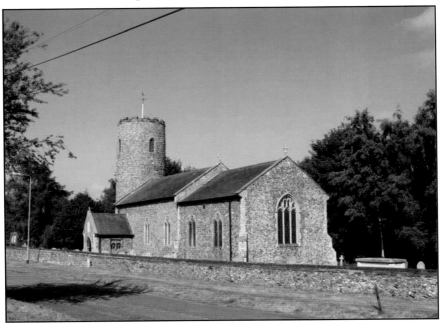

Colney has one of the few remaining Saxon round towers which were probably originally used as defendable lookouts or watch-towers. Once there were double splayed windows, but these have been blocked up. This church was built against the tower in the 14th c. possibly on the site of a Norman church. A simple south porch was added a century later. Appearing quite pristine is the 15th c. font which has Evangelistic emblems and foliage on the corona of the octagonal bowl. The wagon-style roof is modern with crown posts. At the east of the nave is a wall monument to Richard Browne (1674). Much earlier is a chalice brass to a past Rector, Henry Alikok 1507. Set into the wall of the chancel is a tomb beneath which is interred the body of John Tomson Jentilma ((sic) = *gentleman*) (1575).

COLTON St Andrew

No of Bells: 3

19th c. Deanery: Hingham

Hundred: Forehoe

Union house: Wicklewood

21st c. Deanery: Dereham & Mitford

Benefice: Easton

8 m W of Norwich. South of the village turn right and follow road for ½ mile, the church is clearly seen on your left.

O.S. grid ref: TG 104094

Post Code: NR9 5DE

Built in the 13th c. the well proportioned embattled tower still retains its original Y tracery windows. The rest of the church is early 14th c. and it is very apparent that the chancel is much narrower than the nave and probably built sometime beforehand. The windows are all of the Decorated period with curvilinear tracery. Entered by the attractive north porch the visitor is met by the 14th c. octagonal font with crisp quatrefoil designs around the bowl and therefore not mutilated by the Puritans. West of the font is the organ gallery; adjacent to it is a faded wall painting of 'The Gossips', two women with a devil above their heads. The screen has unusual wheel tracery and dates back to the 15th c. One of the bench ends is worthy of close examination, depicting two horses. The Royal Arms are of George III, after 1816.

CORPUSTY St Peter

No of Bells: 1
19th c. Deanery: Ingworth
Hundred: South Erpingham
Union house: Aylsham
21st c. Deanery: -
Friends of Friendless Churches.

5 m WNW of Aylsham.
The church stands on the
top of a hill just south of
the village on the B1149
very near a lay-by.
O.S. grid ref: TG 115295
Post Code: S of NR11 6QE

I don't believe I have ever felt so emotional about a redundant church. It is pitiful to see a church in this state with corrugated iron sheets blocking the windows. I was unable to gain access so I have to rely on information from other sources. The church was built in the 15th c. but like most other churches was restored in the Victorian era. It was made redundant in 1974; the result is the pathetic site we see today. It stands in a prominent position on the top of a hill and would make a fine home for some wealthy businessman. I do not know whether or not the following items are still in the church. A 15th c. font was recorded by Cautley in 1949, along with a simple square headed screen of the same period, and an altar rail dating back to the 17th c. were object of interest on his brief list.

COSTESSEY   St Edmund
No of Bells: 5
19th c. Deanery: Hingham
Hundred: Forehoe
Union house: Wicklewood
21st c. Deanery: Norwich South
Benefice: Costessey

4 m W of Norwich south of the A1067 Drayton Road. Signposted 'Costessey'. The church is in 'The Street' on the right.
O.S. grid ref: TG 177125
Post Code: NR8 5DG

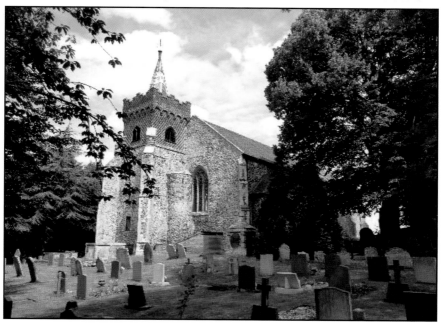

Pronounced Cossy! The 14th c. tower has a circular turret to the belfry and a spire atop the 1800 belfry stage. There is a scratch dial on a south buttress. The 15th c. octagonal font has shields with billet decoration around the top and bottom of the bowl, which in turn is supported on a central shaft with engaged columns. The 15th c. screen is from Booton St Michael: it has fine tracery and end brackets which were designed to support the rood loft; the original rood beam is still in place. You will, if you look carefully, find a 'green man' carved into the screen. Above is a modern arch-braced roof. Standing on a stone base is the Jacobean pulpit, the panels are also from Booton. The benches are Victorian and have decorative poppy-head ends. The names Jernegan and Waldergrave feature on monuments.

COSTON St Michael & All Angels
No of Bells: 1
19th c. Deanery: Hingham
Hundred: Forehoe
Union house: Wicklewood
21st c. Deanery: -
The Churches Conservation Trust

4 m NW of Wymondham.
From Norwich take the B1108
west towards Hingham. Turn
onto B1135 at Kimberley and
keep straight on over x-roads
O.S. grid ref: TG 062063
Post Code: NR9 4DT

Virtually unchanged since the 13th c. when it was built, this lovely
little church survives as witness to the past. Almost unmolested by
Victorian hands it still has much charm. The tower is 13th c. from the
ground up, but the parapet is a later addition. A string course
circumnavigates the whole building. The apex of the old thatched
roof which reached almost to the belfry window is easily apparent;
this much lower profile was the work of the Victorians who probably
saved the church from ruination. A small brick porch clings to the
south wall protecting the doorway. The rood stairs are still open. A
plain octagonal font, a few old benches and a Jacobean pulpit are all
that is left in the way of furnishings, leaving a rather sterile space.
Three small corbels are embedded into the east wall. Shelf brackets?!

CRANWORTH   St Mary

No of Bells: 3
19th c. Deanery: Hingham
Hundred: Mitford
Union house: Gressenhall
21st c. Deanery: Dereham & Mitford
Benefice: Reymerston

5 m NE of Watton. From the A1075 at Shipdham turn south at Shipdham church. Continue 2½ miles to Cranworth.
O.S. grid ref: TF 983044
Post Code: IP25 7SH

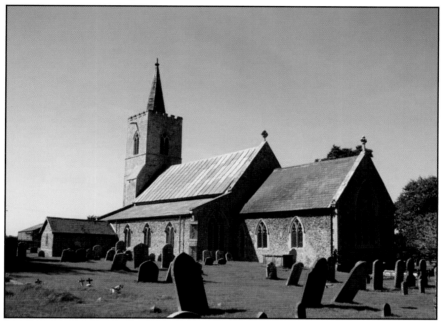

Cranworth church was built in the 14th c. The tower has a well proportioned leaded spire. Entry is via the north door; a vestry added in 1921 occupies the south door. The tracery in the windows is quite different, with more use of mouchettes and quatrefoils. The 14th c. font is octagonal and plain. The arcades are coeval with the building of the church, as is the lovely double piscina and triple arched graduated sedilia. The colourful Victorian stone reredos deliberately complements the design. Most of the furnishings and fittings are 19th c., including the wine-glass pulpit. Memorials to various members of the Gurdon family adorn the walls and are themselves enhanced with many painted family crests. A fine collection of eleven family crests has also been incorporated into the design of the east window.

CRINGLEFORD   St Peter

No of Bells:	3	
19th c. Deanery:	Humbleyard	
Hundred:	Humbleyard	
Union house:	Swainsthorpe	
21st c. Deanery:	Humbleyard	
Benefice:	Cringleford	

2½ SW from Norwich. In Newmarket Road, turn off just before the dual carriageway and follow the road into Cringleford.
O.S. grid ref: TG 198058
Post Code: NR4 6UE

Parts of the church date back to the Saxon period as can be seen from the small windows which have splays inside and out. In the 15th c. the Norman north aisle was demolished and a south aisle was added during the Victorian 'restoration' period. Much of the character and interest of the building was removed at the same time and has left the church rather sterile. The octagonal font which stands on a plinth in the form of a Maltese cross has survived the ravages of time (and Victorians) and has good carvings of foliates around the bowl, which is complemented by smaller examples on the panelled shaft. In the chancel the simple piscina surprisingly retains its original credence shelf. A redundant squint from the demolished north aisle is another surprising survivor of the ancient history of this old church.

CROWNTHORPE St James

No of Bells: 1 removed
19th c. Deanery: Hingham
Hundred: Forehoe
Union house: Wicklewood
21st c. Deanery: Humbleyard
A Private Residence

2 m NW of Wymondham.
Just off the B1135. From
Kimberley to Wymondham
road. Turn right 300 yds
after the railway bridge.
O.S. grid ref: TG 083031
Post Code: NR18 9EU

Now a private residence, so do not expect to see inside. Nothing remains of the original fittings or furnishings. The owner will be pleased to allow you to look round the outside, but please ask first. Anciently a chapel of ease for Wymondham, it was made redundant in the 1970s together with many others in the county, having stood ruinous for many years. Cautley tells us that there is no chancel arch and that there was a plain 16th c. hexagonal font. The pulpit once had Flemish carved panels depicting the Ascension, the Samarian woman at the well and the Sermon on the Mount. The present whereabouts of these items is unknown to me. A 13th c. double arched twin piscina was also recorded. In the external walls are signs of north and south transepts but they were demolished centuries ago.

DEOPHAM St Andrew

No of Bells: 5 (to be re-hung)

19th c. Deanery: Hingham

Hundred: Forehoe

Union house: Wicklewood

21st c. Deanery: Humbleyard

Benefice: High Oak & Hingham

4 miles W of Wymondham. From the B1108 at Hackford follow the signposts to Deopham. Church is in Vicarage Road.

O.S. grid ref: TG 050005

Post Code: NR18 9DT

This is a grand church which indicates that the parish was at one time very wealthy. Now, sadly, the five bells have had to be removed from the belfry and are awaiting the financial resources to re-hang them. The 15th c. tower itself is unusual in that it has pedimented gables on each face of the parapet and octagonal turrets on each corner. Inside the nave, entered through 600-year-old doors, much of the richness has disappeared over the years leaving us to imagine the red, green and gold leaf decoration that used to adorn the screen and reredos. Corbels hang below the wall-posts from which the roof was supported before the clerestory was added. Also the piscinæ to be seen here are quite exceptionally decorated. This is a very interesting church and is well worth a visit if you can find a keyholder at home.

DICKLEBURGH   All Saints

No of Bells:	6
19th c. Deanery:	Redenhall
Hundred:	Diss
Union house:	Pulham
21st c. Deanery:	Redenhall
Benefice:	Dickleburgh & the Pulhams

5 m NE of Diss. Turn off the A140, at the sign for Dickleburgh and you will find the church on the west side of The Street.

O.S. grid ref: TM 167824
Post Code: IP21 4NR

This is quite a large church and has some interesting points to view. On the east wall are two unusual stooled niches each side of the window. The south porch, for instance, has good flush-work and three niches, one of which has a tracery canopy, all sadly lacking their saints. Inside the spacious nave most of the roof is Victorian but that near the chancel is much older. A traditional East Anglian font with wodewoses around the shaft, stands on an octagonal base. Behind the lovely carved 17th c. pulpit are the redundant stairs to the rood loft. There are two piscinæ, both with cinquefoil arches, one in south aisle the other in the chancel, the former more elaborate, having a pinnacle. A good selection of quite impressive monuments, the one to Dame Frances Platers (1659) is the most elaborate. Royal Arms of Charles I.

DISS	St Mary	22 m SSW of Norwich. In
No of Bells:	8	the centre of Diss, close to
19th c. Deanery:	Redenhall	the shopping centre.
Hundred:	Diss	Parking can be found but is
Union house:	Pulham	not always available.
21st c. Deanery:	Redenhall	O.S. grid ref: TM 117800
Benefice:	Diss	Post Code: IP22 4QS

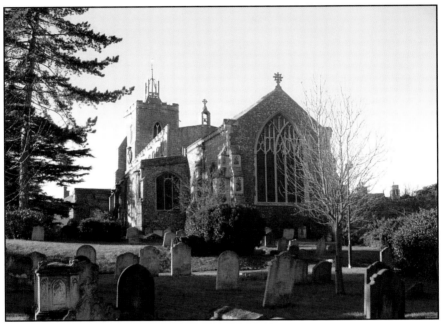

The early 14th c. tower of Diss church with its processional arches is almost insignificant in comparison with the extravagant Victorian chancel. However, the nave holds the interest here. Grotesques and niches on the buttresses add to the charm of the exterior. Inside the nave everything is crisp and clinical. The 15th c. octagonal font is simply decorated with quatrefoils and carries a good font cover of no great age. The chancel arch is dated circa 1300 and some other parts of the church can be similarly dated such as the doorways. There is an arch-braced roof with cambered tie-beams above the ten-window clerestory of the nave, but the interior on the whole is quite austere and holds little of great interest. The beauty of this church lies on the outside in my opinion, but do have a look inside while you are there.

DRAYTON St Margaret

No of Bells: 6

19th c. Deanery: Taverham

Hundred: Taverham

Union house: Horsham St Faith

21st c. Deanery: Norwich North

Benefice: Drayton

4 m NW of Norwich, in School Road, Drayton. From the A1067, NW out of Norwich, turn right towards Thorpe Marriot.

O.S. grid ref: TG 180138

Post Code: NR8 6PP

The church with its thatched nave and un-buttressed tower is almost hidden behind the trees on the village green. If it is locked the key-holder is not far away. The church is entered by a simple small south porch; the visitor is immediately greeted by a plain font which stands on Norman shafts, but I believe the octagonal bowl to be a little later. There is a wide north aisle incorporating the vestry which extends to the west wall of the tower. The arch-braced roof of the nave and that of the aisle are quite recent. Adjacent to the Victorian pulpit are stairs which may have led to an external turret to allow access to the rood loft before the north aisle was added. In the chancel is a restored 13th c. trefoil piscina which is adjacent to a dropped-sill sedilia, just large enough for three. A pleasant, peaceful and well used church.

DUNSTON St Remigius 4 m S of Norwich. Turn left
No of Bells: 3 off the A140 just after the
19th c. Deanery: Humbleyard railway bridge and follow
Hundred: Humbleyard ½ mile. Turn off on right
Union house: Swainsthorpe up an unmade trackway.
21st c. Deanery: Loddon O.S. grid ref: TG 228023
Benefice: Venta Post Code: NR14 8AB

If you want to have a look around in Dunston church you will need to make an appointment to obtain the key from the Rectory and leave your name and address. The church is remote and that may be why. Architecturally interesting from the outside. Disappointingly, most of what is inside is Victorian and is of little interest for the historian or architectural student. The 15th c. traditional font is no different from any other, the pulpit is uninteresting and the roofs are plain and boring. Victorian poppy-head decorations on the bench-ends do little to improve the situation. The only compensation is the square-headed screen which has some original colour and ogee tracery decoration. The centre section has interesting spandrels with depictions of a wodewose one side and a dragon scrapping with a lion on the other.

EARLHAM	St Mary	2½ m from Norwich city
No of Bells:	1	centre on the B1108 to
19th c. Deanery:	Norwich	Colney. There is a lay-by
Hundred:	Norwich	opposite Earlham Park. The
Union house:	Norwich	church gate is in the lay-by.
21st c. Deanery:	Norwich South	O.S. grid ref: TG 190083
Benefice:	Earlham	Post Code: NR5 8BL

Earlham is one of the nine hamlets of Norwich and was supported as such by the city. Basically the church is a small 14th c. one with modifications and restructuring over the centuries. The brick crow-stepped gabled porch has a tiny parvise above and matching brickwork on the crenellated parapet of the flint tower. Quatrefoils decorate the octagonal bowl of the 14th c. font. Stairs which once led to the rood loft are still open, the screen that remains is well traceried and dates from the 15th c. The lectern is a carved wooden statuette of, I believe, a musician or choirboy. A nice cusped piscina and carved wood reredos are in the sanctuary. Interestingly, a wall monument to his siblings was brought here from St Giles in Middlesex by Waller Bacon to be near where their parents lie buried in the vault.

EAST CARLETON   St Mary

No of Bells: 1
19th c. Deanery: Humbleyard
Hundred: Humbleyard
Union house: Swainsthorpe
21st c. Deanery: Humbleyard
Benefice: Swardeston

5 m SW of Norwich on the B1113.Turn right ¾ south of Swardeston and continue 1 mile. The church is on the right but easily missed.
O.S. grid ref: TG 180021
Post Code: NR14 8HT

Situated opposite Nursery Cottage. To the right of the church is the old churchyard in which can be found the remains of East Carleton St Peter's church. A short wall is now all that remains of this church, which was demolished in the mid 16th c. St Mary's church was possibly rebuilt about the same time, using materials from the former. It has a continuous roof-line, which indicates that no chancel arch exists. However, most of what is to be seen here today is 19th c. re-build, including the tower. Off the chancel is a north transept containing the organ. The font is probably Victorian with shield shapes around the otherwise plain octagonal bowl. The piscina as it used to be has been converted to a simple plain niche, a similar fate to the sedilia. Unfortunately there is little of interest to the historian.

EAST DEREHAM   St Nicholas

No of Bells:	8 in the bell tower *
19th c. Deanery:	Hingham
Hundred:	Mitford
Union house:	Gressenhall
21st c. Deanery:	Dereham & Mitford
Benefice:	Dereham & District

16 m W x N of Norwich and north of the A47. Head into the town centre via the A1075 and St Withberga's Lane.

O.S. grid ref: TF 989133
Post Code: NR19 1ED

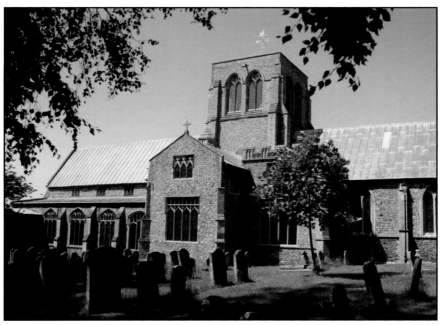

Saint Withberga's well is a few feet west of the church. She died here in 655. Her remains were stolen by the Ecclesiasts at Ely cathedral. I think it is about time they were returned. This is a splendid cruciform church, full of history, and usually open. The lovely Seven Sacrament 15th c. font still has some of the original paint, as do the ceilings of the 15th c. transepts. There was obviously a church here before the present building as the chancel is 13th c. and has a fine trefoil arched double piscina with a central column and graduated sedilia. Unfortunately the base of the 15th c. screen has suffered from terrible restoration of the paintings. A chest in the south aisle originally came from Flanders. A few yards away is the 16th c. *The nearby bell tower has eight bells, the church tower has only a Sanctus bell.

EAST HARLING Sts Peter & Paul *****

No of Bells: 8

19th c. Deanery: Rockland

Hundred: Guiltcross

Union house: Kenninghall

21st c. Deanery: Thetford & Rockland

Benefice: Harling

8 miles ENE of Thetford. South of the A11 take the B1111, beside which is the church 2½ m on the left.

O.S. grid ref: TL 990867

Post Code: NR16 2NA

This is a very interesting church. As well as its external appearance the interior holds many delights for the church crawler. Above the tower are crocketted flying buttresses supporting the leaded spirelet. On the central merlon of each face is a statuette of a saint. Entry is by the 15th c. south porch and 14th c. doorway, coeval with the rest of the building. Above the lofty arcades are a clerestory and a beautiful hammer-beam roof. The once magnificent rood screen still has many carvings. The Herling or Harling family obviously feature greatly here; the family bull and unicorn are depicted in the tracery of the south aisle. There are fine tombs of Sir Thomas Lovell (1551) another to Anne his daughter. The earliest is the Chamberlain tomb of 1462. There is much more to see here and is well worth a visit.

EAST RUNTON   Holy Trinity

No of Bells:	0	
19th c. Deanery	Repps	
Hundred:	North Erpingham	
Union house:	Sheringham	
21st c. Deanery:	Repps	
Benefice:	Aylmerton	

1 m W of Cromer turn left into Felbrigg Road, past & opposite Beach Road the church is on the right just before the railway bridge.
O.S. grid ref: TG 197426
Post Code: NR27 9PQ

East Runton has historically, never had a parish church. When the Victorian school (built in 1854) was made redundant in 1959, the local PCC purchased it for £500 and used the main hall as a church room. However, costs were high and it was decided in the 1960s to utilise what was once the infant school-room instead. The apsidal end was added as a chancel in the 1980s to alleviate the cramped conditions and to make it more church-like. In 2004 a new entrance porch and toilets were incorporated into the building at the southern end. Inside, the walls and ceiling are painted white throughout. The sparsely decorated room which is the nave has comfortable modern chairs. It is obviously well used and much cared for. The old school is the building now behind the church with the bell turret.

EAST TUDDENHAM All Saints

No of Bells:	2	
19th c. Deanery	Hingham	
Hundred:	Mitford	
Union house:	Gressenhall	
21st c. Deanery:	Dereham & Mitford	
Benefice:	Mattishall	

9 m W of Norwich. From the A47 turn left 3 miles after dual carriageway ends and follow ¾ m. Turn left and church is on the left.
O.S. grid ref: TG 085115
Post Code: NR20 3NB

The tower has a 13th c. base and is 15th c. above. Above the entrance of the porch are the words 'GLORIA TIBI TR' *(Glory to thee O Trinity),* the Annunciation is depicted in the spandrils. Above the porch is a small parvise. The lovely south doorway with engaged columns is late 12th c., as is the circular font which is, curiously, decorated with foliage. Nearby in the corner, is a stone effigy of a 13th c. knight who holds his heart in his hands. The Victorian restoration of 1876 removed many of the old benches and poppyheads. Two notable 19th c. poppy-heads can be seen: a man 'mooning' above two shocked faces, and a green man. In the sanctuary is a corner piscina with a square label opening into a dropped-sill sedilia. The Royal Arms are without doubt those of Charles I (1625-1649).

EAST WRETHAM   St Ethelbert   6 m NNE of Thetford.
No of Bells: 1   Leave Thetford on the
19th c. Deanery   Rockland   A1075 & turn left for ¾
Hundred: Shropham   mile after Wretham Camp
Union house: Thetford St Mary's   and before Stonebridge.
21st c. Deanery: Thetford & Rockland   O.S. grid ref: TL 915906
Benefice: Thetford   Post Code: IP24 1RJ

Unmistakable by the strange pseudo Norman top of the tower, this church was built in 1865 by Wyrley Birch and designed by George Street. Another example of his work can be seen at Roydon All Saints near Kings Lynn. The only part of the original church is the Norman south doorway which has three orders of decoration and engaged columns. There is nothing of any great age to be seen here. The octagonal font with tracery decoration has a tall coeval tabernacled and crocketted cover. Depicted in the eight niches are twelve saints, some rarely encountered. Scissor beams span the roof of the nave which is plastered; a boarded wagon roof in the chancel is varnished. A corner piscina with a pointed arch adjoins a dropped-sill sedilia. The traditional style pulpit with tracery panels stands on a stone base.

EASTON	St Peter	6 m W of Norwich off the
No of Bells:	1, above the porch	A47. At the first round-
19th c. Deanery	Hingham	about past the Norfolk
Hundred:	Forehoe	Showground take first exit
Union house:	Wicklewood	and immediate right.
21st c. Deanery:	Dereham & Mitford	O.S. grid ref: TG 130110
Benefice:	Easton	Post Code: NR9 5EP

The tower fell in 1771 and a bellcote was added in 1848 but has since disappeared. Some interesting flush-work can be found and inside the porch is a rare doorway. Built in the period of transition from Norman to Early English and quite elaborately and unusually decorated. In the nave, an arch of the same style can be seen almost hidden by a horrible modern staircase which leads to a gallery. Strangely, too, the clerestory only has windows on the north side and no sign of there ever having been any on the south. The roof is simply arch-braced with floral bosses. Shallow arcading on the otherwise plain octagonal font bowl supported by a central shaft and eight columns indicates a 13th c. date. In the chancel is a plain piscina and a graduated sedilia. Lying on the floor is what I think may be an old stoup.

ECCLES St Peter
No of Bells: 3
19th c. Deanery Rockland
Hundred: Shropham
Union house: Kenninghall
21st c. Deanery: Rockland
Benefice: Quidenham

5 m SSW of Attleborough. Take Hargham Road out of Attleborough and follow for 5 miles. Turn right ½ m past Eccles railway Station. O.S. grid ref: TM 019893
Post Code: NR16 2PA

Do not confuse this parish with Eccles-by-the-Sea. The round Norman tower has a later crenellated upper storey. The appearance of the semi-circular windows in the nave is simply explained once inside; the lower part of the old 14th c. arcade which once formed the south aisle was only partially filled and the upper part transformed into windows. Between the north and south door which, incidentally, is also set into one of the arcade arches, is the 14th c. plain octagonal font. The roofs, seating and other furnishings are Victorian but in the chancel is a double piscina and, most unusual, is the mensa almost ten feet in length supported on eight columnar legs. It was recovered from the graveyard in the 1940s having been discarded, probably by Victorian restorers or perhaps earlier, by Puritans.

EDGEFIELD Sts Peter & Paul
No of Bells: 4, now removed
19th c. Deanery Holt
Hundred: Holt
Union house: West Beckham
21st c. Deanery: -
Benefice: -

3 m S of Holt. From Holt take the B1149 and bear right after Edgefield Hall, then take the next left. Park near the old farmyard gate.
O.S. grid ref: TG 085348
Post Code: NR24 2AE

The 14th c. tower of the abandoned Edgefield church is an irregular octagon from top to bottom, one of only a few in the county. The church was abandoned in 1883 and a new church built nearer to the more densely inhabited part of the parish. Most of the materials were moved by horse and cart to the new site about ¾ of a mile away (*see next page*). Although this ruin is very overgrown with trees in the nave, it is still possible to see the 14th c. north and 15th c. south arcades in the new church as they were rebuilt there exactly as they originally stood in this old one. The screen and font were salvaged too and can also be viewed in the new church. Some of the old walls remain and it is not difficult to make out the footprint of the old building.

EDGEFIELD   Sts Peter & Paul

No of Bells: 1
19th c. Deanery   Holt
Hundred: Holt
Union house: West Beckham
21st c. Deanery: Ingworth
Benefice: Seven Churches Itteringham

3½ m S of Holt. Leave
Holt on the B1149 and
once in the village proper
bear right & right again
into Church Road.
O.S. grid ref: TG 093343
Post Code: NR24 2AF

There is far more here than came from the old church. A fine five window clerestory and south aisle almost gives it the appearance of a warehouse from the south. From the north less so, but having the tower at the north-eastern corner it still looks wrong. It was built in 1883, as explained on the previous page, in the style of the 15th c. Much of that which is to be seen here however is recycled 13th to 15th c. A Norman font, beautifully simplistic with very shallow arcading, supported on eight new columns; the 14th c. represented by the north arcade, the 15th c. by the south arcade and the lovely screen, which still has the original artwork carefully preserved, even though it was mutilated by the Puritans. The early piscina has been re-installed and a sedilia beneath a simple arch. A 'new' church with unusual history.

ELSING	St Mary	****	5 m ENE of Dereham.
No of Bells:	5		Midway between North
19th c. Deanery	Sparham		Tuddenham on the A47 &
Hundred:	Eynesford		Bawdeswell on the A1067.
Union house:	Gressenhall		Many avenues of approach.
21st c. Deanery:	Sparham		O.S. grid ref: TG 052166
Benefice:	FLEBBS		Post Code: NR20 3EA

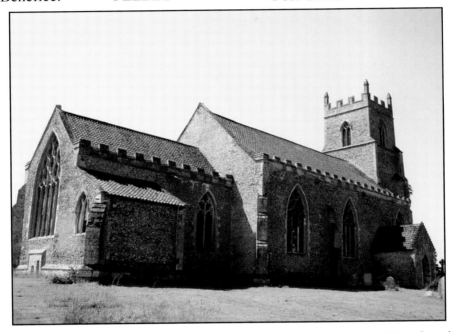

What a splendid church this is! Well proportioned and with a lovely crenellated parapet around both nave and chancel. Dating from the 14th c. it has been re-roofed and stripped of all the old benches. The lovely coeval font with a deep base rests on a single short shaft. Sitting upon it is the finest tabernacled 14th c. font cover in Norfolk, partially and lovingly restored. In the chancel are four matching arches; beneath the lesser is a piscina and beneath each of the others is a sedile. The visitor cannot have missed, by this time, the case situated in the centre of the chancel with a copy of the brass of Sir Hugh Hastyngs (1347), founder of the church. It is of national importance and good to see it on display. The Royal Arms are attributed to George III dated 1794, but the Arms are post-1801 with the Electoral Bonnet.

ERPINGHAM St Mary the Virgin

No of Bells:	2
19th c. Deanery	Ingworth
Hundred:	South Erpingham
Union house:	Aylsham
21st c. Deanery:	Ingworth
Benefice:	Scarrowbeck

3 m N of Aylsham.
Leaving Aylsham on the
A140, in 2 miles turn left at
the x-roads, then left again
in about 400 yds.
O.S. grid ref: TG 198313
Post Code: NR11 6PL

The 15th c. tower is worthy of closer inspection. Around the base is a string of armorial shields and above on the parapet more can be seen as well as the crowned M of the BVM. Note the layering of the cobbles and compare it with those on the rubble-built porch. Originally from St Benedict's in Norwich, the 15th c. font has good carvings which are explained in the comprehensive guide. The nave arcade dates from at least 100 years earlier. An iron-bound 15th c. chest is nearby, and leaning against the south wall are statues of the Four Latin Doctors which were at one time pinnacles on the tower. At the east end of the south aisle is a piscina and double sedilia. In the chancel is a corner piscina and triple sedilia. A goblet-style pulpit and the portrait of King Charles are other items of interest here.

FELBRIGG	St Margaret	3 m SSW of Cromer in the
No of Bells:	1	grounds of Felbrigg Hall.
19th c. Deanery	Repps	Go to the Hall and park and
Hundred:	North Erpingham	walk to the church.
Union house:	Sharingham	There is a parking fee.
21st c. Deanery:	Repps	O.S. grid ref: TG 198391
Benefice:	Roughton	Post Code: NR 11 8PR

This is one of the few churches that you have to pay to visit although it is only a parking fee. Built in the 14th c., probably financed by the Felbrygge family, it is not therefore surprising that their names are on monuments and brasses galore, dating from the mid-part of that century. An early brass to Sir Simon de Felbrygge (1416) is one of only eight known to a Knight of the Garter. Other names mentioned on memorials are Ketton-Cremers and Windhams, all of the same stock. The octagonal font supported on a broad shaft is 14th c. as is the piscina in the chancel. The nave is lined with painted box-pews, which insinuates inequality, quite honestly they look very out of place in such lovely surroundings. The Royal Arms are of George III. A very interesting church although overwhelmed by competing monuments.

FELTHORPE St Margaret

No of Bells: 1

19th c. Deanery Taverham

Hundred: Taverham

Union house: Horsham St Faith's

21st c. Deanery: Norwich North

Benefice: Horsford

7 m NW of Norwich off the B1149. Turn right at the x-roads after Horsford woods, 2nd left and bear right, near Church Farm, Felthorpe.

O.S. grid ref: TG 163179

Post Code: NR10 4EA

Although the church may look ancient and perhaps mediaeval, it is not. Most of it is from 1846 when among other rebuilding works a south aisle was added, all at the expense of a Mrs Fellows. Other adornments such as the stumpy pinnacles on the tower were added and the whole building was re-roofed and re-glazed. 'Modern' seating was installed and all the lovely old pews were destroyed. Parts of the church still date back to the 14th c., however, and the piscina in the chancel is witness to the fact. There is sadly very little here of historical or architectural interest; and the church is always locked with the nearest keyholder about twenty minutes walk or more away. Not very encouraging or welcoming to the occasional visitor! I suppose the PCC will have the usual excuses about vandalism and theft if asked.

FERSFIELD   St Andrew ****   4½ m WNW of Diss. From

No of Bells:	1	the A1066 turn off to
19th c. Deanery	Redenhall	Fersfield east of South
Hundred:	Diss	Lopham and continue 1½
Union house:	Kenninghall	miles to destination on left.
21st c. Deanery:	Redenhall	O.S. grid ref: TM 065828
Benefice:	Upper Waveney	Post Code: IP22 2BL

A strange-looking and curious church by all accounts! The slender tower with its pyramidal cap adds to its charm. Parts of the building are Norman but later rebuilding has obliterated much of the evidence. Removed from its original resting place, in the arched recess tomb nearby is the glass-encased coloured wooden effigy of Sir Robert de Bois (1311). A second recess has a female figure, carved in stone, said to be Amicia, his mother. Above the lancet-like tower arch is a small Sanctus bell window, and cut into the chancel arch is a cross-shaped squint. The square Norman font with chamfered corners and rope-work carved around the rim of the bowl is quite different although it sits on a later shaft. Royal Arms are of Queen Anne, dated 1703, before the union with Scotland when the fleurs de lys were removed.

FIELD DALLING   St Andrew

No of Bells:	5
19th c. Deanery	Holt
Hundred:	North Greenhoe
Union house:	Great Snoring
21st c. Deanery:	Holt
Benefice:	Stiffkey & Bale

5 m W of Holt. From the A148 west of Holt, go north via Saxlingham or Bale to the village centre and the church.

O.S. grid ref: TG 006390
Post Code: NR25 7LG

The dominating tower is 14th c. and for some reason slightly out of alignment with the nave. Alterations to the nave a century later created a grand north arcade and aisle with traceried spandrils to the arch-braced roof. Box pews are currently utilised as a storage area and contain an old chest among other detritus. A lovely old bier stands nearby. Beneath the similar style roof of the nave (with Tudor bosses at the intersections) old benches with poppy-heads provide the seating. At the west end is the 15th c. font with emblems of the Passion and Sts James and Andrew. Beyond the tall chancel arch is a simple piscina and dropped-sill sedilia. The pre-1801 Hanoverian Royal Arms, seem to have been painted on a hatchment and lack the Crown of Charlemagne. Good 15th c. glass and a brass dated 1485.

FLORDON   St Michael & All Angels

No of Bells:	1	
19th c. Deanery	Humbleyard	
Hundred:	Humbleyard	
Union house:	Swainsthorpe	
21st c. Deanery:	Humbleyard	
Benefice:	Mulbarton	

7½ m S of Norwich. Best accessed via the A 140 turning west at Newton Flotman. In Flordon take the Mulbarton Rd.
O.S. grid ref: TM 189972
Post Code: NR15 1RP

Set back off the road between houses up an unmade track you will find this modest little church at the edge of a green. It was once the proud possessor of a round Norman tower which fell and was never re-built. Instead a small turret was erected, and the four bells sold to Tasburgh church. The scruffy appearance of the exterior is deceptive and the 700 year-old porch almost blocks an earlier double-recessed lancet window (it is charming). Even the door knocker is 13th c. A late Norman or early English plain octagonal font stands at the west end of the nave. In the walls are the signs that early low windows and seating have been replaced. Above the chancel arch hang the Hanoverian Royal Arms. Unhappily, the ancient beauty of the church is somewhat marred by modern benches, but that's progress!

FORNCETT END　　St Edmund

No of Bells:	1
19th c. Deanery	Depwade
Hundred:	Depwade
Union house:	Pulham St Mary
21st c. Deanery:	Humbleyard
Benefice:	Upper Tas Valley

11 m SSW of Norwich. On the B1113 travelling in a southerly direction, turn left immediately south of the village. Church on the right. O.S. grid ref: TM 140938 Post Code: NR16 1LE

The foundation stone was laid on St Peter's Day 1904 making this an Edwardian church. Built entirely of brick and tile it was never finished as can be seen from the photograph taken from the southeast, where shiplap boarding fills the gap where the chancel should have been built. Above the porch is the single bell turret and inside the nave is the most elaborately carved octagonal font I have ever seen. Around the rim are human and animal faces, with a wolf and a king; most seem to be pertaining to the legend of St Edmund. Below is deep-cut tracery and below that another rim of animal faces. As one would expect, all the fittings and furnishings are coeval with the building of the church. It is very much a living church and although not mediaeval, it does have its points of interest.

FORNCETT ST MARY St Mary

		11 m SSW of Norwich.
No of Bells:	once 3 now removed	From the B1113 just south
19th c. Deanery	Depwade	of Tacolneston turn east
Hundred:	Depwade	then 2nd right. The church
Union house:	Pulham St Mary	is set well back on the left.
21st c. Deanery:	-	O.S. grid ref: TM 166938
Benefice:	-	Post Code: NR16 1JG

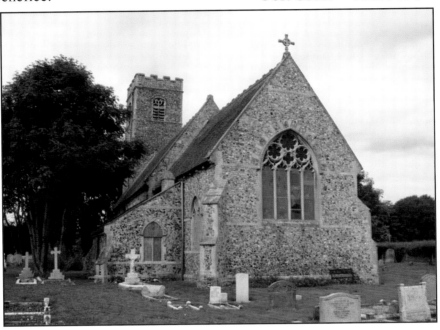

St Mary's has been redundant since 1981 after which time it was vandalised and heavily overgrown with vegetation. Thanks to the intervention of members of the Coleman family, now living in Gloucestershire, the task of clearing the graveyard and preserving the building has been ongoing. Although the interior of this lovely 15th c. church is still in a mess it is due to ongoing restoration and not neglect. It is a tribute to those who care about redundant churches that what we see today is a fine sound building and not a ruin. Although the roofs are Victorian, the wall-posts which support it are slender columns with floral capitals on carved corbels. The octagonal font, no longer in the church, was 15th c. and had four sides deeply recessed. In restoring this grade I listed building I wish them every success.

FORNCETT ST PETER   St Peter

No of Bells:	6	
19th c. Deanery	Depwade	
Hundred:	Depwade	
Union house:	Pulham St Mary	
21st c. Deanery:	Humbleyard	
Benefice:	Upper Tas Valley	

12 m SSW of Norwich. Follow instructions for Forncett St Mary *(p.91)* and continue ¾ mile further on until 2nd 'T' junction.

O.S. grid ref: TM 165928

Post Code: NR16 1HY

The church and tower are Saxon, built about the turn of the 1st millennium. The tower has round windows splayed inside and out, the crenulated parapet is much later. The upper (belfry) windows are distinctive of that period. The church itself has been rebuilt and modified a number of times over the intervening centuries. The three window clerestory, for instance, was added in the 14th c. Larger windows were inserted into the walls, along with arcades forming the aisles, during the 15th c. The Victorian era saw new roofs and slate replace the lead. In the nave is a wonderful set of bench ends with carvings that illustrate the saints, seasons and the Seven Deadly Sins. A delightful church, with loads to interest any visitor, and a good comprehensive guide book from which the above is extracted.

FOULSHAM   Holy Innocents   8 m SE of Fakenham. Turn
No of Bells: 3   off the A1067 and follow
19th c. Deanery   Sparham   the signposts where you
Hundred: Eynesford   will find the church north
Union house: Aylsham   of the village centre.
21st c. Deanery: Sparham   O.S. grid ref: TG 033251
Benefice: Foulsham   Post Code: NR20 5SF

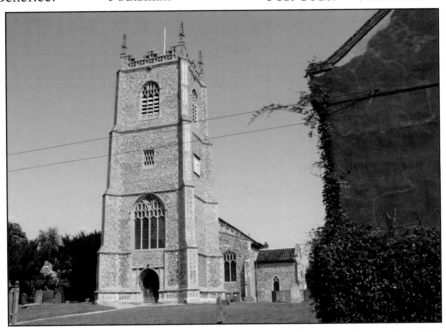

This is a most magnificent 15th c. tower standing at almost 100 feet including the crocketted pinnacles. A band of flushwork around the base with the arms of the benefactor in the spandrils above the door. The double stepped-parapet is decorated with quatrefoils, shields and 'M's. In the nave the 14th c. arcade, which was re-built after a disastrous fire in 1770, divides the nave and supports a good ten-window clerestory. The chancel arch reaches the apex of the nave roof. In the chancel is a beautiful 14th c. arcaded piscina and sedilia but that too had to be restored after the fire. The font is a copy of the original and has a tall elaborate cover with doors so it doesn't have to be raised. The roof has been plastered and has a central rose. There is much to see here, particularly details in the various carvings.

FOXLEY   St Thomas

No of Bells:	5
19th c. Deanery	Sparham
Hundred:	Eynesford
Union house:	Gressenhall
21st c. Deanery:	Sparham
Benefice:	FLEBBS

7 m NE of Dereham. Just off the A10674 and 4 miles W of Reepham turn east into the centre of the village and the Themelthorpe road.
O.S. grid ref: TG 039218
Post Code: NR20 4QP

The tower dominates the church with its panelled parapet and truncated pinnacles. On the south side are the stairs leading to the belfry. All the roofs are plastered over including the porch. In the nave below the western gallery is a quite plain 14th c. font, decorated with simple quatrefoils on each facet; the conical cover is surmounted by a dove. Ancient benches with poppy-heads lead down to the simple double-decker pulpit and screen which is arguably the most interesting thing to be found here. The front panels, I believe, show traces of having once been painted, but on the doors, one of which may have been removed during the Commonwealth are the four Latin Doctors. At the feet of two are the donors, with the mediaeval equivalent of speech bubbles, asking for prayers for their souls.

FRENZE	St Andrew	2 m E of Diss. Just off the
No of Bells:	1	A1066. First left once over
19th c. Deanery	Redenhall	the bridge on the way to
Hundred:	Diss	Scole and follow road past
Union house:	Pulham St Mary	office complex to the Hall.
21st c. Deanery:	-	O.S. grid ref: TM 136804
The Churches Conservation Trust		Post Code: IP22 4XW

A remote but interesting church that has stood here for 600 years. There is no trace of there ever having been a tower, only a single bellcote with a weather-vane. Before entering the 15th c. porch glance up on the left side and you will see the needle end of the tie-beam, through which is passed a bar to prevent the walls spreading. Another can be seen on the opposite wall. In the nave is a 14th c. octagonal font with designs reflecting the window styles of the period. The central shaft is fluted. On the wall nearby are what remains of the Royal Arms of James I. Three of the vertical boards are missing. The Blennerhasset family is well represented here with good brasses and memorials. There is a lovely Jacobean pulpit complete with back-board and tester. This little church is well worth seeking out.

FUNDENHALL St Nicholas

No of Bells:	5
19th c. Deanery	Depwade
Hundred:	Depwade
Union house:	Pulham St Mary
21st c. Deanery:	Humbleyard
Benefice:	Upper Tas Valley

4½ m SSE of Wymondham. West of the B1113 between Wreningham & Tacolneston. Turn W at the x-roads S of the Ashwell Thorpe turnoff.

O.S. grid ref: TM 152969
Post Code: NR16 1AH

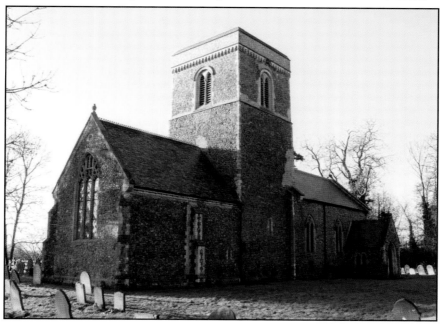

The Norman central tower has recently undergone costly restoration and the church is worth a visit for a number of reasons. First, it is unusual because of the central tower; although only the lower part is Norman. Secondly, the narrow south doorway with its engaged columns and capitals is also Norman. Lastly, although the screen has gone, the coving to the rood loft still survives, which is in itself quite rare. Despite most of the fixtures and fittings being of Victorian manufacture they are of fine quality and interesting. Some older benches remain and the interior of the church has not lost any of its charm although the reredos is somewhat morose. The delicate 15th c. octagonal font is an exception and is quite uncommon in its design and decoration. Interesting, and well worth a visit.

GARBOLDISHAM All Saints

No of Bells:	-	
19th c. Deanery	Rockland	
Hundred:	Guiltcross	
Union house:	Kenninghall	
21st c. Deanery:	-	
Benefice:	-	

3½ m S of East Harling.
Follow directions for St John's
(overleaf) Down the hill left
into Harling Road then left
into Water Lane.
O.S. grid ref: TM 004818
Post Code: IP22 2SB

In 1734 the east side of the 14th c. tower collapsed onto the nave and
the church was subsequently abandoned. By all accounts up to the
time of the disaster it was a well endowed church with good
patronage. Fortunately for the parish there were already two churches
and the Rectory was consolidated with that of St John's. The site was
completely cleared and today only the tower stands as sentinel as to
what once stood here. The screen was salvaged and can still be seen
set up at St John's church today. It is certainly unusual in that it has
paintings of St Germanus and a rare St William. It is said to be
William of York but could possibly be St William of Norwich as
there seem to be representations of four nails in his gown and signs of
stigmata on the left hand. A little puzzling.

GARBOLDISHAM St John the Baptist 3½ m S of East Harling.

No of Bells:	6
19th c. Deanery	Rockland
Hundred:	Guiltcross
Union house:	Kenninghall
21st c. Deanery:	Thetford & Rockland
Benefice:	Guiltcross

Garboldisham is bypassed by the A1066 but the church is easily found on entering the village.

O.S. grid ref: TM 004817
Post Code: IP22 2SE

As mentioned on the previous page the screen is intriguing, but that is only one of the delights that can be found here. The 15th c. tower may at one time have had a Galilee or perhaps just a porch, but clearly something has been demolished from its west face. As well as a flushwork base the parapet is well decorated. A peal board tells that the tower had a peal of 6 bells in 1773. The early octagonal font is quite plain. Above the north door are the post-1707 Royal Arms of Queen Ann. The roof of the nave is an arch-braced construction with tie-beams. In the chancel, a double piscina and dropped-sill sedilia have undergone some Victorian restoration as has the rest of the church. Most of the benches are 'modern', as is the pulpit, the former having tracery from the old screen incorporated in the back-rests.

GARVESTON St Margaret

No of Bells: 6
19th c. Deanery   Hingham
Hundred: Mitford
Union house: Gressenhall
21st c. Deanery: Hingham
Benefice: Barnham Broom Upper Yare

5 m SSE of East Dereham.
Head out of Dereham on
the B1135 and the church
can be spotted in Dereham
Road. Difficult parking.
O.S. grid ref: TG 024074
Post Code: NR9 4AD

It is the dull north side of this church that presents itself to the road. The southern aspect is much better, showing the Perpendicular south aisle and 15th c. embattled tower to its best advantage. Much restoration has gone on here over the centuries, but the body of the church is much as it was when first constructed in the 14th c. The occasional blocked doorway and particularly the height of the piscina and sedilia from the floor tell their own story. The lovely arcade which forms the south aisle for instance and the matching chancel arch however, are unchanged. A neat 15th c. octagonal font, with shields on a foliate background decorating the bowl, stands against the inner wall of the tower. Almost all the furnishings are of mid-Victorian date. See the doors and locks for some good craftsmanship.

GASTHORPE St Nicholas
No of Bells: -
19th c. Deanery: Rockland
Hundred: Guiltcross
Union house: Kenninghall
21st c. Deanery: -
Benefice: -

6½ m E of Thetford. 2½ m west of Garboldisham on the A 1066 between two houses on the left. ½ m walk up a grassy track between fields. O.S. grid ref: TL 982812
Post Code: IP22 2SX

You should be able to park off the main road, near the five-barred-gate as long as you don't block it. Originally known as Gatesthorpe, the church has been ruinous for centuries and the parish consolidated with Riddlesworth which is to the west. The remains of the tower are quite distinct but I have marked with an arrow the east wall of the chancel. The site is completely overgrown with dense vegetation. Wellington boots and stout trousers are the order of the day. The relatively small church was built in the 14th c. and ruinous by the beginning of the 19th c. Most of the walls and window spaces can easily be distinguished but nothing remains of monuments within the ruins. There is more to see than indicated in the photograph above and it is a good ruin to explore but only with care.

GISSING	St Mary	*****	5 m N of Diss. Either from
No of Bells:	5		Diss via Burston or from
19th c. Deanery:	Redenhall		the B1134; turn 2nd left
Hundred:	Diss		west of the crossing gates,
Union house:	Pulham St Mary		bear left then right.
21st c. Deanery:	Redenhall		O.S. grid ref: TM 146852
Benefice:	Winfarthing		Post Code: IP22 5UJ

This is a beautiful 10th-13th c. Saxon-Norman church with a spectacular double hammerbeam roof in the nave and is a must for all church crawlers. Round Saxon splayed windows in the tower and Norman doors both east and west are another noteworthy feature of the church. The north porch which formerly had a parvise has two canopied niches and good flushwork. The font is early 15th c. and the pulpit Victorian. Beneath two 13th c. arches, and housing the organ, is the rebuilt (1879) south 'Kemp' chapel. There really is so much of interest here that it is impossible to describe everything in the space allowed, so I suggest a visit with binoculars and even a torch to see the roof detail. Many memorials adorn the walls, chiefly to the Kemp family; Cockerham, Dade and Kerridge families are also included.

GLANDFORD St Martin *****

No of Bells:	1 + 8-bell carillon	
19th c. Deanery:	Holt	
Hundred:	Holt	
Union house:	Erpingham	
21st c. Deanery:	Holt	
Benefice:	Glaven Valley (Blakeney)	

2½ m NW of Holt. From the A149 coast road head south between Blakeney & Cley. Follow the signs for the Shell Museum.

O.S. grid ref: TG 0444415

Post Code: NR25 7JR

This building was ruinous in 1864 (White's Norfolk) and had been for some time. It is due to the grief and enthusiasm of Sir Alfred Jodrell that we see a well loved church instead of a ruin. After his wife Adela died in 1898, he made it his business to rebuild the ruin. He had already spent thousands on nearby Saxlingham. Entry is by the north porch. The interior smells of like and French polish and a carpenter's workshop. Everywhere you look are beautiful wood-carvings; in the roof, on the benches, pulpit, reredos, everywhere! The Seven Sacrament font is a 20th c. example, carved in a different style to the mediaeval. A splendid statue of an angel in the north chapel bears witness to Jodrell's work and is his memorial to Adela. An hour can be easily spent here, and still there will be things you have missed.

GREAT ELLINGHAM St James the Apostle

No of Bells:	6	2 m NW of Attleborough
19th c. Deanery:	Rockland	on the B1077 in
Hundred:	Shropham	Attleborough Road at the
Union house:	Rockland All Saints	eastern end of the village.
21st c. Deanery:	Thetford & Rockland	O.S. grid ref: TM 021972
Benefice:	Great Ellingham (Shelrock)	Post Code: NR17 1LE

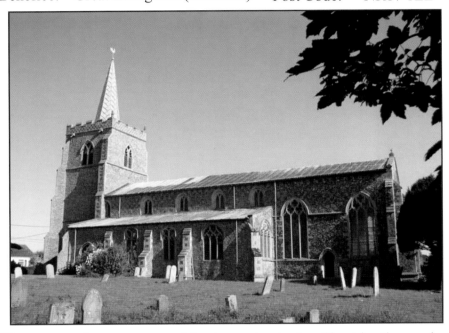

The truncated appearance of the tower is nicely off-set by the modest leaded spire. Dating from the 14th c. the church seems stripped of its character by the removal of the pews which have been replaced with scores of chairs when the money could have been better spent on the interior of the church. Although scruffy it does have its points of interest. The roof of the nave is an arch-braced and tie-beam type. Between the wall-posts are the clerestory windows. Shields in octofoils decorate the bowl of the 15th c. font. There are indistinct traces of wall paintings and a 14th c. niche in the south aisle still has traces of original colouring. Remains of a parclose screen enclose a south aisle chapel. In the chancel a larger window has destroyed a once beautiful piscina and dropped-sill sedilia under a single arch.

GREAT MELTON All Saints

No of Bells:	3
19th c. Deanery:	Humbleyard
Hundred:	Humbleyard
Union house:	Swainsthorpe
21st c. Deanery:	Humbleyard
Benefice:	Hethersett

5½ m W of Norwich. From the A47 turn off at Little Melton and follow through to Great Melton. The church is in Market Lane.
O.S. grid ref: TG 141062
Post Code: NR9 3BH

Although the 14th c. un-buttressed tower is ancient, the church itself was completely rebuilt in the 1880s around the old foundations using material from St Mary's. It used to be derelict, but when its sister church of St Mary's fell into disrepair it was decided to rebuild All Saints. Being Victorian it holds little interest; that which is worthy of note has been consigned to the porch. On either side is a stone coffin lid, each carved with 'Celtic' decoration, and two 15th c. benches with carved poppy-heads. The benches inside the church hold no interest. In the chancel is the large square-headed piscina and the sedilia both of which have also been restored. The PCC have a 'trust nobody' policy and you will be supervised while you have a look round. Not really worth the hassle, as all the interest is in the porch.

GREAT MELTON   St Mary

No of Bells:	-	
19th c. Deanery:	Humbleyard	
Hundred:	Humbleyard	
Union house:	Swainsthorpe	
21st c. Deanery:	-	
Benefice:	-	

5½ m W of Norwich. From the A47 turn off at Little Melton and follow through to Great Melton. The tower is beside All Saints.
O.S. grid ref: TG 141062
Post Code: NR9 3BH

Standing sentinel over the graveyard and outline of the nave and chancel, this fine 14th c. tower has been well preserved. The church which was once part of it was in use up to the 1880s. All Saints *(p 104)* had been in a ruinous state since the end of the reign of Queen Anne (1714). It was a grander church than that of All Saints and it is therefore surprising that the lesser took precedence over the greater. Parts of the church, I understand, were Early English built in the latter part of the 13th c. It was only relatively recently that the walls were completely demolished and the site cleaned up. Railings protect the foundations of the church which are clearly marked. On the east face of the tower there are two distinct roof lines indicating that re-roofing took place at some stage during its life.

GREAT MOULTON St Michael

No of Bells:	1	
19th c. Deanery:	Depwade	
Hundred:	Depwade	
Union house:	Pulham St Mary	
21st c. Deanery:	Depwade	
Benefice:	Pilgrim	

9 m NNE of Diss. From Long Stratton go to Wacton and follow the road to Aslacton. The church is north of Great Moulton before crossing the railway bridge.

O.S. grid ref: TM 165908

Post Code: NR15 2LD

Sometimes referred to simply as Moulton. But do not confuse with Moulton near Yarmouth. The dark flint and red brick of the embattled tower which was re-built in 1887 complement each other well. On the wall of the chancel the outline of a Norman window over the lancet which replaced it. A small scratch dial can be seen on the jamb of another. So although extensive restoration has taken place some evidence of the early origins can still be found. Over the chancel arch is what is supposed to be St Michael overwhelming the devil, looking to me like St George standing on a dead dragon. A Norman pillar piscina can be seen in the sanctuary. Unfortunately it is all offset by the overwhelming presence of Victorian furnishings. The excellent guide deals with everything in greater detail.

GREAT WITCHINGHAM St Mary

No of Bells:	2, unused	
19th c. Deanery:	Sparham	
Hundred:	Eynesford	
Union house:	Horsham St Faiths	
21st c. Deanery:	Sparham	
Benefice:	Wensum	

10 m NW of Norwich. From the A1067 turn north at Lenwade to Great Witchingham and the church is in 1 m on the left.
O.S. grid ref: TG 123202
Post Code: NR9 5PE

This is a grand looking church with its 14th c. tower dominating the clerestoried nave. Externally there are points of interest but inside there is much more. Note the crowned Ms over the porch as you enter and the carvings in the spandrels. Still bearing some original pastel colouring is the splendid Seven Sacrament font. Around the shaft are saints between engaged columns, each one named by angels around the corona. 14th c. arcades support the roof which appears plain but note the small angels and the carved decoration on the cornice. Like the pulpit the benches are of no great age. An old chest has poker-work depicting birds and exotic creatures. Hanging on the wall are the Royal Arms of Charles II, dated 1660, a gift of Oliver le Neve. His memorial slab tells us he died in 1678 at the age of 77.

GRESHAM	All Saints	5 m SW of Cromer. From
No of Bells:	2, at one time 3	Cromer take the A148 and
19th c. Deanery:	Repps	turn left to Aylmerton.
Hundred:	North Erpingham	Straight on at the x-roads &
Union house:	Sheringham	left at the next x-roads.
21st c. Deanery:	Repps	O.S. grid ref: TG 167386
Benefice:	Aylmerton	Post Code: NR11 8RE

Signs of an earlier Saxon church can still be found. The present tower is 13th c. with a Norman base, the upper part was re-built in 1887 and the parapet added. A Cotman drawing of how it was in 1818 is inside. The porch, which has two scratch dials on the jamb, although small, has a tiny parvise above. In the nave is one of the finest Seven Sacrament fonts of the 15th c. anywhere in East Anglia. In the 14th c. chancel is a simple piscina with a pointed arch. The nave is crammed with lovely simple box-pews nearest the pulpit and plain benches towards the back. A blocked doorway in the west wall once led to the rood loft access turret. In the chancel there are many memorials to various members of the local Batt family as well as memorials to members of the Spurgin and Dewing families. The oldest is 1658.

GRISTON   Sts Peter & Paul

No of Bells:	5
19th c. Deanery:	Breckles
Hundred:	Wayland
Union house:	Rockland All Saints
21st c. Deanery:	Breckland
Benefice:	Wayland

2 m SE of Watton. Leave Watton on the A1075 for 2½ m and take the first left then left again and follow the road to the church.

O.S. grid ref: TL 943993

Post Code: IP25 6QA

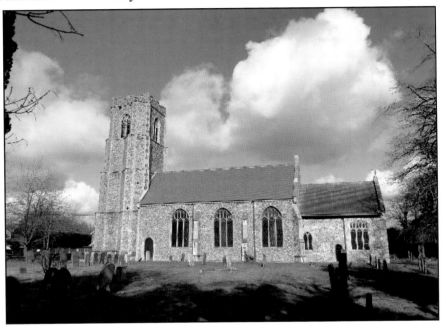

At the base of the 14th c. tower is a course of carved stone of crossed keys and swords representing Sts Peter and Paul and repeated on the parapet. At the east end of the new tiled roof is an empty sanctus bell turret. At the west end of the nave the plain 14th c. octagonal font with one facet has an inscription referring to the tower, written in 1568. Above hung on the Jacobean ringing gallery are the pre-1801 Hanoverian Royal Arms updated in 1902 and incorrectly coloured. As well as the figures in the roof, two have been hung on the wall after restorations. The 17th c. pulpit is complete with backboard and tester and is beautifully carved. The roof is arch-braced with cambered tie-beams and tracery in the spandrels. In the raised chancel are a piscina and dropped-sill sedilia. Some interesting old bench-ends, too.

GUESTWICK St Peter

No of Bells: 1
19th c. Deanery: Sparham
Hundred: Eynesford
Union house: Aylsham
21st c. Deanery: Sparham
Benefice: Foulsham

5 m NW of Reepham.
Follow the winding minor
road heading NW out of
Reepham for 5 miles until
you see the church.
O.S. grid ref: TG 061270
Post Code: NR20 5QD

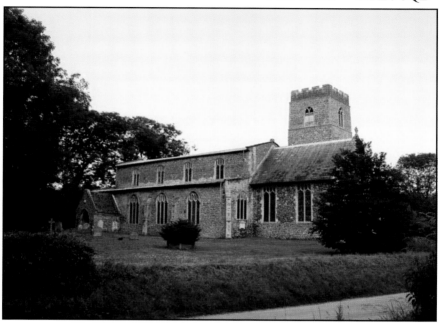

A Saxon church stood here before the Conquest. The Normans raised this tower on its foundations, apart from the belfry stage which is later. This 15th c. edifice was built to the SW of the Saxon church, hence the unusual NE position of the tower. Shields with emblems of the saints decorate the facets of the 15th c. octagonal font. In the north aisle is a rare staircase with a handrail which used to lead up to the rood loft. The chancel roof is 15th c. arch-braced, the others are modern. In the SE corner is a small angle piscina with delicate tracery and original colour. On the wall are three hatchments of the Bulwer family. Various memorials to them are scattered throughout the church. Two monumental brasses (Richard & James Athill) from the early 16th c. and a chalice brass to John Robertson (1504).

GUIST	St Andrew	6 m SE of Fakenham.
No of Bells:	1	Standing slightly set back
19th c. Deanery:	Sparham	beside the A1067, Norwich
Hundred:	Eynesford	to Fakenham road just east
Union house:	Gressenhall	of Guist village.
21st c. Deanery:	Sparham	O.S. grid ref: TG 000256
Benefice:	Elmham	Post Code: NR20 5PQ

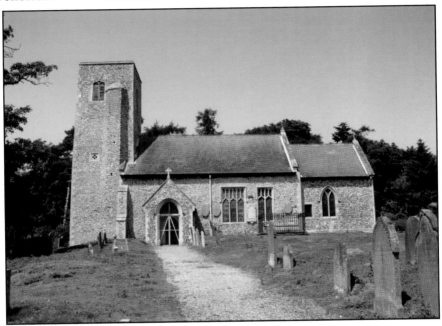

What is seen here today is mostly Victorian restoration, the church was almost ruinous by the mid-1800s. The tower is 14th c. and has 15th c. upper level. Just inside the porch is the original 13th c. doorway which intriguingly has a scratch dial on the top of the arch. When White visited pre-1864 he mentions an ancient font, but this is nowhere to be found today. Instead, a modern replica in the style of the 16th c. is to be seen. All the fittings and furnishings are crisp and 19th c. but note on the pulpit a small head of a green man, keeping pagan traditions alive. The old parish chest has been retained; dated 1636 it is decorated with floriated scrolls. Many of the 17th to 19th c. monuments to be found here are to the Wiggett family, but the most touching is to a baby, Boley Rice Wickes aged 1 month.

GUNTHORPE St Mary

No of Bells:	1 (at one time 4)
19th c. Deanery:	Holt
Hundred:	Holt
Union house:	Great Snoring
21st c. Deanery:	Holt
Benefice:	Stiffkey & Bale

5 m WSW of Holt. From the A148 SW of Holt turn left at the Bale / Gunthorpe x-roads. The church is well north of the village.
O.S. grid ref: TG 012353
Post Code: NR24 2NY

On seeing this church for the first time, I somehow had the feeling that it was all too neat and tidy to be interesting. The chequered parapet to the 15th c. tower didn't do much to allay my fears. The church, I found, was interestingly different, not all of it to my taste. Built in the 13th c. some parts still survive from the period. The Victorian south porch protects a 13th c. doorway into a 19th c. nave where saintly emblems on the bowl of the 15th c. octagonal font catch the eye. There is much coloured glass; the east window casts light onto the marble columns of the chancel arch. The tiled 'screen' is hideous. I found the 17th c. black memorial slabs more to my taste. Outside near the tower is a small headstone to Augustine Andrews age 24 (1743), a mason. Did he die while repairing the tower?

HACKFORD	All Saints	12 m NW of Norwich. The
No of Bells:	-	parish is integrated with
19th c. Deanery:	as Whitwell	Reepham which is situated
Hundred:	as Whitwell	along the B1145 and
Union house:	as Whitwell	adjoins the Market Place.
21st c. Deanery:	-	O.S. grid ref: TG 102229
Benefice:	-	Post Code: NR10 4JW

The church, now a ruin, once stood alongside two other churches at the point where three parishes conjoin in the same common churchyard. A unique situation! The other two are still standing, although Whitwell St Michael *(page 244)* is now redundant. The other, Reepham St Mary *(page 178)* is only a stone's throw away. The church became ruinous in the 16th c. and the material was used over the course of time to repair the other two. Very little is known about the church. Almost hidden by trees and shrubs today it is still just possible to imagine the problems when, on a Sunday, two churches were ringing their respective bells and the other was trying to conduct a service. Reepham Market Place is actually in Hackford. The two parishes of Whitwell and Hackford were consolidated.

HACKFORD St Mary the Virgin

No of Bells: 1

19th c. Deanery: Hingham

Hundred: Forehoe

Union house: Wicklewood

21st c. Deanery: Humbleyard

Benefice: High Oak & Hingham

2 m E of Hingham off the B1108 between Hingham & Kimberley turn off towards Wicklewood & take the first right.

O.S. grid ref: TG 059023

Post Code: NR18 9HN

Do not confuse this place with the other Hackford on the previous page, they are two separate parishes. This pleasant little church is tucked away down a narrow country lane and when I visited was undergoing some interior restoration. Inside the porch is a most unusual canopied pillar stoup, arguably the most interesting object to be found here. The 15th c. octagonal font is decorated with shields representing the Trinity and saints. At the eastern end of the nave behind the pulpit is another curiosity. The rood stairs are simply a set of steps built against the wall with a newel post once supporting a handrail. Close by are two canopied niches set into the chancel arch. Within the chancel a simple angle piscina opening into the dropped-sill sedilia. The Royal Arms are pre-1801 Hanoverian.

HANWORTH	St Bartholomew	5 m N of Aylsham. Just off
No of Bells:	5 (only 4 in use)	the A140 midway between
19th c. Deanery:	Repps	Roughton & Erpingham.
Hundred:	North Erpingham	Turn west for ½ mile at
Union house:	West Beckham	Hanworth Cross.
21st c. Deanery:	Repps	O.S. grid ref: TG 203350
Benefice:	Roughton	Post Code: NR11 7HP

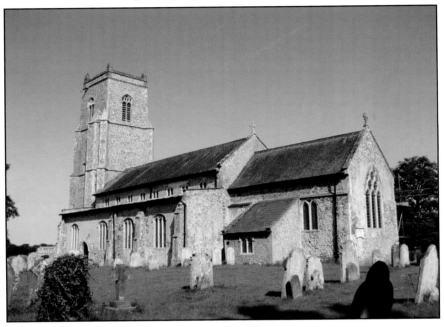

This is a very interesting church and is well maintained. Someone has ensured the architectural student has plenty of information; on a door are the plans for the church in every fine detail. There is plenty of interest to discover here. The 14th c. tower is surmounted by fine brick pinnacles. There is a good clerestory letting plenty of light filter into the interior. The octagonal font is crudely hewn and stands on four splayed legs and a central shaft. An iron-bound parish chest that must weigh a ton stands close by. On the chancel arch the fixing points for the rood loft can be clearly seen. In the chancel is a simple piscina adjacent to a rudimentary stepped sedilia with a pointed arch cut into the wall. The post-1707 Royal Arms are those of Queen Anne after the union with Scotland. Well worth seeking out!

HAPTON	St Margaret	9 m SW of Norwich. From
No of Bells:	1	the B1113 heading north,
19th c. Deanery:	Depwade	first right after Tacolneston
Hundred:	Depwade	Church and first left into
Union house:	Pulham St Mary	Church Lane, Hapton
21st c. Deanery:	Humbleyard	O.S. grid ref: TM 176966
Benefice:	Upper Tas Valley	Post Code: NR15 1SE

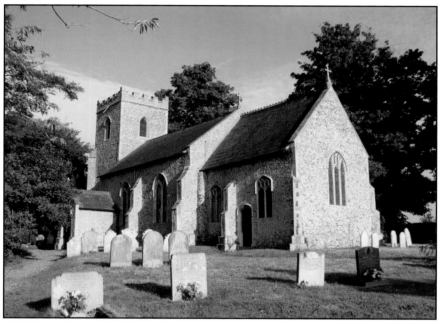

When I first visited this church I was unable enter. However, it was worth a return visit. Disregarding the tower, which is wholly Victorian, parts of the church date from the 13th c. The blocked north door and the handle on the south door confirms this; the south porch was added a century later. The chancel arch is 14th c. and deserves close inspection of the carving on the capitals, where you will find a 'green man'. Representing the 15th c. is the plain octagonal font. An ogee design of cover is Jacobean but has been modified with ogee supports. Parts of the old mediaeval screen have been utilized as a back support in the sedilia. Other parts of the salvaged screen have been converted into a credence table. A 15th c. heavy iron-bound parish chest has found a resting place in front of the pews.

HARDINGHAM St George

No of Bells: 1
19th c. Deanery: Hingham
Hundred: Mitford
Union house: Gressenhall
21st c. Deanery: Dereham & Mitford
Benefice: Barnham Broom Upper Yare

2½ m N x E of Hingham.
From Hardingham village
head N, bear left at Y junc
and turn left at x-roads for
¾ mile into Church Road.
O.S. grid ref: TG 035051
Post Code: NR9 4EW

The church is well to the north-west of the village it serves. The tower
sits at the south west corner of the church and serves as the entrance
into the nave with its lovely hammerbeam roof. The belfry of the
splendid 13th c. tower seems to be a later addition, with the buttresses
being terminated with small gables below the upper stage. Most of the
building seems to be from the same period with early doorways,
windows and niches. In the chancel there is an unusual double piscina
with interlacing arches and an asymmetrical double arch over the
stepped sedilia. An early 13th c. font, supported on a later central
shaft and eight columns, has cusped arcades on each facet. Although
most of the furnishings are Victorian there are plenty of 17th c. black
slab memorials to various members of the Grigson family.

HARGHAM   All Saints
No of Bells: 0
19th c. Deanery: Rockland
Hundred: Shropham
Union house: Rockland All Saints
21st c. Deanery: -
The Norfolk Churches Trust

3 m S of Attleborough, just
½ m off the A11 on the
left-hand side of the road to
Old Buckenham, before the
crossroads.
O.S. grid ref: TM 020914
Post Code: NR16 2JN

Pronounced Harfam. Poor, desolate and neglected. That is how I
would describe this church. The church is supported by the Norfolk
Churches Trust, and the key is two miles away in Attleborough. The
nave is semi ruinous by virtue of a partial fall of the tower centuries
ago. A wall has been built and a door inserted on the west wall of
what is left of the nave. Through the curious little squint near the
chancel door one can see the altar. There is also a low side window.
There are plain benches in the restored Victorian interior with its
stencilled walls. In the chancel is a corner piscina and adjacent
dropped-sill sedilia. A plain octagonal font stands forlornly near the
west doorway. Seating for about 24 persons is divided from the
chancel by a horrible stone barrier. The church is always kept locked.

HAVERINGLAND St Peter

No of Bells:	3	
19th c. Deanery:	Sparham	
Hundred:	Eynesford	
Union house:	Horsham St Faiths	
21st c. Deanery:	Ingworth	
Benefice:	Cawston	

9 m NNW of Norwich From the B1149 north of Horsford turn left and follow towards Cawston. Church is on right across old airfield runway.
O.S. grid ref: TG 151209
Post Code: NR10 4PN

Normally kept locked with keyholders. The church stands at the edge of the disused airfield but was once surrounded by the park's woodland. Apart from the tower, it was rebuilt in the mid-1800s in the traditional style, probably a close copy of what stood here before. Quite large for a small parish, it has a north and south aisle as well as a south transept. The roof of the nave is a graceful arch-braced construction with long wall posts supported on carved corbels. A 15th c. font has cusped arcading on both bowl and shaft. An old chest with a heavily carved front stands in the nave. Obviously all the fixtures and fittings are Victorian and carvings on some of the bench ends are interesting with crowned lions here and there. There is a carving on the altar rail. The chancel is tiled and has a traceried holy table.

HEMPSTEAD All Saints
No of Bells: 1 (originally 3)
19th c. Deanery: Holt
Hundred: Holt
Union house: Erpingham
21st c. Deanery: Holt
Benefice: Barningham Northwood

2 m SE of Holt. Leave the A148 at Holt and take the road to Baconsthorpe and in 1 mile bear right, then take the 2nd on the right.
O.S. grid ref: TG 104371
Post Code: NR25 6TW

Although the church is marked on the map with a tower, it is very truncated and barely reaches the height of the nave. It was rebuilt of brick in 1744. The lovely thatched apsidal chancel was added as late as 1925. The church started its life before the Conquest as a Saxon church and the changes that have taken place over the last millennium are well explained diagrammatically inside. At the west end is a gallery containing the small organ on which someone has carved graffiti. Most of the fixtures and fittings are Victorian with one or two exceptions, particularly two benches. On the wall is a brass plaque commemorating the life of Edmund Hunt who died in 1610. A most beautiful lectern in the form of an angel stands just in front of the pulpit. A lovely, clean and much loved church.

HETHEL	All Saints	7 m SSW of Norwich off
No of Bells:	6	the B1113. After Mulbarton
19th c. Deanery:	Humbleyard	and before Bracon Ash turn
Hundred:	Humbleyard	right. Continue over the
Union house:	Swainsthorpe	crossroads for 500 yds.
21st c. Deanery:	Humbleyard	O.S. grid ref: TG 172004
Benefice:	Mulbarton	Post Code: NR14 8HE

Hethel church is set well back off the road and from outward appearances could do with some attention. The tower is, in the lower portion, Norman. The upper parts are later embellishments. The first impression as you enter the gate is the hideous mausoleum stuck on the side. It is the last resting place for members of the Branthwaite family. Inside the nave however, the memorial to Myles Branthwaite (1612) and his wife is quite stunning. He reclines stiffly on one arm just above her. A very plain 14th c. font and a ghastly white painted pulpit clash in the otherwise serene atmosphere. Hatchments hang in the tower beyond the arch. In the 1730-ish chancel is a simple arch over a piscina beside which is a dropped-sill sedilia. The last man to be hanged at Norwich in 1848 (James Rush) lived in this parish.

HETHERSETT St Remigius
No of Bells: 5
19th c. Deanery: Humbleyard
Hundred: Humbleyard
Union house: Swainsthorpe
21st c. Deanery: Humbleyard
Benefice: Hethersett

5 m WSW of Norwich. From the outer ring-road take the B1172 at the Thickthorn roundabout. Standing well back on left of Norwich Road. O.S. grid ref: TG 161049
Post Code: NR9 3AS

The tower, which has a spirelet, is 14th c. and has niches in the buttresses. Unusually there are three parts to the roof of this church. When the chancel was rebuilt in 1898, part of the roof of the nave roof was also re-constructed at a lower pitch allowing a small window to be inserted in the gable. Inside one can observe the influence of the Victorian restoration everywhere. Quotations from the Bible adorn every arch of the 14th c. arcades, insistent on getting the message across; but a picture paints a thousand words and these are to be found in the splendid Victorian stained glass. The 14th c. octagonal font bowl stands on eight hexagonal columns and is decorated with floriated crosses. There has been, in my opinion, too much restoration here but it is a lovely and well loved church which is worth visiting.

HEVINGHAM St Mary the Virgin & St Botolph

No of Bells:	5	3 m S of Aylsham. Next to
19th c. Deanery:	Ingworth	a lay-by on the A140
Hundred:	South Erpingham	between Marsham &
Union house:	Aylsham	Hevingham village.
21st c. Deanery:	Norwich North	O.S. grid ref: TG 201224
Benefice:	Horsford	Post Code: NR10 5QU

Situated very close to the A140 and quite vulnerable, this church is understandably locked. Six stooled niches decorate the south face of the porch. Above the porch is a parvise which at one time was used as a school-room. Adjacent to the porch is the featureless south transept, looking shed-like in comparison with its small windows. A rather mutilated 14th c. hexagonal font has seen better days but has a good carving of the crucifixion. West of the large chancel arch are the four stone brackets which once supported the rood loft, now dismantled. In the sanctuary is an angle piscina and adjacent dropped-sill sedilia with graduated seating. Some sun-bleached benches are said to have been used in the parvise as school desks for the children. A few items of interest, but 19th c. restoration has spoiled the character.

HEYDON Sts Peter & Paul

No of Bells: 6
19th c. Deanery: Ingworth
Hundred: South Erpingham
Union house: Aylsham
21st c. Deanery: Ingworth
Benefice: Cawston

5 m W of Aylsham. Best approached from west of the B1149, Norwich to Holt road. The church is quite central to the village.
O.S. grid ref: TG 114275
Post Code: NR11 6AD

From the moment you see the fine crocketted pinnacles on the 15th c. tower, you know this church is something quite special. Look up as you enter the porch at the lovely groined ceiling before opening the 15th c. door. Tall 14th c. arcades line the central aisle, which is illuminated by a 15th c. clerestory. Inside is an unusual 13th c. round font on an octagonal step. Nearby on the wall are the post-1707 Royal Arms of Queen Anne, strangely (with the fourth quarter reversed). The graceful 15th c. wine-glass pulpit, complete with a beautifully carved back-board and tester, stands to the right of the screen. On the north wall are paintings of the martyrdom of John the Baptist. Notices regarding the main features of the church are posted close by. The church has many unusual features and is worth a visit.

HIGH KELLING   All Saints

		4 m SW of Sheringham just
No of Bells:	1	off the A140. Unseen from
19th c. Deanery:	Holt	the road. In woodland,
Hundred:	Holt	almost directly opposite
Union house:	Erpingham	Avenue Road.
21st c. Deanery:	Holt	O.S. grid ref: TG 089418
Benefice:	Holt	Post Code: NR25 6RD

High Kelling has not, nor has ever had any church other than this. Strictly speaking, this is a chapel of ease but it is also designated a church and is therefore worthy of inclusion in this guide. Built in the 1920s and formerly a chapel to the TB hospital which stood nearby, it was bought for £500 by the community. It is, despite its barrack-like appearance, a much loved and well maintained church. The walls are clad with flint and the tranquil setting is ideal. The small wooden font stands on the window sill at the west end of the building, which is open to the sanctuary and without altar rail or screen. Set neatly between are rows of comfortable looking bench-style seats. Interestingly, I understand the bell was bought on eBay for the sum of £200 and a bell-cote subsequently erected to house it.

HINDOLVESTON St George (old)   8 m E. of Fakenham. From
No of Bells: -   the new church (facing page)
19th c. Deanery: Sparham   continue ¼ m on the left
Hundred: Eynesford   branch of the Y junction in
Union house: Aylsham   which the church sits.
21st c. Deanery: -   O.S. grid ref: TG 030292
Benefice: -   Post Code: NR20 5BT

In 1864 William White described this church in White's Norfolk, as having a nave, chancel, porch and square tower with one bell. Nothing was mentioned about its condition. The inset is Ladbrooke's drawing made before the east face of the tower crashed onto the nave in 1892. What caused the fall no one knows, but the man inside the church at the time lived to tell the tale. In the foreground is what used to be the vestry at the eastern end of the church. The tower is still at its original height but only the western face is relatively whole. The church and tower were 14th c. and many of its contents, including the font, pulpit, parish chest and a good number of niches can be seen today in the new church featured on the opposite page. The graveyard is still in use and is a peaceful and tranquil place to sit and reflect.

HINDOLVESTON St George (new)

No of Bells:	1
19th c. Deanery:	Sparham
Hundred:	Eynesford
Union house:	Aylsham
21st c. Deanery:	Holt
Benefice:	Briston

8 m E. of Fakenham. The nearest main road is the B1110. Turn east 2 m S of the B1354 intersection. The church is 1 mile further.

O.S. grid ref: TG 031293

Post Code: NR20 5BS

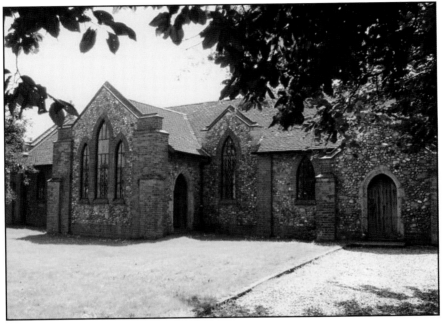

The dedication is correctly 'St George the Martyr' who bled milk instead of blood when he was decapitated. This well designed little church was built to replace the one featured on the previous page. I was pleasantly surprised to find it open. Building started in 1930 and it was opened in 1932. It contains many features salvaged from the old church, image niches on almost every wall, the old 14th c. font (scarred, but clearly depicting the Crucifixion). Several brass inscriptions have been rescued; a good figure brass for Edward (1558) and Margaret (1568) Hunt with their 14 children is attached to the wall. I hope there is never a fire here: it will melt like butter, not being on the floor. A real effort has been made to retain the essence of the old church and although relatively new is very interesting.

HINGHAM St Andrew ******** 6 m W of Wymondham. Off
No of Bells: 8 + 1 clock bell the B1108 in the centre of
19th c. Deanery: Hingham Hingham, in Attleborough
Hundred: Forehoe Road. South of the x-roads.
Union house: Wicklewood
21st c. Deanery: Humbleyard O.S. grid ref: TG 022021
Benefice: High Oak & Hingham Post Code: NR9 4HP

This is an impressive church! The 14th c. tower is 120 feet tall and
has a good tracery and trail base course. The beautiful 14th c. arcaded
nave of clustered columns has a single hammerbeam roof which was
constructed in 1871. The octagonal font is mid-Victorian. There are
two superb reasons to visit this church, the beautiful stained glass in
the windows which is some of the best I have seen; and the Morley
tomb. The former, especially in the spectacular east window is 16th c.
and was gifted to the church in 1813 by Lord Wodehouse, lord of the
manor. The latter dominates the church, as intended; it is the
memorial to Thomas Morley (1435) and his wife Isabel, née de la
Pole. Like the piscina and sedilia it was severely knocked about by
the Puritans, but the magnificence is preserved in the craftsmanship.

128

HOCKERING St Michael

No of Bells:	1
19th c. Deanery:	Hingham
Hundred:	Mitford
Union house:	Gressenhall
21st c. Deanery:	Dereham & Mitford
Benefice:	Mattishall

5 m E of East Dereham & 9 m W of Norwich. Just off the A47 at the W end of The Street, Hockering. Visible from the A47.

O.S. grid ref: TG 071132
Post Code: NR20 3AJ

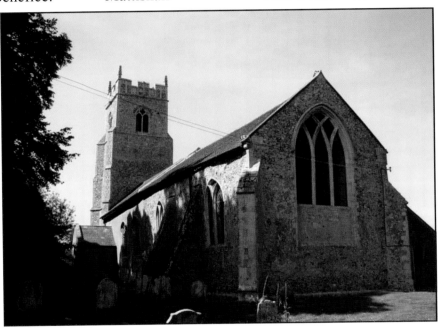

Fine pinnacles point skyward from the flush-worked parapet of the 15th c. tower. The nave and heavily buttressed chancel are about a century earlier, the 14th c. arcade is made up of clustered columns. Interestingly the modern font has its best carving, those of various saints etc., depicted on the 15th c. shaft rather than on the bowl. Hanging above, on the face of the western gallery are the pre 1801 Royal Hanoverian Arms. On some of the benches there are carvings of dogs and deer. On the ends are ermine crests of the Berney family, and five plumes in a coronet carved into the poppyheads. The wine-glass pulpit is Jacobean. The piscina and graduated sedilia have been well restored. Set into the floor beneath the piscina is a 13th c. coffin slab which predates the present church by a century or more.

(GREAT) HOCKHAM Holy Trinity

No of Bells: 1
19th c. Deanery: Rockland
Hundred: Shropham
Union house: Rockland All Saints
21st c. Deanery: Breckland
Benefice: Wayland

5 m NW by N of East Harling. From the A1075 head to the south of the village to Hockham Hall, the church is in the grounds.
O.S. grid ref: TL 951921
Post Code: IP24 1NZ

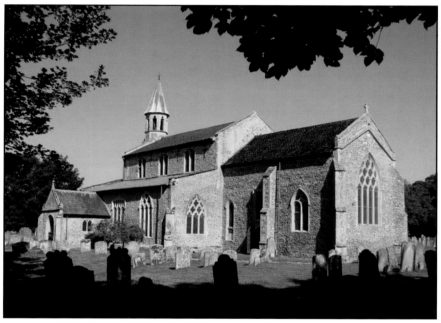

Hockham church has been without a tower since the old one collapsed centuries ago. The solitary bell is in a small but attractive turret which replaces an earlier model, erected at the west end of the nave roof. A simple three-window clerestory illuminates the interior. It is an early church with many phases of restoration but the 13th c. arcades are unchanged. Both north and south aisles have squints to the chancel altar, and the wall painting is quite fresh. There is yet another large painting of significance on the tympanum of the chancel arch. Deserving special mention are the early bench ends which are very interesting and well carved, although the years have taken their toll. In the chancel is a good 13th c. piscina and sedilia, in the south aisle is a nice 14th c. example of the same. Interesting but usually locked!

HOE	St Andrew	2 m N of East Dereham.
No of Bells:	1	From the B1110, 2 m N of
19th c. Deanery:	Brisley	Dereham, turn right to Hoe
Hundred:	Launditch	and follow the road to near
Union house:	Gressenhall	the Hall.
21st c. Deanery:	Dereham & Mitford	O.S. grid ref: TF 997164
Benefice:	Swanton Morley	Post Code: NR20 4BB

With only a broken tower and being surrounded by trees it is not easy to recognise this edifice as a church; the clean lines of the roof don't help to resolve the situation. Only the porch and windows distinguish this from a tithe barn. Inside the barn-like nave is a large 15th c. font with rose and quatrefoil designs around the bowl. It stands on a heavily carved shaft, which in turn stands on four sections of octagonal column, probably from an earlier phase of building. There is nothing very attractive about this Victorianised church. It is bare and generally unadorned and somewhat clinical; even the simple pulpit has a heavy and unattractive stone base. A 1706 wall monument to Roger Lestrange breaks the monotony of the bare white-washed walls.

HOLT	St Andrew	24 m NNW of Norwich.
No of Bells:	8	Turn off the bypass (A148)
19th c. Deanery:	Holt	towards the town centre. St
Hundred:	Holt	Andrew's is to the south,
Union house:	Erpingham	just off the main street.
21st c. Deanery:	Holt	O.S. grid ref: TG 081388
Benefice:	Holt	Post Code: NR25 6BB

This lovely church has been surrounded by trees and walls and is hidden from the road, which is a shame. Usually open, with someone in attendance to answer questions, it is a pleasure to visit. Parts of the church are as early as the 12th c. but much of what is to be seen here today is much later. The lovely circular 12th c. font is a small part of the delights to be found here. Tall 14th c. arcades line the nave and support a clerestory of modest proportions. The nave roof is relatively modern but has elegant tracery in the frames above the tie-beams. Further east the roof is unusual with heavy arch-braced beams spanning the width of the chancel. Below is a piscina and double sedilia with multi-cusped arches. The Royal Arms are Hanoverian but I feel may have been over-painted on a much earlier Stuart canvas.

HONINGHAM St Andrew

No of Bells:	6
19th c. Deanery:	Hingham
Hundred:	Forehoe
Union house:	Horsham St Faith
21st c. Deanery:	Dereham & Mitford
Benefice:	Honingham

7 m W of Norwich. The church is easily found beside the road on an incline the Norwich side of a new roundabout.

O.S. grid ref: TG 103119
Post Code: NR9 5BT

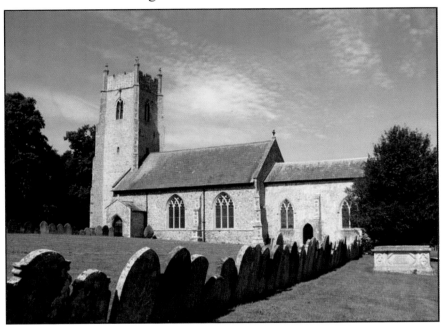

The proportions of this church are beautifully balanced. The tower especially is very attractive with the four evangelists perched on octagonal extensions of the buttresses on each corner of the flush-worked parapet. Standing close to the road it is disappointing, although understandable, that the church is always locked. I do feel the PCC could make an effort to open to visitors, if only at weekends. Inside you will find that almost everything is Victorian restoration on a grand scale and very little of the original interior remains. Exceptions include the 14th c. font with its carved bowl and clustered columns. A few old bench-ends remain and some carvings are noteworthy. A tour around the outside and a glance through the windows may be enough to see all that there is to see here.

HORSFORD   All Saints

No of Bells: 1

19th c. Deanery: Taverham

Hundred: Taverham

Union house: Horsham St Faith

21st c. Deanery: Norwich North

Benefice: Horsford

4 m NNW of Norwich just off the B1149. Situated at the southern end of Horsford on the road towards Horsham St Faith.

O.S. grid ref: TG 196154

Post Code: NR10 3DB

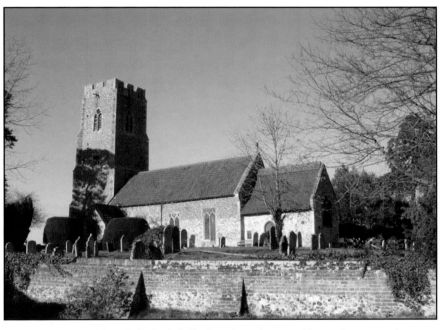

You will find this delightful little church standing close to the road and is well worth taking a look inside. Perhaps the most interesting thing to look out for is the 900-year-old square font which has shallow arcading around the sides of the Purbeck bowl. There is no south aisle but the north aisle is formed by a nice early arcade. All the fixtures and furnishings are Victorian and are rather plain and disappointing, including the pulpit. The 16th c. screen which at one time was vaulted on both sides, has been spoiled with brown paint, leaving only the outlines of the lovely tracery of a once beautiful screen. A nice new western gallery houses the organ. Worth a look around as long as expectations are not too high. Some of the glass in the windows is interesting although of no real historical interest.

HUNWORTH   St Lawrence
No of Bells: 1
19th c. Deanery: Holt
Hundred: Holt
Union house: Erpingham
21st c. Deanery: Holt
Benefice: Brinton

2 miles S of Holt. From the
B1149 turn off right
towards Hunworth. Turn
right towards Thornage,
then left after 400 yards.
O.S. grid ref: TG 065355
Post Code: NR24 2EQ

Time has stood still for many years at Hunworth church. The old
sketch hanging on the wall inside shows the outside of the church
almost exactly as it is today. Unfortunately the same can't be said for
the inside; electricity has been installed in the most unsympathetic
way possible and has marred the appearance of the interior with ugly
meter boxes and sockets. The fitting and furnishings are all Victorian
and lack any charm or interesting features. The octagonal mediaeval
font is very plain and unadorned. In the south transept is a small
piscina with what I assume is a credence shelf at the side. A good
carved eagle lectern is worth a second glance but the only real unusual
thing about this rather poorly maintained church is a panel of tracery
just below the weathering of the southwest tower buttress.

ILLINGTON   St Andrew

No of Bells: 0 (originally 2)

19th c. Deanery: Rockland

Hundred: Shropham

Union house: Rockland All Saints

21st c. Deanery: Thetford & Rockland

Benefice: Thetford Team Ministry

5 m WNW of East Harling. From the A1075 at Stonebridge turn east to Illington. The church is near Hall Farm.

O.S. grid ref: TL 947900

Post Code: IP24 1RP

To all intents and purposes this church is redundant. Supported by the Norfolk Churches Trust it holds only the minimum services to allow it to remain active. This is a lovely, though sadly inactive church The tower which was built in the late 14th c. underwent considerable restoration in 1997. The west doorway, set into the attractively decorated tower, has two niches which once held statuettes: virtually unused since the 1980s, it has declined steadily ever since. The church was rebuilt from an earlier Norman church in the 14th c. it still retains slit windows in the nave which were opened during restorations in the 1880s. The window seating is still in evidence. In the base of the tower is a wafer oven, a rare survival from mediaeval times. The plain octagonal font is coeval with the building of the church.

INGWORTH   St Lawrence

No of Bells:	1
19th c. Deanery:	Ingworth
Hundred:	South Erpingham
Union house:	Aylsham
21st c. Deanery:	Ingworth
Benefice:	Scarrowbeck, Erpingham

2 m N of Aylsham. From Aylsham head north on the A140, after 2 miles turn left to Ingworth and follow 1 mile to the T junction.
O.S. grid ref: TG 194297
Post Code: NR11 6AE

In 1822 the Norman round tower fell and was never rebuilt. It now serves as a vestry and office. The whole church is beautifully thatched. On the crow-stepped gable of the parvise of the porch is a small niche, above which is a stone head set into the brickwork. On entering the nave the 15th c. font is the first thing you will see. With quatrefoils around the bowl with a carved corona, it is supported on a traceried shaft. (Cautley suspects it was once a Seven Sacrament font). Past the old box-pews of the north aisle is what remains of the once splendid 15th c. screen, unfortunately painted sometime in the Victorian era. In the chancel is a piscina with an unusual drainage hole. Placed high on the west wall of the nave, in pristine condition, are the splendid carved Royal Arms of William and Mary.

INTWOOD	All Saints	3½ m SW of Norwich. Just
No of Bells:	5	off the A47 take the B1113
19th c. Deanery:	Humbleyard	to Swardeston and head
Hundred:	Humbleyard	north to Intwood. The
Union house:	Swainsthorpe	church is at the T junction.
21st c. Deanery:	Humbleyard	O.S. grid ref: TG 196742
Benefice:	Swardeston	Post Code: NR4 6TG

A church has stood on this site since Saxon times, and some vestiges of the original still remain. The church was substantially rebuilt and an octagonal top was added to the tower by Henry Hobart who lived at the Hall in the late 16th c. Nearby Keswick was demolished to supply the building materials. Further restoration by heavy-handed Victorians destroyed much of this church and most of what is seen today, especially the interior, was financed by the Muskett and Unthank families. Even the octagonal font is from this period (1854). Benches adorned with elaborately detailed poppyheads, some of which have figures on the armrests, fill the aisle but these too are Victorian. A western gallery gives a good view of the nave and carved reredos behind the altar.

ITTERINGHAM St Mary the Virgin

No of Bells: 1
19th c. Deanery: Ingworth
Hundred: South Erpingham
Union house: Aylsham
21st c. Deanery: Ingworth
Benefice: Seven Churches Itteringham

4 m NW of Aylsham. From Aylsham head towards and through Blickling into Itteringham. The church is just north of the village.
O.S. grid ref: TG 145310
Post Code: NR11 7AX

A very plain church with a simple but substantial tower which dates from the early 13th c. The list of rectors starts in 1227. On the north side is a ruinous guild chapel which was added in the 14th c. A very plain hexagonal font of uncertain vintage greets the visitor. Box-pews which line both sides of the aisle have, rather uncommonly, poppy-heads of an 18th c. style. Strangely, too, the otherwise plain pulpit is adorned with a bare-breasted angel facing the congregation. The dark trusses of the roof are eye-catching against the white plastered ceiling but detract from the otherwise interesting surroundings. A decorated parish chest is dated 1716 although its design is at least 100 years earlier. The Royal Arms which hang above the north door (painted in an unusual style) are those of William IV and are dated 1833.

KELLING	St Mary	3 m N of Holt. From the
No of Bells:	1	A140 coast road turn south
19th c. Deanery:	Holt	near the Muckleburgh
Hundred:	Holt	Museum. The church is 1
Union house:	Erpingham	mile further, near the Hall.
21st c. Deanery:	Holt	O.S. grid ref: TG 088417
Benefice:	Weybourne	Post Code: NR25 7EW

The south transept was in ruins by 1864 but the rest of the church was restored about this time. What is here today is a lovely building with clean lines that is a credit to the community. Atop the tower is a parapet with very distinctive chequering. A tiny quatrefoil window penetrates the wall of the porch. Inside the nave is an octagonal font with a 15th c. dedication to its donor, de Kelling, around the top of the bowl; its facets display emblems of religious significance. The Royal Arms are Stuart and those of Queen Ann, but have been modified to G R and re-dated 1797. The large expanse of the nave is accentuated by the lack of wall monuments but in the chancel is a lovely Easter Sepulchre which is probably the oldest thing in the church, slightly spoiled by the chancel floor having been raised.

KENNINGHALL St Mary

No of Bells:	8
19th c. Deanery:	Rockland
Hundred:	Guiltcross
Union house:	Kenninghall
21st c. Deanery:	Thetford & Rockland
Benefice:	Guiltcross

3 m ESE of East Harling. Turn south off the A11 at Snetterton and head through Quidenham to Kenninghall Street.

O.S. grid ref: TM 041860
Post Code: NR16 2EP

Before entering the church a look around the 15th c. knapped flint tower is essential. It is finely decorated with a good base-course. A buttress, too, has a stone shield of the Duke of Norfolk. A scratch dial can also be found. The chancel is really quite large in comparison to the nave which has a good 14th c. five-window clerestory above the arcade and some excellent tracery (part of the arch-braced cambered tie-beam roof). While scanning the roof you will notice the Royal Arms of Elizabeth filling the tympanum of the chancel arch. The Arms of King Charles I are also to be seen. The plain octagonal font has an enormous cover reaching to almost ten feet. In the chancel is a plain piscina and sedilia. This is a lovely church to look around. However, most of the furnishings are of the Victorian era.

KESWICK	All Saints	3 m SSW of Norwich.
No of Bells:	1	From the A140 N of the
19th c. Deanery:	Humbleyard	A47 take the B1113 after
Hundred:	Humbleyard	the railway bridge and
Union house:	Swainsthorpe	continue ½ mile (on right).
21st c. Deanery:	Humbleyard	O.S. grid ref: TG 214046
Benefice:	Upper Tas Valley	Post Code: NR4 6DY

Keswick church was dismantled in the 16th c. to supply materials for the rebuilding of Intwood All Saints. It stood as a ruin until 1922 when it was partially rebuilt by the Gurney family after being used as a private mortuary chapel. The small apsidal end was added incorporating a War Memorial in the 1950s. Part of the old chancel still stands ruinous. Inside is small, being less than twenty feet long and slightly wider. The strange font appears to have been purchased from the local garden centre but everything here with the possible exception of the east window is well loved and cared for. The window in question, in the apse, which seems to be a bone of contention among the congregation was designed by the William Morris workshop and supposedly depicts Hope. Always kept locked!

KETTERINGHAM St Peter

No of Bells: 6
19th c. Deanery: Humbleyard
Hundred: Humbleyard
Union house: Swainsthorpe
21st c. Deanery: Humbleyard
Benefice: Swardeston

3 m E of Wymondham.
From there take the B1172
to Hethersett where you
turn south to Ketteringham.
The church is near the Hall.
O.S. grid ref: TG 164025
Post Code: NR18 8RS

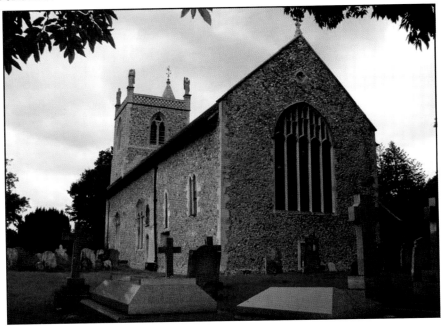

This much restored barn-like church has lovely chequer-work on the tower parapet which one cannot help noticing as outstanding. There are two statuettes of angels and a saint acting as pinnacles. The church dates from Norman times and small lancet windows are still evident behind glass. Inside the building more early work is to be found, such as the 13th c. piscina and a coeval double lancet window in the chancel. Close to the former is a fine table-tomb of Thomas Hevenyngham and his wife Anne. The font is 15th c. bearing armorial shields at the base. Beneath the bowl is vine tracery still retaining traces of the original colouring. In the grounds is a mausoleum which is notable for its construction and is highly prized as one of Norfolk's finest buildings. There is much to see here and it is well worth a visit.

KILVERSTONE   St Andrew

No of Bells: 1
19th c. Deanery: Rockland
Hundred: Shropham
Union house: Thetford St Mary's
21st c. Deanery: Thetford & Rockland
Benefice: Thetford

1½ m ENE of Thetford.
Leave Thetford on the
A1075 and follow ¾ m to
Kilverstone Hall. 200 yds
past the Hall, turn right.
O.S. grid ref: TL 894890
Post Code: IP24 2RN

I adore this lovely little church. The stout round tower is probably as early as 10th c. at its foundations and has some very interesting features, although they have all been restored to some degree. A good look around the outside is essential to appreciate the age and beauty of the architecture and the external cinquefoil piscina indicating an earlier south aisle. Inside the small porch is a Norman doorway with one engaged shaft either side. Unfortunately, severe restoration has left little of the Norman period to see. A rather unusual circular 19th c. font looks totally out of place. Above on the tower wall are Hanoverian Royal Arms donated by Charles Wright. In the chancel is a fairly plain piscina and a small sedilia for two. Set into the floor is a black marble tablet to Ann Wright (1691), the wife of Charles.

KIMBERLEY St Peter
No of Bells: 2
19th c. Deanery: Hingham
Hundred: Forehoe
Union house: Wicklewood
21st c. Deanery: Dereham & Mitford
Benefice:Barnham Broom / Upper Yare

3 m NW of Wymondham.
Off the B1108 at Kimberley
on the Wymondham road
just behind the 'Village
Green' on the left.
O.S. grid ref: TG 072042
Post Code: NR18 9EY

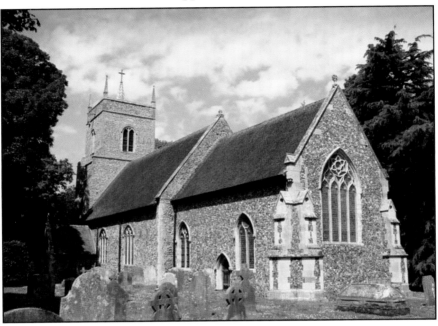

This lovely church has a spirelet on the top of the tower which was reconstructed in 1631 after a partial fall; the date can be clearly seen in the brickwork of the west face. Set in the wall of the north side of the nave is a late 13th c window which indicates the date of the church. Inside the nave is a beautiful hammerbeam roof, constructed in the early 20th c. after the completion of other restoration work during the Victorian period. The Royal Arms are those of James I, bearing his unique motto. There are many monuments to view here, including that of the Wodehouse family who are buried in a vault. Dame Elizabeth Strutt (1651), daughter of Sir Thomas Wodehouse, has her own splendid wall monument. Brasses also record the importance of the family and its influence within the parish.

LANGHAM	Sts Andrew & Mary	5 m WNW of Holt. From
No of Bells:	3	the A140 at Morston, head
19th c. Deanery:	Holt	south for 2 miles. The
Hundred:	Holt	church is at the crossroads
Union house:	Great Snoring	in the village centre.
21st c. Deanery:	Holt	O.S. grid ref: TG 007413
Benefice:	Stiffkey & Bale	Post Code: NR25 7BX

The full name of Langham Magna or Episcopi is indicative that at one time there was a Langham Parva (St Mary) but the two parishes were consolidated centuries ago. The porch has been recently re-built as can be seen by the lines in the cement rendering. The large arcaded octagonal bowl of the font almost certainly came from St Mary's, although I believe the columns upon which it stands are of a later date. In the south aisle is a chapel with its own simple piscina and sedilia, only slightly less elaborate than that in the chancel. The Royal Arms are Stuart and much earlier than the date of 1742 suggests. They are attributed to Anne but her motto (Semper Eadem) does not appear. While most of the furnishings and fittings are Victorian it is an interesting church to visit, especially to those interested in glass.

LARLING	St Ethelbert	2 m NNW of East Harling.
No of Bells:	3	Directly off the A11, 2 m
19th c. Deanery:	Rockland	west of Snetterton circuit,
Hundred:	Shropham	turn left then right under
Union house:	Rockland All Saints	the A11 and 2nd right.
21st c. Deanery:	Thetford & Rockland	O.S. grid ref: TL 982898
Benefice:	East Harling	Post Code: NR16 2QZ

A remote church, never open and no keyholder is listed. Poor show! The church has undergone much restoration over the centuries and has left the tower unfinished and without a parapet. Inside the locked porch is a beautiful Norman doorway with two engaged shafts and unusual decoration on the arch. Through the west window you will be able to see (if you are tall enough) the organ and the arcade of the 14th c. south aisle and the simplest of benches. If you are fortunate enough to gain access there is a lovely plain 12th c. font and a superb double arched piscina of the same period. Much of the church has been Victorianised but there are some parts which retain the original features. It is a great shame that nobody is willing advertise their name as keyholder or that the interior is not more easily accessible.

LETHERINGSETT St Andrew

No of Bells:	3
19th c. Deanery:	Holt
Hundred:	Holt
Union house:	Erpingham
21st c. Deanery:	Holt
Benefice:	Glaven Valley (Blakeney)

1½ m W of Holt. From Holt head west on the A148 and follow the road for 1½ miles. The church is close to a bend in the road.

O.S. grid ref: TG 060389
Post Code: NR25 7AR

A lovely round tower which is almost certainly Norman sets off this church to perfection. The continuous line of the roof may appear boring from the outside but wait until you see the inside! The north and south aisles stretch as far as the chancel giving an impression of great space. The simple clerestory casts light upon the clean lines of the interior. The octagonal 13th c. font set on eight columns and a central shaft has shallow arcading around the bowl. In the north aisle is a stoup and a chapel, the south aisle has a small piscina. In the chancel the reredos is of stone and so well carved with canopied niches containing saints and crocketted pinnacles that it seems totally out of place in a small rural church. There are the remains of a corner piscina and a sedilia which I was very pleased to find preserved.

LITTLE BARNINGHAM St Andrew

No of Bells:	1
19th c. Deanery:	Ingworth
Hundred:	South Erpingham
Union house:	Aylsham
21st c. Deanery:	Ingworth

Benefice: Seven Churches Itteringham

6 m NW of Aylsham. From the B1149 at Saxthorpe church head north to Little Barningham and turn right at the crossroads.

O.S. grid ref: TG 142333
Post Code: NR11 7AG

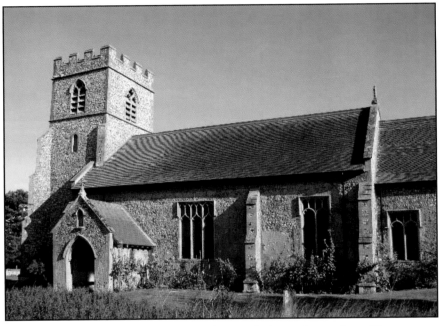

This is a lovely little church which stands just above the village street, has hollyhocks growing around the south walls, and sturdy buttresses supporting the embattled tower. Beneath the tower is the organ which must have been the largest to be had for the available space. 19th c. Victorian restoration has unfortunately left the interior rather uninteresting except for the 18inch high carved skeleton which stands on the corner of a box pew dated 1640. It bears a verse for married couples and reminds them '......As I am soe shall you be'. The skeleton is a copy of an original which was stolen in 1995. Probably the reason why the church is now kept locked. A decorated altar frontal depicts flowers, birds and other living things, creating a welcome contrast to death. Different if nothing else!

LITTLE ELLINGHAM   St Peter
No of Bells: 1
19th c. Deanery: Breckles
Hundred: Wayland
Union house: Rockland All saints
21st c. Deanery: Thetford & Rockland
Benefice: Great Ellingham (Shelrock)

5 m E of Watton. Leave Watton on the B1108 and turn right at Scoulton and follow the road into the village centre.
O.S. grid ref: TM 005993
Post Code: NR17 1JH

An uncommon configuration in Norfolk, with the 14th c. south tower also serving as a porch. The church suffered a disastrous fire in 1867 and was rebuilt and is why Cautley, in his 'Norfolk Churches' gives it no mention. Obviously much of the mediaeval aspect has disappeared but there is still interest here. The font is Victorian and carved from an expensive porphyry marble, and is totally out of place. What is nice to see are the re-used carved corbels in the chancel which create a shelf next to the trefoil piscina. Set into the floor below is a Norman stone slab with zigzag decoration, giving an indication of the possible date of the original building of the church. On the north side of the nave is a restored recess, a tomb of someone long forgotten. So although Victorian it does retain some of its history.

LITTLE MELTON   All Saints   5 m W of Norwich. From there
No of Bells: 3   take the A47 and turn left at the
19th c. Deanery: Humbleyard   Hospital roundabout and 1st exit
Hundred: Humbleyard   to Barford. Take 2nd left then
Union house: Swainsthorpe 1st left towards Little Melton.
21st c. Deanery: Humbleyard   O.S. grid ref: TG 153069
Benefice: Hethersett   Post Code: NR9 3NS

This church is more often locked than not, which is a pity because
there are a number of items of interest and nothing worthwhile for the
thief except some personal belongings which ought not to be left
there anyway. Most of the building dates from the 14th c. but traces
of an earlier church remain. The 13th c. font for instance; typical of
its period with short columns around a central shaft. Traces of very
early wall paintings are to be seen although somewhat faded since
their discovery. Modern roofs protect the mostly original interior and
14th c. arcades reveal the date of its final major stage of building. The
pulpit stands on a stone base. A splendid double piscina and a
graduated sedilia (divided by the altar rail) have been preserved in the
chancel. A nice screen, parts of which were used to create the pulpit.

LITTLE WITCHINGHAM St Faith

No of Bells: 1
19th c. Deanery: Sparham
Hundred: Eynesford
Union house: Horsham St Faiths
21st c. Deanery: -
The Churches Conservation Trust

2½ m SSE of Reepham.
From the A1067 at
Attlebridge turn north to
Alderford, bear right to
Reepham, then 2nd left.
O.S. grid ref: TG 115203
Post Code: NR9 5PA

For many years this church stood empty and superfluous to parochial requirements, but thankfully the CCT now looks after its welfare. Some very important wall paintings have been discovered here and when I visited preservation work was well under way. They are mostly made up of scrolls, vines and art-work, quite unusual. When H. Munro Cautley visited here he described the church as 'a poor little disused church with only a few simple old benches'. If he had been able to see under the whitewash I am sure he would have enthused for half a page. Although at the time of writing it is locked due to on-going work, it may be open every day, but if not the key is only a few yards away. The octagonal font is decorated with simple quatrefoil designs, but the paintings alone are well worth a visit.

LONG STRATTON St Mary

No of Bells:	6
19th c. Deanery:	Depwade
Hundred:	Depwade
Union house:	Pulham St Mary
21st c. Deanery:	Depwade
Benefice:	Long Stratton

10 m S of Norwich. To be found on the southern side of the valley in which Long Stratton is situated on the A140 Ipswich Road.
O.S. grid ref: TM 196922
Post Code: NR15 2TA

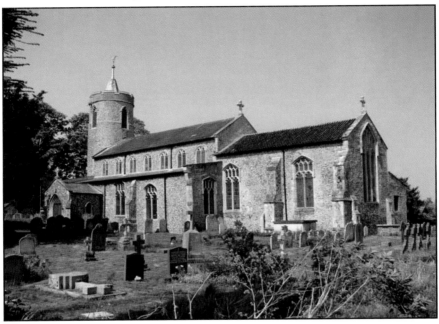

The church is very close to the main road which runs through the parish and has stood there since Norman times, or perhaps earlier. Certainly the lower portion of the round tower is Norman but the spirelet is comparatively recent. The nave has a simple arch-braced roof and that of the chancel has been plastered. The most interesting item in the church however, is the Sexton's wheel and a candle bracket, which are protected in a glass case. The former is somewhat inferior to the one to be found at Yaxley in Suffolk but the latter is unique this side of Hertfordshire. In the chancel opposite the piscina and sedilia is the splendid monument to Sir Edmund Reve (1647). Elsewhere there is another to Robert de Swaffham (1361). High on the west wall of the nave can be found the Royal Arms of Charles II.

LYNG   St Margaret

No of Bells:	6 once now 5
19th c. Deanery:	Sparham
Hundred:	Eynesford
Union house:	Gressenhall
21st c. Deanery:	Sparham
Benefice:	FLEBBS

5 m SW of Reepham. From the A1067, 2 m east of Bawdeswell head south to Lyng and turn at the 'Fox & Hounds' P.H.

O.S. grid ref: TG 069178

Post Code: NR9 5RE

Almost concealed from the main road behind the pub, stands Lyng church with its tall porch and as can be seen by the presence of a nice three-light window, there was once a parvise above. 15th c. tracery adorns the entrance door to the nave and inside a lovely old 13th c. Norman font standing on eight round columns and a central shaft. To the west are the stairs to the ringing gallery. Nearby, behind the pews is a well maintained bier. The church is renowned for its mediaeval altar cloth *(The Lyng Pall)* now preserved in a glass case and protected from the light by a roller blind. Most of the fixtures and fittings are Victorian, including the hammerbeam roof of the nave. Beyond is the chancel, re-built in 1905. A Benedictine nunnery dedicated to St Edmund was once also within the parish boundary.

MANNINGTON   St Mary

No of Bells: -
19th c. Deanery: Ingworth
Hundred: South Erpingham
Union house: Aylsham
21st c. Deanery: -
On private land, access is permitted.

5 m NNW of Aylsham. Take the road from Saxthorpe to Mannington Hall which is well signed. Then walk 300 yds east of the visitor centre.
O.S. grid ref: TG 142319
Post Code: near NR11 7BB

This building has a rather complicated history. Never, I believe, actually a parish church in the strictest sense of the word, but important enough to be included in this guide. It seems to have been more a chapel of ease for the use of the parish, with the main church at Itteringham. Having stood ruinous for many centuries it has been landscaped into the gardens of Mannington Hall and stands serenely on the opposite side of the road amongst the rhododendrons. In the 19th century the Earl of Orford was living at the Hall and made a feature of the ruin, surrounding it with ephemera and various objets d'art; even installing his own memorial, but he was eventually buried at Itteringham. It is a pleasant and tranquil place to visit but has little significance in the overall scheme of Norfolk churches.

MARLINGFORD Blessed Virgin Mary

		6 m W of Norwich from where take the A47 and turn left at the Hospital roundabout and 1st exit. Then 3rd right then left.
No of Bells:	1	
19th c. Deanery:	Hingham	
Hundred:	Forehoe	
Union house:	Wicklewood	
21st c. Deanery:	Dereham & Mitford	
Benefice:	Easton	

O.S. grid ref: TG 128083
Post Code: NR9 5HP

When I visited Marlingford I was astonished that so many headstones have been moved, not by vandals, but by the PCC who have removed stones and kerbs to facilitate easier mowing. The timbered porch protects a simple Norman doorway which has been recently rebuilt, probably in Victorian times. The octagonal 13th c. Norman font has arcading on the facets of the bowl which stands on eight Victorian columns. A monster of a stone pulpit sits inelegantly at the front of the pews. Behind it is a commandment board featuring Moses, Aaron and Joshua, which I think must have been restored. An hour glass bracket is attached to the opposite wall. A wall memorial to Mary Cullyer (1672), wife of John and daughter of Clement Jermy, was the oldest I could find but there are others from the 17th c.

MARSHAM	All Saints	10 m N of Norwich. Just
No of Bells:	8	off the A140. The church is
19th c. Deanery:	Ingworth	signposted just south of the
Hundred:	South Erpingham	village centre. There is a
Union house:	Aylsham	car park off the main road.
21st c. Deanery:	Ingworth	O.S. grid ref: TG 197238
Benefice:	Bure Valley	Post Code: NR10 5RB

A few treats await the visitor to Marsham All Saints. Built mainly in the 14th c. the arcades support a good five-window clerestory which illuminates the angels in the arch-braced hammerbeam roof of the nave. Great tie-beams were added to prevent the spreading of the walls with the added weight of the roof. A lovely Seven Sacrament font with a fine corona of angels stands at its west end. Close by is the organ, upon which are the Royal Arms of James I. At the eastern end of the nave a badly situated modern pulpit blocks the view of part of the beautiful painted screen base which depicts fourteen saints, including a rare Saint Faith holding her saw. The upper part of the once canopied screen has unfortunately been pruned to a minimum of tracery. Victorian benches with poppy-heads fill the nave.

MATLASK	St Peter	6 m SE of Holt. Midway
No of Bells:	1 (at one time 3)	between the B1149 at
19th c. Deanery:	Repps	Edgefield & the A140 at
Hundred:	Repps	Roughton. South of
Union house:	North Erpingham	Barningham Hall.
21st c. Deanery:	Holt	O.S. grid ref: TG 151348
Benefice:	Barningham Winter	Post Code: NR11 7JG

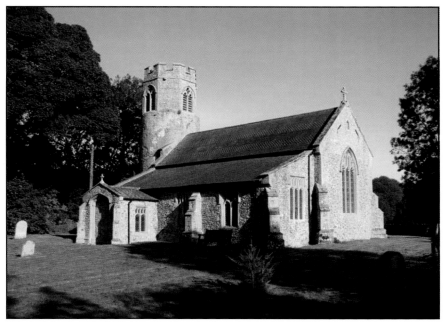

Situated in a well maintained churchyard this lovely little church has a single roof for nave and chancel, the latter having collapsed during a service in 1726. It was never rebuilt, but instead the nave was reduced in length. A plain asymmetrical octagonal font from the 15th c. stands on a low plinth at the west end, with a cover of the same date. Beneath the Norman tower (with a later octagonal top) is a 14th c. parish chest of English oak; the old bier is nearby. Although the roof is modern the old corbels with faces that support the wall posts are as old as the church itself. Benches which fill the nave are said to be 15th c. and have poppy-head carved ends which I believe are somewhat later. A good set of Royal Arms attributed to George III hang on the wall, as do hatchments to members of the Gunton family.

MATTISHALL All Saints ****

No of Bells:	6 (only 2 in use)	
19th c. Deanery:	Hingham	
Hundred:	Mitford	
Union house:	Gressenhall	
21st c. Deanery:	Dereham & Mitford	
Benefice:	Mattishall	

11 m W of Norwich. Turn west off the A47 through East Tuddenham, the church is on the crossroads in Church Plain, Mattishall. O.S. grid ref: TG 053111
Post Code: NR20 5QF

'I am here and here I will stay' is the bold statement this church makes. The stout 14th c. tower with its bell turret dominates the 15th c. nave with its four-window clerestory and chancel. Inside, a number of delights await, not least the hammerbeam roof of the nave with angels and bosses and stencilled stars on ceiling and tie-beams. Above the chancel arch is an east window which once spread morning sunlight onto the rood and canopy of honour. Beyond the 15th c. arcades are aisles north and south with stone seating for the congregation before benches became popular. In the sanctuary is a piscina and sedilia clearly illustrating that the floor of the chancel has at some time been raised. The base of the painted screen is quite spectacular and is a 'must', with all twelve apostles depicted.

MATTISHALL BURGH St Peter

No of Bells:	6
19th c. Deanery:	Hingham
Hundred:	Mitford
Union house:	Gressenhall
21st c. Deanery:	Dereham & Mitford
Benefice:	Mattishall (Redundant)

1 m NE of Mattishall. From Mattishall church *(see previous page)* head north for ½ m then turn right into Church Lane.

O.S. grid ref: TG 055118
Post Code: NR20 3QU

Mattishall Burgh church has little to offer the visitor, no welcome, no open door. It is a very beautiful 13th c. shed containing a coeval Purbeck font and arcade. Through the grimy windows I could make out a jumble of benches and a couple of wall monuments. I could see a 15th c. screen which appears to be painted a horrible brown instead of being varnished. An angle piscina in the sanctuary opens into the side of the adjacent sedilia. This is a lovely church that is spoiled by a locked door and a bad attitude. No effort has been made to make the key available and to make visitors welcome. It is overlooked by houses all around and the chances of theft are remote. However, the windows which are very expensive to replace are left vulnerable to the annoyed visitor and the determined vandal. Poor show!

MELTON CONSTABLE St Peter

No of Bells: 1
19th c. Deanery: Holt
Hundred: Holt
Union house: Local support
21st c. Deanery: Holt
Benefice: Briston

6½ m ENE of Fakenham. At Melton Constable on the B1354 turn south to Melton Hall. The church is in the Hall driveway.
O.S. grid ref: TG 038310
Post Code: NR24 2NE

Here is a church that is well loved, well attended and much visited. It has stood here since just after the Conquest although many changes and much rebuilding has taken place. The only truly original part of the building is the tower with its pyramidal cap and lovely windows although I must say the nave may also be virtually unaltered. None of the original doorways remain. The chancel arch, being part of the tower is quite interesting as is the whole of the interior of the building. In the south transept are scores of memorials to various members of the Astley family dating from the 17th c. to the present day. The family have obviously been great benefactors to the church and parish over the centuries. There are number of curios to see here although most of the fittings and furnishings are modern and spotlessly clean.

MENDHAM All Saints (Suffolk)
No of Bells: 6
19th c. Deanery: Hoxne
Hundred: Hoxne
Union house: Stradbroke
21st c Deanery: Hoxne
Benefice: Redenhall

6 m SW of Bungay
between Harleston,
Norfolk & Homersfield: in
The Street, 50 yds from the
River Waveney.
O.S. grid ref TM 269829
Post Code: IP20 0NH

This 14th c. church has been heavily restored over the centuries, particularly by the Victorians after it fell into disrepair. The clerestory is 15th c. but the roofs were virtually replaced in 1868 following partial collapse. The tower was repaired at the same time and crenulations restored. The rebuilt chancel and arch are most notable, being constructed in wood as part of the chancel roof. The corbels and other carved figures were the work of local artisan Mr. Godbold of Harleston in Norfolk. There are portrait brasses dating back to the 17th c. of Cecily and two Richards of the Freston family. The trefoil piscina is restored and is flanked by a sedile. There was a priory in the parish founded by William de Huntingfield in 1140. Two-fifths of the parish are in Norfolk, but the church is in Suffolk.

METTON	St Andrew	3½ m S of Cromer. From the
No of Bells:	3	A10 at Roughton head west
19th c. Deanery:	Repps	on the BB1436 and take the
Hundred:	North Erpingham	1st left to Metton. The church
Union house:	West Beckham	is in the High Street.
21st c. Deanery:	Repps	O.S. grid ref: TG 199373
Benefice:	Roughton	Post Code: NR11 8QX

Why the tower was built right up to the western boundary of the churchyard is difficult to understand, but it was necessary to create an ambulatory pathway around the church for processions, and archways were built into the base of the tower for this purpose. It could easily have been built to the north or south of the nave. A wander around the exterior will reveal the very limited size of the churchyard. Inside the church are strange carved faces staring down from the hammers of the now concealed roof timbers. Even more bizarrely is the corbel head which forms part of the bowl of the piscina. An adjacent dropped window sill sedilia has been filled in after a replacement window was inserted. A modern font has replaced what must have been a 15th c. model, the period when the church was constructed.

MORLEY St Botolph 3 m WSW of Wymondham
No of Bells: 1 (3 before 1959) from where take the B1172.
19th c. Deanery: Hingham Turn off right to Morley
Hundred: Forehoe then 3rd right, opposite the
Union house: Wicklewood telephone kiosk.
21st c. Deanery: Humbleyard O.S. grid ref: TF 069003
Benefice: High Oak & Hingham Post Code: NR18 9TH

In 1959 this church was virtually destroyed by fire and all that remained was the 14th c. tower and the walls. Almost a complete rebuild was necessary and that is why today there is nothing of historical and little of architectural interest to see here. That does not mean however, that there is nothing to see. James Fletcher Watson was the architect who brought the church back to life. (His other major work was Bawdeswell which is entirely different in its design.) It is once again a fine building with a modern hammerbeam roof which has been painted in two tones of blue. Obviously the furnishings and fittings in the church are new too, even the font, but everything is still in the traditional style which is nice. This is an attractive church and well loved and cared for by the community.

MORLEY St Peter

No of Bells:	1
19th c. Deanery:	Hingham
Hundred:	Forehoe
Union house:	Wicklewood
21st c. Deanery:	Humbleyard
Benefice:	High Oak & Hingham

2½ m NNE of Attleborough. From Attleborough head to the A47, but turn left just over the flyover, then left again and follow for 1 mile.
O.S. grid ref: TG 063987
Post Code: NR18 9TU

Situated on a sharp bend in the road this church has a large churchyard, well maintained and attended. However, it is kept locked and no key-holder listed at the time of writing. The tower, which is 15th c., has lost its upper half and is now capped with a pyramidal roof. Much of the exterior has been cement-rendered and has started to deteriorate, giving the church an unjustified shabby appearance. Inside the nave is an unusual 16th c. font with an undercut bowl bearing quatrefoil designs and standing on a slim central shaft. A Victorian pulpit and plain benches furnish the nave, which terminates in a lovely traceried screen. In the choir are some poppy-head benches while a Stuart holy table can be found in the sanctuary. An early 17th c. wall monument makes very interesting reading.

MORSTON   All Saints
No of Bells: 1
19th c. Deanery: Holt
Hundred: Holt
Union house: Great Snoring
21st c. Deanery: Holt
Benefice: Stiffkey & Bale

6 m E of Wells. The church can be found quite close to the A149 coast road. Just west of Langham Road in The Street.
O.S. grid ref: TG 008438
Post Code: NR25 7AA

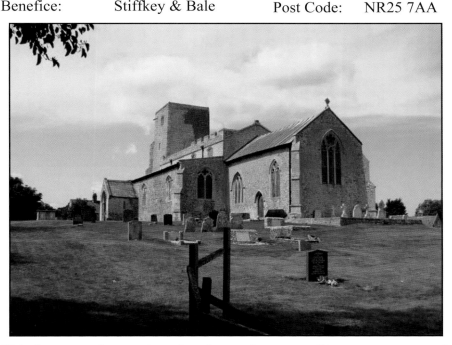

This is a most interesting church, not because of its greatness, nor its patronage, but because of its unusual architecture and traditional style interior. Parts of the church date back to the 14th c. and possibly earlier judging by its position. The clerestory is partially embattled and appears to have been designed that way. Why? The tower has suffered a partial collapse over the years and the scar is very apparent, but that couldn't have been the cause. Inside the nave, in the tympanum of the chancel arch are the Royal Arms of 1823 , I believe in the 17th c. style, so it may have been over-painted since Elizabeth's time. The lovely screen has the Four Doctors and saints in full colour; and a brass to Richard Makyngs (1596) as a rector, is unique for this period in the county. Much more to see than I have space for here!

MORTON-on -the-HILL St Margaret

No of Bells:	0	
19th c. Deanery:	Sparham	
Hundred:	Eynesford	
Union house:	Horham St Faiths	
21st c. Deanery:	Sparham	
Benefice:	Wensum Group	

10 m NW of Norwich.
From the A1067 turn S at
Attlebridge on a minor road
and enter the Morton Hall
estate, and follow the road.
O.S. grid ref: TG 127159
Post Code: NR9 5JS

The round tower, if not the church, is almost certainly pre-Conquest.
It is obvious from the picture above that the tower has suffered a
serious collapse which has since been consolidated. The small porch
protects a door with early mediaeval tracery on its upper part. This
however is not the entrance. That is on the north side. Inside what
remains of the nave are all the usual trappings of a normal church, but
this is nothing of the sort. It is the dedication and perseverance of one
woman, Lady Prince-Smith, which has kept this lovely little church
open and active. It was in the 1970s that she set to work restoring the
church with help from the Norfolk Churches Trust. Robert Southwell,
who once lived at the Hall, was hung drawn and quartered for being a
Jesuit, and was canonised as a martyr Saint by Pope Paul VI in 1970.

MULBARTON   St Mary Magdalene   5 m SSW of Norwich. Leave
No of Bells: 6   Norwich on the A140
19th c. Deanery: Humbleyard   heading south and turn right
Hundred: Humbleyard   at Swainsthorpe. Follow road
Union house: Swainsthorpe   taking left - right - right.
21st c. Deanery: Humbleyard   O.S. grid ref: TG 195011
Benefice: Mulbarton   Post Code: NR14 8JS

It is unfortunate, to my mind, that this church is used for secular
purposes as well as worship. Because drum-kits and other musical
instruments are left in the church, it is kept locked. However, the
rectory next door does hold the key if you care to enter. A metal strap
holds the broken bowl of the 15th c. font together and a hatchment
hangs on the wall nearby. Benches and other furnishings are modern
and lack any interesting qualities except those in the choir which have
poppy-heads. A Victorian pulpit stands in front of the chancel arch. In
the chancel a cusped piscina has been preserved but the sedilia have
been removed. On the opposite wall is a 17th c. memorial to Sir
Edwin Rich and his son and others; another is to Rev. Benjamin Lany
(1766) and there are more to other members of his family.

NEW BUCKENHAM St Martin

No of Bells:	8
19th c. Deanery:	Rockland
Hundred:	Shropham
Union house:	Kenninghall
21st c. Deanery:	Thetford & Rockland
Benefice:	Quidenham

4 m SE of Attleborough. The church is almost on the B1113 as it passes through the village and is almost impossible to miss.

O.S. grid ref: TM 088905
Post Code: NR16 2BA

On my second visit to this church I noticed things I hadn't seen before. So I recommend an hour is needed to see all there is to see here. The significant 15th c. tower has huge pinnacles and gargoyles and a good base course and tracery on the buttresses. Ten windows in the clerestory complement the four larger versions in the south aisle and spill light throughout the interior. The font, dated 1619, has wodewoses around the shaft. Above, a hammerbeam roof is supported on wall posts resting on carved corbels. In the chancel is a beautiful stone reredos, intricately carved and in contrast to the simple piscina and dropped-sill sedilia. To the north is a fine altar tomb of high quality. Set into the floor are some early ledger slabs; one to John Kendall is dated 1672.

NEWTON FLOTMAN St Mary

No of Bells:	3
19th c. Deanery:	Humbleyard
Hundred:	Humbleyard
Union house:	Swainsthorpe
21st c. Deanery:	Depwade
Benefice:	Tas Valley

7 m S of Norwich. The Church stands elevated, by the side of the A140 just as you enter the village from the Norwich direction.
O.S. grid ref: TM 212984
Post Code: NR15 1PN

Stepped battlements are perhaps the only real external distinguishing feature of this church. Set into the battlements is a plaque to Ralph Blundeville (1503). There are a few things to excite the visitor, and it is a living church a with good congregation. Originally re-built in 1385 it was restored in 19th c. The 15th c font has a traceried bowl with blank shields on each facet. Coeval benches have poppy-heads and a handful have animals carved on the armrests. Most of the remaining fixtures and fittings are however modern as are the timbers in the roofs. On the north wall of the chancel is a large memorial to various members of the Blundeville family, primarily Thomas. An interesting brass is also to be found nearby. Thomas was a man of note and his many achievements are well recorded.

NORTH LOPHAM   St Nicholas

No of Bells:	8
19th c. Deanery:	Rockland
Hundred:	Guiltcross
Union house:	Kenninghall
21st c. Deanery:	Redenhall
Benefice:	Upper Waveney

5 m WNW of Diss. From Diss on the A1066 turn right past South Lopham church and continue just over 1 mile to destination.
O.S. grid ref: TM 036825
Post Code: IP22 2LP

North Lopham church stands very close to the road and is very prominent. The early 14th c. tower has diagonal buttresses which give it a bulky appearance. Around the tower is a stringcourse with a good example of flush-work with initials of saints. On the tower are the initials of the benefactors. Inside the 14th c. porch there is a cusped niche above the door. There is shallow tracery on the tapering octagonal font which dates from the same period. Close by is the old parish chest which Cautley has also dated as 14th c. New roofs and pulpit were installed by the Victorians during restoration work but the simple piscina and sedilia have been unmolested. A well carved lectern and a bench-end or two are worth seeking out. Royal Arms of George III hang on the wall. Architecturally quite interesting.

NORTH TUDDENHAM St Mary

No of Bells:	1
19th c. Deanery:	Hingham
Hundred:	Mitford
Union house:	Gressenhall
21st c. Deanery:	Dereham & Mitford
Benefice:	Mattishall

12 m W of Norwich. Turn south off the dual carriageway just east of the flyover. Turn left, right, left then left into the driveway.
O.S. grid ref: TG 056130
Post Code: NR20 3DH

This church is well worth a visit for a number of reasons. Generally dating from the 14th c. the building is surprisingly grand and purposeful for a small parish. A scratch dial can be found on a south buttress. Over the 14th c. porch is a small parvise, now used for storage. Beneath the tower arch is part of a screen believed to date from about 1390, rescued and installed here. The 15th c. font is deeply cut with shields and has angels around the corbel. An old parish chest is nearby. A good hammer-beam roof covers the nave. The most interesting and exciting thing to see is the screen which dates back to the 15th c. and has well restored paintings of eight saints which are fully described in the guide book. A well built tomb stands in the tiled chancel and many memorials adorn the walls.

OLD BUCKENHAM   All Saints

No of Bells:	6	
19th c. Deanery:	Rockland	
Hundred:	Shropham	
Union house:	Kenninghall	
21st c. Deanery:	Thetford & Rockland	
Benefice:	Quidenham	

3 m S by E of Attleborough from where take the B1077 heading south and into Old Buckenham. The church is close to Church Green.

O.S. grid ref: TM 067914
Post Code: NR17 1RP

The 14th c. octagonal tower once had a spire as can be seen from the sketch in the nave; the stepped parapet is Tudor. Notice the quoin stones have been carved to form a shaft on each angle of the tower. Very little has changed over the centuries and this lovely little church is thatched from end to end. On the door is some mediaeval ironwork. The font is 15th c. and has simple quatrefoil and shield decoration. Bench ends are well worth close examination; figures and exotic creatures sit on the armrests. The lion on the Royal Arms of George III has the strangest grin on his face I think I have ever seen. A wall plaque states that restorations took place in 1858 when all the seating was replaced. A bier bears the date 1666. There is a nice pictorial window and a well carved modern pulpit.

OULTON   Sts Peter & Paul

No of Bells: 1

19th c. Deanery: Ingworth

Hundred: South Erpingham

Union house: Aylsham

21st c. Deanery: Ingworth

Benefice: Seven Churches Itteringham

3½ m NW of Aylsham. From the B1149 near Heydon turn north to Oulton. Next right, and 100 yards over crossroads.

O.S. grid ref: TG 136285

Post Code: NR11 6NS

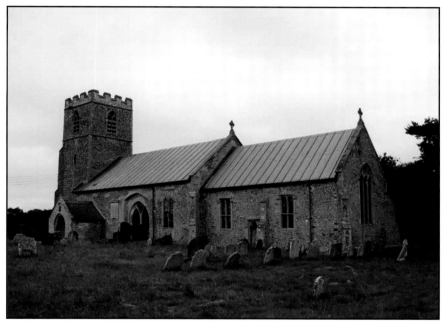

This is a lovely little church where a little restoration has been carried out but the character of the building remains intact. Cautley had little to say about the church and stated that the Arms were Hanoverian. They are in fact Stuart and initialled C R, but in terrible condition; they could even be of Queen Anne judging by the quarterings. The off-centre tower is 14th c. and the church slightly earlier. A plain octagonal font sits on a broad shaft. Unfortunately somebody has seen fit to remove all the pews and turn the church into something of a dance hall with impermanent seating but happily the character of the church is strong enough to offset the deficiency. The lovely Georgian pulpit stands on a thin stem of a foot and looks quite precarious. The names Bell and Pitman appear on monuments in the chancel.

OXNEAD St Michael 3 m SSE of Aylsham. From
No of Bells: 1 the A140 at Aylsham head
19th c. Deanery: Ingworth to Buxton. At crossroads in
Hundred: South Erpingham 2 m turn left and right 200
Union house: Aylsham yds after the river bridge.
21st c. Deanery: Ingworth O.S. grid ref: TG 229241
Benefice: Bure Valley Post Code: NR10 5HP

It is sad to see a church falling into decline and that seems to be what was happening here when Cautley passed this way last century. He remarked that there was nothing of interest here except the Paston tombs. The north chancel chapel was ruinous then and will forever more remain so. The interior, as Cautley remarked, has suffered from unsympathetic Victorian restoration. A plain octagonal font devoid of decoration does nothing to lift the spirit. However, the church is clean and well maintained. The quaint crow-step gable on both east end and porch and the slender appearance of the 14th c. tower add charm to the scene. The Paston tombs are still the only really interesting things to come here to visit, and the rich detail in the carving of the effigies with traces of the original paint is worthy of close examination.

PLUMSTEAD St Michael

No of Bells:	1 (3 prior to 1738)	
19th c. Deanery:	Repps	
Hundred:	North Erpingham	
Union house:	West Beckham	
21st c. Deanery:	Holt	
Benefice:	Barningham Winter	

4 m SE of Holt. From the B1149 at Edgefield head east for 2 miles to Plumstead. The church is central in the village.
O.S. grid ref: TG 132349
Post Code: NR11 7LG

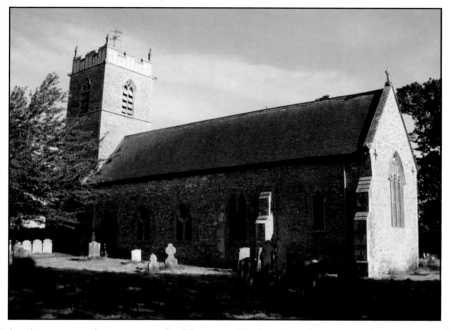

The large continuous roof offers no distinction between the nave and chancel and there is no chancel arch. Atop the 15th c. tower is a parapet with some good flush-work and pinnacles. Traces of Norman architecture can be found on the north wall. A plain octagonal font creates no excitement. A hammer-beam and arch-braced roof has small angels on the ends of the hammers and tracery in the spandrels creating a somewhat cluttered appearance. At one time there was a south aisle and clerestory but these were demolished in the 18th c. Most of the fixtures and fittings are Victorian and hold little interest for the historian. In the chancel is a simple piscina and dropped-sill sedilia. The Royal Arms are of George VI, put up after his death and I believe because of that are unique in Norfolk.

QUIDENHAM St Andrew

No of Bells:	8
19th c. Deanery:	Rockland
Hundred:	Guiltcross
Union house:	Kenninghall
21st c. Deanery:	Thetford & Rockland
Benefice:	Quidenham

2 m E of East Harling. Turn south off the A11 onto the B1111 to East Harling church. After which turn left for 2½ m then left again.
O.S. grid ref: TM 028877
Post Code: NR16 2JP

For almost a thousand years a church has stood on this site, maybe more. The tower is Saxon at the base and a later octagonal top has been added. The 1857 shingled spire makes it easily recognisable. The font is plain and uninteresting, but above it hangs a lovely set of Stuart Royal Arms carved in wood. In the nave and chancel can be found much evidence of 13th and 14th c. building work and are both thought to date from around that period. Subsequent restorations and restructuring works have taken place and the purpose of the three small columns in the north wall of the chancel are unknown, but are thought to have once been part of a pre-Conquest font. Why they should be preserved in such a manner is anybody's guess. On the opposite wall is a piscina and sedilia group within four cusped arches.

REEPHAM St Mary

No of Bells:	1	
19th c. Deanery:	Sparham	
Hundred:	Eynesford	
Union house:	Reepham	
21st c. Deanery:	Sparham	
Benefice:	Reepham	

12 m NW of Norwich. From Norwich, on the A1067, take the B1145 to Reepham. The church is just south of the centre of the town.

O.S. grid ref: TG 102229
Post Code: NR10 4JW

In the background is St Michael's Whitwell. To the left of the picture are the remains of Hackford All Saints. St Mary's has a strange configuration with the tower being central to the south aisle while the porch is slightly to the west. The south arcade dates from the 13th c., when the church was built. A coeval square font with arcading around the bowl stands on four octagonal columns around a central round shaft. A fine altar tomb of Sir Roger de Kerdiston (1337) is the most outstanding feature here; he rests on a bed of stones with a lion at his feet. Eight weepers decorate the arcaded sides of the monument. A brass to William Kerdiston, his son, is dated 1391. The Hanoverian Royal Arms are dated 1745 Cautley believed were Stuart and re-dated, but I think they are Hanoverian in the style of Stuart Arms.

REYMERSTON   St Peter

No of Bells: 5
19th c. Deanery: Hingham
Hundred: Mitford
Union house: Gressenhall
21st c. Deanery: Dereham & Mitford
Benefice: Reymerston

4 m SE of E. Dereham from
where take the B1135 to
Garveston then right to
Reymerston. The church is
in Church Road.
O.S. grid ref: TG 020060
Post Code: NR9 4AG

This sturdy looking church dates from the Norman period; the tower is little changed since it was built. A 13th c. clerestory and aisles have been added to the 12th c. nave. The north doorway has dog-tooth decoration over two engaged columns. The 15th c. octagonal font has some good bold carvings of saintly emblems around the bowl upon which stands a tall pinnacled font cover. A simple 16th c. arch-braced roof void of decoration covers the nave. A Jacobean three-decker pulpit complete with back and sounding board stands near the chancel arch and a few feet away is an eagle lectern. Beautifully carved Flemish altar rails require close examination to appreciate all the elements of the design. Although Victorian restoration has obviously taken place here I found it had been very sympathetically carried out.

RIDDLESWORTH St Peter

No of Bells:	1	
19th c. Deanery:	Rockland	
Hundred:	Guiltcross	
Union house:	Kenninghall	
21st c. Deanery:	Thetford & Rockland	
Benefice:	Guiltcross	

4 m SW of East Harling.
From the A1066 between
Thetford and Diss turn into
Riddlesworth School grounds
and follow just past the Hall.
O.S. grid ref: TL 966813
Post Code: IP22 2TA

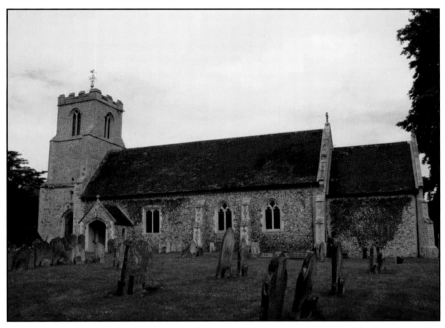

A simple church with a stout 14th c. tower, beneath which, is a processional arch. The south porch leads directly into the nave. On the left on the wall of the tower are the Royal Arms of Charles I dated 1632, although clearly the date has been over-painted 1666. Close by is the 14th c. font, with its plain tapered octagonal bowl and late 17th c. cover. The keen eye will notice that the rood stairs seem to be misplaced. This is because originally, the nave east of here was the chancel; the chancel as it is today is a later add-on. At the east end of the nave, in what was the chancel, is a quite spectacular monument to Drugo Drury (1617) on the north wall. It is flanked by lesser monuments to various members of the Thornhill, and Champion families. An interesting history and association with the Hall.

RINGLAND   St Peter

No of Bells:	5
19th c. Deanery:	Sparham
Hundred:	Eynesford
Union house:	Horsham St Faith
21st c. Deanery:	Sparham
Benefice:	Wensum

7 m NW of Norwich. From Norwich turn right off the A47; alternatively left off the A1067 to Ringland just outside Taverham.

O.S. grid ref: TG 133141

Post Code: NR8 6JJ

Built on an acclivity overlooking the village is this charming church which is well worth a look around if the key-holder (200 yds away) is at home. Above the roofs of the north and south aisles is a lovely seven-window clerestory which spills light into the interior of the nave and illuminates the wonderful roof. Comparable to that in St Peter Mancroft, the hammerbeam and arch-braced roof is supported on long wall-posts. Angels and Tudor roses form part of the overall effect. The whole is supported on 14th c. arcades with octagonal columns and is really something special for a small parish church. The typical East Anglian style font is 15th c. with lions around the base. A few old benches remain and it would seem that Victorian restoration was kept to a sympathetic minimum.

ROCKLAND All Saints

No of Bells: 5

19th c. Deanery: Rockland

Hundred: Shropham

Union house: Rockland All Saints

21st c. Deanery: Thetford & Rockland

Benefice: Great Ellingham (Shelrock)

4 m W of Attleborough. Take the B1077 west to Rockland St Peter, then 1st left and follow straight on for 1 m, then left again to destination.

O.S. grid ref: TL 995961

Post Code: NR17 1XW

This is a church with a long history. There is a thousand-year-old sepulchral slab dating from Saxon times in the chancel, and long and short work can be seen in the structure of the nave. The church we see today is mainly 13th to 15th c. and was built on the site utilising part of the much older church. The Norman influence can be seen in the construction of the north doorway. There is a well carved octagonal font of 1880 depicting various religious scenes and saintly emblems. The barrel roofs leave a lot to be desired, somehow out of place here, and looking too new in ancient surroundings. A small font bowl circa 1100 was found in a garden in the parish some years ago. Most of the fixtures and fittings are Victorian in date, the Edwardian pulpit even later. The Royal Arms of Queen Victoria are dated 1860.

ROCKLAND St Andrew

No of Bells: -
19th c. Deanery: Rockland
Hundred: -
Union house: -
21st c. Deanery: -
Benefice: -

See directions for Rockland All Saints which is 200 yards west of this church. The ruin is only about twenty-five feet from the road.
O.S. grid ref: TL 997959
Post Code: NR17 1XW

The ruin of St Andrew's church has been part of the local scenery for centuries Abandoned in the early 1700s it was originally built in the 14th c. as the parish or manor church for the manor neighbouring All Saints. In ancient times manors were more of a division than parishes, and each would have its own church and display of wealth and prosperity. Some parishes had many manors and grew into large towns and cities. Stories surrounding this church are included in the guide to All Saints. One tells of rector, Baldwin de Rosey, who in 1286 assaulted a parishioner. A successor Simon att Wode (Attwood) was found guilty of burglary in 1332. From these tales it would appear that not everyone practised what they preached, even then. Rockland All Saints is seen in the distance.

ROCKLAND   St Peter
No of Bells: 2
19th c. Deanery: Rockland
Hundred: Shropham
Union house: Rockland All Saints
21st c. Deanery: Thetford & Rockland
Benefice: Great Ellingham (Shelrock)

4 m W of Attleborough, on the main road (B1077) through the village. After the crossroads turn left into the road to the church.
O.S. grid ref: TL 990971
Post Code: NR17 1TT

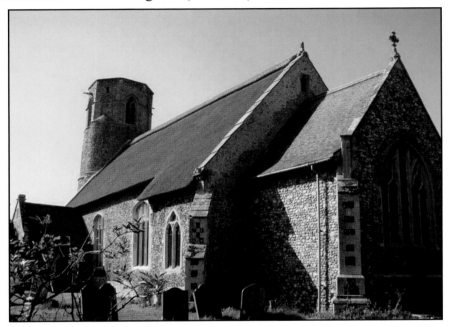

The 13th c. tower is round with a stair turret leading up to the belfry stage, above which is an octagonal top. Just inside the nave, set in the wall, is half a stoup bowl, broken as a result of a fire in 1947 which gutted the church and destroyed almost everything in it. Consequently most of the furnishings and fittings are salvaged from other churches either redundant or unused. The screen, for example, is from Tottington St Andrew in the battle area and looks completely wrong here. The pulpit was from there too, but has been since reclaimed. At the time of writing the church has no pulpit. Because the original benches were burned, the seating is now individual chairs, giving the unfortunate appearance of a schoolroom. The large octagonal 14th c. font with quatrefoil tracery designs was undamaged in the fire.

ROUDHAM   St Andrew
No of Bells: -
19th c. Deanery: Rockland
Hundred: -
Union house: -
21st c. Deanery: -
Maintained by the local people.

11 m SW of Attleborough.
Turn off the A11 to East
Harling follow 1 m then
left for 2 miles. The ruin is
beside the road.
O.S. grid ref: TL 954872
Post Code: NR16 2RJ

Roudham church is a well maintained ruin. It has important historical significance. The church was destroyed by fire on 16th August 1736. The bell from the 14th c. tower is kept at Bridgham, where it sits on the nave floor. The tower itself is situated at the south-west corner and doubled as a porch. It has a variety of openings and unusually, large circular sound holes. The graveyard is still in use and a mausoleum which was created shortly after the fire is at the east end of the nave, cordoned off with railings Family ledger stones are laid as a pavement. It is a pleasing building to explore as it has a good variety of architectural styles, and the putlog holes which once supported the scaffolding are easily distinguishable in the flint-work of both tower and walls inside and out. Not officially declared a ruin!

ROYDON St Remigius

No of Bells: 3
19th c. Deanery: Redenhall
Hundred: Diss
Union house: Pulham St Mary
21st c. Deanery: Redenhall
Benefice: Upper Waveney

2 miles west of Diss on the main road at the western end of the village. Plenty of parking available at the front of the church.

O.S. grid ref: TM 096803
Post Code: IP22 3RU

The base of the tower is Norman, which has been horribly cement-rendered, the upper two-thirds is a 19th c. addition. The nave has a community room, built onto the south side, and although sympathetically constructed of flint and stone, spoils the exterior appearance. It was made possible by the transference of the south porch to its present position, creating a 'transept' to house the organ in 1864. Five niches adorn the north porch and entrance to the nave, in which is a 13th c. arcade with grotesque heads below the capitals, and a Victorian hammer-beam roof which has been in-filled with plaster between the beams. There are simple quatrefoil designs on the basic octagonal font. The undated Royal Arms of King George I are painted on planks of wood and hung in a plain frame.

RUNHALL   All Saints
No of Bells: 1 (unusable)
19th c. Deanery: Hingham
Hundred: Forehoe
Union house: Wicklewood
21st c. Deanery: Dereham & Mitford
Benefice: Barnham Broom Upper Yare

12 m W of Norwich. Leave the A47 onto the B1108; 4 m through Barford take the B1135 through Coston, in 1 mile turn left at T junction.
O.S. grid ref: TG 057069
Post Code: NR9 4DR

Runhall is a small parish church in unspoiled surroundings with a super round tower dating from the Conquest or just after. The 800-year-old ironwork on the inside west door is original and worth taking a look at. The chancel became ruinous centuries ago and was removed completely. Today the east end of the nave serves as the chancel. On the north side of the nave is an unused Norman doorway. The font is octagonal and decorated with tracery from bowl to shaft The pulpit partially hides a niche set into the north side of what was the chancel arch which would at one time have contained a statuette; there may be another behind the organ to the south. The structure of the roof is quite unusual and is supported on story posts to contend with the wide span of the nave. Quaint as well as interesting.

RUSHFORD   St John the Evangelist   3½ m E x S of Thetford.
No of Bells: 6   From Thetford on the
19th c. Deanery: Rockland   A1066 turn left after 2½
Hundred: Guiltcross   miles and follow the road
Union house: Thetford St Mary's   for ½ mile then turn left
21st c. Deanery: Thetford & Rockland   O.S. grid ref: TL 923813
Benefice: East Harling   Post Code: IP24 2SE

The parish of Rushford is partly in Suffolk; the church, however, stands in Norfolk. Somehow mysterious with its lovely thatched roof and tall stair turret reaching all the way to the top of the 13th c. tower This was the church featured in the film 'The Witchfinder General'. At one time the church had north and south transepts, but having stood ruinous for a century or more it is virtually a Victorian re-build. Close by is the old college for priests founded by Edmund Gonville in 1342, now a private house. There is a tiny 'modern' apsidal chancel. The 19th c. font has been somewhat over-decorated. The church has a very interesting history but is very difficult to access, and because of this fact I cannot recommend a visit unless you can find some means of making an appointment. A sad situation.

SALLE   Sts Peter & Paul *****
No of Bells: 8
19th c. Deanery: Sparham
Hundred: Eynesford
Union house: Aylsham
21st c. Deanery: Sparham
Benefice: Reepham

1½ m N of Reepham. From
Reepham turn north
towards Salle and follow
the road signs. Bear left
then turn left to The Green.
O.S. grid ref: TG 110249
Post Code: NR10 4SE

Every church crawler should include this beautiful church in their
itinerary. Pronounced Saul (never Sale) it is the pride of the parish
and rightly so. There is much to see here. Cautley calls it the finest
church in Norfolk and who am I to argue? I certainly found it
inspiring and welcoming. Enter by the west door beneath the lovely
tower and note the carvings as you pass by and beneath them. The
Seven Sacrament font is a fine example. At the other end of the nave
is the three-decker wine-glass pulpit which retains its back and tester.
Misericordes fill the choir, and splendid carved bosses adorn the roof.
Genuine and unchanged 15th c. history and architecture surrounds
you wherever you look. Note the painting on the tympanum of the
chancel arch and good contemporary iron-bound chest. Very special!

SALTHOUSE St Nicholas
No of Bells: 1 (unused)
19th c. Deanery: Holt
Hundred: Holt
Union house: Erpingham
21st c. Deanery: Holt
Benefice: Weybourne

4 m N of Holt. From the A149 coast road, the church is signposted to the south and is best accessed from Cross Street.
O.S. grid ref: TG 076438
Post Code: NR25 7XQ

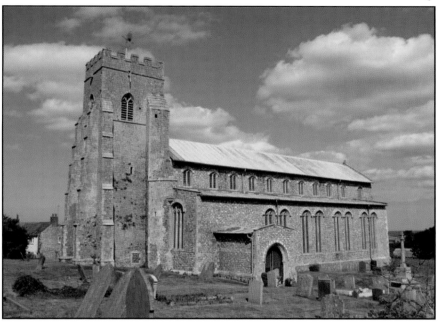

This church was re-built in the early 16th c. (the tower is 13th c.) on high ground and serves as a beacon to seafarers. Much of the original building survives. Here is the most splendidly carved 15th c. font I have seen to date; carvings of instruments of the Passion and other saintly and religious emblems, from the brim to the foot of the stem. The lower part of the rood screen which has mutilated, yet fine paintings of 16 saints, has been moved to the west end of the nave. The bench-ends have some lovely carved poppy-heads and graffiti scratched into the woodwork give us a glimpse into the past. The modern pulpit stands on a plain stone base. The central aisle has many monumental slabs. Beautiful tall arcades support a superb twenty-two window clerestory which pours light into the nave.

SAXLINGHAM   St Margaret

No of Bells: 1
19th c. Deanery: Holt
Hundred: Holt
Union house: Great Snoring
21st c. Deanery: Holt
Benefice: Stiffkey & Bale

3 m W of Holt. From Holt take the A148 through Letheringsett then turn off right to Saxlingham and continue to destination.
O.S. grid ref: TG 026396
Post Code: NR25 7JY

Do not confuse with Saxlingham Nethergate or Saxlingham Thorpe. The graveyard is mainly to the north of the mostly 15th c. much restored cruciform church. The roof is continuous over both the nave and chancel. Inside it is simple arch-braced with the wall-posts sitting on plain corbels. The 15th c. font has geometric decoration. In the west window are armorial shields. In the entrance of the north transept is a canopied niche with a statuette of an Elizabethan lady; possibly from a memorial, now missing as a result of the 1898 modernisation by Jodrell of nearby Bayfield Hall. There are three piscinæ all quite plain. The pulpit and benches are all Victorian, as is much of the structure, for in the mid-1800s the church was in a ruinous state. The Heydon family were also great benefactors here.

SAXTHORPE   St Andrew
No of Bells: 6
19th c. Deanery: Ingworth
Hundred: South Erpingham
Union house: Aylsham
21st c. Deanery: Ingworth
Benefice: Seven Churches Itteringham

6 m NW of Aylsham.
Saxthorpe church is at the junction of the B1149 heading north and the B1354 heading east.
O.S. grid ref: TG 116305
Post Code: NR11 7BL

The church was built about 1490 on the site of St Dunstan's chapel. The tower, I believe, is about a century older. On the south side is the external stair turret. Tie-beams prevent the walls spreading and the arch-braced roof is supported on plain corbels.   A plain 14th c. font bowl stands on a delicately traceried shaft. A scrolled ogee cover rests on top. The front stall on the north side has a traceried back, on the ends of which are small carvings of faces and the Agnus Dei, the emblem of the Page family. The emblem also appears elsewhere in the church on family monuments. Rood loft stairs are adjacent to the pulpit and only the lower half of the screen remains, the loft having been removed centuries ago. There is a plain piscina, and a sedilia which has been made unusable by the raising of the chancel floor.

SCOLE St Andrew

No of Bells:	5
19th c. Deanery:	Redenhall
Hundred:	Diss
Union house:	Pulham St Mary
21st c. Deanery:	Redenhall
Benefice:	Scole

2 m E of Diss. Leave Diss via Frenze and head east; go straight over the roundabout and into the village. Turn north at 'The White Hart Inn'.

O.S. grid ref: TM 151790

Post Code: IP21 4DY

This church was almost totally destroyed by fire on January 7th 1963.The tower and walls were left standing and the church was rebuilt and re-consecrated in September 1964 so it is not surprising to find that all the furnishings in the church are modern. The 15th c. font with religious emblems and lions at the base survived unscathed; as did the corner piscina and sedilia. During the re-building a blocked Norman window was discovered in the north wall of the nave, still retaining some decorative colour. Much new woodwork has been used in the reconstruction of the interior, especially the lined roof, pulpit and choir stalls. The east window is quite spectacular, being a multitude of strong colours. A modern church in an old shell doesn't do much for me but the church is well attended and well loved.

SCOULTON Holy Trinity
No of Bells: 3, (unusable)
19th c. Deanery: Breckles
Hundred: Wayland
Union house: Rockland All Saints
21st c. Deanery: High Oak & Hingham
Benefice: Humbleyard

5 m E of Watton. Leave Watton on the B1108 and head east for 3 miles. Take the 2nd left after the B1077 turn-off, continue 50 yards.
O.S. grid ref: TF 973010
Post Code: NR9 4NZ

The octagonal upper stage to the otherwise square 14th c. tower makes this church easily recognisable. There is a scratch dial on the wall of the south aisle. Inside is a 13th c. arcade. The octagonal font has an exceptionally deep bowl but devoid of decoration, the cover is Jacobean as is the lovely pulpit complete with back-board and tester. On the opposite wall is a second pulpit, somewhat younger. A low side window is set below one of the 13th c. chancel windows. Some of the benches have early carvings. Behind the organ is what appears to be an Easter sepulchre with five holes in the sill, which are a mystery. All possibilities have been considered except that the sill, which, when moved, was reinstated upside down. Although the holes may be cressets for an everlasting flame, but that too is controversial.

SHARRINGTON   All Saints   3 m WSW of Holt. Leave
No of Bells: 1   Holt on the A148 and
19th c. Deanery: Holt   through Letheringsett. Turn
Hundred: Holt   left into and through
Union house: Great Snoring   Sharrington to the church.
21st c. Deanery: Holt   O.S. grid ref: TG 030367
Benefice: Stiffkey & Bale   Post Code: NR24 2PF

On the north side of the nave blocked arches can be seen where a north aisle once stood. Differences in the walls also indicate that the church once had transepts which were all removed many years ago. Entry to the nave is via the west doorway of the ancient tower, on the north side of which is a curious small traceried doorway or window at ground level. Inside the nave is the pristine font with Tudor roses and buttresses around the base of the shaft. Nearby is an old parish chest with three clasps for locks. Each of the corbels supporting the arch-braced roof has a demonic face gazing down on the congregation. Victorian pulpit and benches furnish the interior. Particularly interesting are the floor brasses, now mounted on a board and attached to the wall. Christopher Dawbeney's story is told on a large plaque.

SHELFANGER All Saints

No of Bells:　　6
19th c. Deanery:　Redenhall
Hundred:　　Diss
Union house:　Pulham St Mary
21st c. Deanery:　Redenhall
Benefice:　　Winfarthing

2½ m N of Diss. Leave Diss on the B1077 towards Shimpling and Winfarthing. After 2½ m the church is on the right beside the road.
O.S. grid ref: TM 107837
Post Code:　IP22 2DU

A distinctive church. The 13th c. square tower has a tiled pyramidal roof peeking above the chequered embattled parapet. Strangely, the tower is slightly north of the centre of the nave. Entry to the nave is through the 15th c. half-timbered porch which contains a stoup. Part of an early 14th c. screen has been utilised in the ringing gallery. The scissor-braced roof is blatantly noticeable. In 1966, during restoration, wall paintings were discovered behind an inner wall. They are now on display, and are a fine example of mid-13th c. religious art. The 15th c. font is quite ordinary bearing the initials of the donor. Most of the fixtures and fittings are of the Victorian period following heavy restoration during that time. A small piscina and sedilia can be found in the chancel. Beneath the tower are the Royal Arms of William IV.

SHERINGHAM   St Peter
No of Bells: 1
19th c. Deanery: Repps
Hundred: North Erpingham
Union house: Sheringham
21st c. Deanery: Repps
Benefice: Weybourne

5 m W of Cromer. St Peter's is north of the A149. A little to the west of the town centre in 'The Boulevard'.
O.S. grid ref: TG 157433
Post Code: NR26 8LH

(See also **Upper** Sheringham). This modern church is in the town centre and was built in 1895 to accommodate the needs of the growing town and the blossoming holiday trade. It is very barn-like but unmistakeably a church with its spirelet at the west end and Early English- style windows. Within, it is utilitarian with chairs instead of benches and easily adaptable for non-secular uses. Bare brick seems to be the preferred option. The octagonal font standing on a double plinth is void of any decoration. The roof is a somewhat overbearing and complicated mixture of tie-beams, arch-bracing and king posts. A well carved traceried 15th c. goblet style pulpit takes its usual position on the north side, on the south is a carved eagle lectern. Behind them is the chancel and a south chapel enclosed by a screen.

SHIMPLING   St George

No of Bells: 3
19th c. Deanery: Redenhall
Hundred: Diss
Union house: Pulham St Mary
21st c. Deanery: Redenhall
The Churches Conservation Trust

3½ m NE of Diss. From the A140 turn left at Dickleburgh then left again for ½ m. Then left down the track opposite Hall Lane.

O.S. grid ref: TM 156826
Post Code: IP21 4UB

Carefully maintained by the Churches Conservation Trust this is a lovely church spoiled only by the cement rendering on the walls of the nave and chancel. Thankfully the scratch dial has been preserved which indicated the hours from 8 a.m. to 5 p.m. The Norman round tower has a later 15th c. octagonal upper stage surmounted by a well proportioned spire. Entry is through the half-timbered Tudor porch. A traditional East Anglian font is heavily carved with saintly emblems and lions at the base of the shaft. A parish chest with its lid cut from a tree trunk is showing its great age. Benches with good poppy-heads line the nave and choir. The pulpit is Victorian. Part of the old screen has been used to form an arch beneath the tower. There is a piscina and dropped-sill sedilia in the chancel. Well worth a visit.

SHIPDHAM   All Saints

No of Bells:	6
19th c. Deanery:	Hingham
Hundred:	Mitford
Union house:	Gressenhall
21st c. Deanery:	Dereham & Mitford
Benefice:	Shipdham

5 m SSW of East Dereham.
Leave E. Dereham on the
A1075 and into Shipdham
where you will find the
church in the village centre.
O.S. grid ref: TF 957074
Post Code: IP25 7LX

Shipdham church is easily recognisable by its double-domed cupola
and tall sanctus bell turret on the east end of the nave. Unfortunately
the 15th c. tower is marred by cement rendering. A late Norman
doorway leads into the chancel. The porch, which has a parvise, leads
to the 12th c. south doorway and into the nave where stands the
Norman font; another late 14th c. font with tracery around the bowl is
unused. Close by is the old bier, kept in readiness in case it is ever
needed. In the north aisle on the wall above the organ are the Royal
Arms of Charles II, dated 1661. They are Elizabethan in style and
updated after the Commonwealth. The unusual double-width, rotating
lectern is dated around 1500 and is worthy of close examination,
particularly the base with three lions around the foot.

SHROPHAM St Peter
No of Bells: 5
19th c. Deanery: Rockland
Hundred: Shropham
Union house: Rockland All Saints
21st c. Deanery: Thetford & Rockland
Benefice: Great Ellingham (Shelrock)

5 m NNW of East Harling.
Leave the A11 4 m S of
Attleborough and follow the
road signs. At the crossroads
in the village centre turn left.
O.S. grid ref: TL 985928
Post Code: NR17 1EJ

The 16th c. tower has large buttresses with flushwork decoration; a stair turret on the south-east leads directly into the belfry. The north door is 13th c. with dog-tooth decoration; most of the structure of the building is from around the same period. Set into the four chancel buttresses are niches for statuettes. On entering the nave one is greeted by the 17th c. font with billeted decoration and heads beneath the bowl; note the clasp which once held a lock to protect the holy water. Behind the door is the remaining pillar of an early stoup. Octagonal pillars form the 13th c. north aisle. Set into the reveal of a north window is a blocked squint, originally used to view the altar. In the chancel is a beautifully traceried cusped and crocketted piscina and sedilia which alone makes the visit worthwhile.

SNETTERTON   All Saints
No of Bells: (4 removed)
19th c. Deanery: Rockland
Hundred: Shropham
Union house: Rockland All Saints
21st c. Deanery: Thetford & Rockland
Benefice: Great Ellingham (Shelrock)

4 m SW of Attleborough.
From the A11 south of
Attleborough follow the
signs for the I.L.P.H. who
hold the key.
O.S. grid ref: TL 994910
Post Code: NR16 2LR

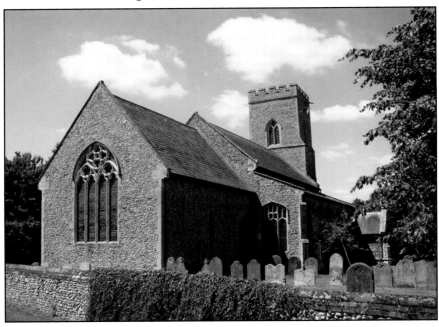

This is yet another of Norfolk's redundant churches of which there are so many. The bells from the 14th c. tower were removed and are now at Barton Turf. Inside there is a complete mess to greet the visitor, with horsehair and bird droppings everywhere. However, there is a good notice board with various bits of useful information about the church and the graves in the churchyard. The fine 13th c. piscina with its double drain and adjacent graduated sedilia are the earliest features in the church. Lovely carved bosses are set at the intersections of the arch-braced roof. The 15th c. font is decorated with double arches and quatrefoils. There is damage to the lovely coved screen. Perhaps more visitors would encourage those in charge to clear up the mess more often. A nice church neglected!

SOUTH LOPHAM   St Andrew *****

No of Bells:	8	
19th c. Deanery:	Rockland	
Hundred:	Guiltcross	
Union house:	Kenninghall	
21st c. Deanery:	Redenhall	
Benefice:	Upper Waveney	

5 m W of Diss. Follow the A1066 to S Lopham and turn right. The church is about 500 yds up the road on the left.
O.S. grid ref: TM 039852
Post Code: IP22 2LW

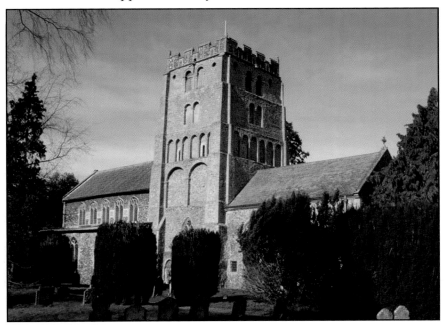

A suburb example of a Norman church standing proudly beside the road. It is the finest example of Norman architecture in the county apart from Norwich cathedral; very grand and is a must for church crawlers. The central tower has blind arcades in five stages reaching to 100 feet; 13th c. doorways on the north and south sides. High on the north wall is a Saxon window of the early 11th c. suggesting perhaps an earlier period of building. Entry is gained through the porch of the south aisle. Inside, is a 14th c. octagonal font similar to that at North Lopham. Behind it, the glorious west window spills the afternoon light into the nave. Above is a lovely hammerbeam roof and most of the interior is 15th c. Much restoration has been carried out here and all of it sympathetic. A well deserved 5 stars.

SOUTHBURGH   St Andrew

No of Bells: 2*
19th c. Deanery: Hingham
Hundred: Mitford
Union house: Gressenhall
21st c. Deanery: Dereham & Mitford
Benefice: Reymerston

3 m NW x N of Hingham.
From Norwich on the B1108
and B1135 continue straight
on. Once over the railway
bridge continue 3½ miles.
O.S. grid ref: TG 003048
Post Code: IP25 7TF

I feel Cautley did this lovely little church an injustice by disregarding it in his 'Norfolk Churches', probably because it was mostly re-built in 1882 after a fire a century earlier. The church was without a tower until that date and the two bells were *temporarily hung under a thatched roof in the churchyard. They were re-installed when the new tower was built with its elegant spire. The interior walls were re-lined with stone and as much as possible of the old church was conserved. The screen is original as it was virtually undamaged. Although the original drains of the piscina were reset into the wall, the arches are Victorian. A new octagonal font is very attractive but devoid of any decoration. As you would expect the furnishings are all late 19th c. but it is a pleasure to visit and a lovely landmark for miles around.

SPARHAM St Mary the Virgin
No of Bells: 3
19th c. Deanery: Sparham
Hundred: Eynesford
Union house: Gressenhall
21st c. Deanery: Sparham
Benefice: FLEBBS

10m NW of Norwich. From the A1067 turn right into Sparham and follow to village centre and destination.
O.S. grid ref: TG 071196
Post Code: NR9 5AQ

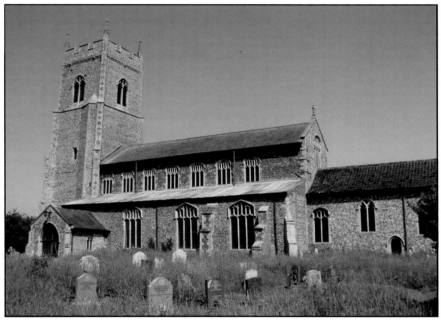

A splendid church with a 15th c. fourteen-window clerestory which spills plenty of light into the nave. Remains of an earlier clerestory can be discerned by the quatrefoil windows which are now blocked. Inside the porch is a mass-dial which proves the porch to be a later addition, probably built at the same time the clerestory was added. The lofty nave has a good arch-braced roof with angels looking down. The screen, which has been removed from its original position, is displayed in the north aisle. One panel depicts skeletal figures from the Dance of Death. Close by is a brass to Sir William Mustarder (1490). A few old 15th c. benches remain but the main seating is new. In the chancel area is a relatively plain piscina and sedilia. The restored Royal Arms of George I hang over the north door.

STODY	St Mary	3 m SSW of Holt. Leave
No of Bells:	1	Holt on the B1111 heading
19th c. Deanery:	Holt	south. Turn left towards
Hundred:	Holt	Hunworth then right, past
Union house:	Erpingham	the church and on to Stody.
21st c. Deanery:	Holt	O.S. grid ref: TG 056351
Benefice:	Brinton	Post Code: NR24 2ED

The round tower may be Saxon in origin although the section with the bell openings and parapet is later. Here is a cruciform church. The roofs match over the whole length and width of the nave, chancel and transepts with cross-vaulting, which is quite uncommon in a small church. A 13th c. octagonal font which sits on a double octagonal plinth is decorated with shallow arches on the bowl and is supported by eight columns and a central shaft. The interior is austere and has little of interest to offer the visitor other than the stained glass, one of the best assemblages of 15th century stained glass in north Norfolk. High in the north windows, and also in the east side of the south transept are depicted various apostles, saints, prophets and kings. Whether you find the church open is down to luck and good timing.

STOW BEDON   St Botolph

No of Bells:	1
19th c. Deanery:	Breckles
Hundred:	Wayland
Union house:	Rockland All Saints
21st c. Deanery:	Breckland
Benefice:	Wayland

4 m SE of Watton. Leave Watton on the A1075, after 3½ m turn left <u>before</u> the B1111 turnoff, bear right and right again & 300 yds.
O.S. grid ref: TL 962957
Post Code: NR17 1EU

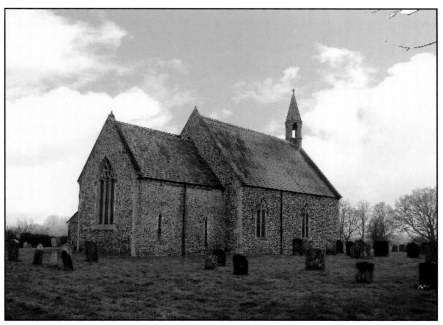

This little church stands on ancient ground, which was possibly a site of worship long before the present building was erected. Sometime between 1740 and 1820 the tower fell down and a bell turret was erected in its stead. A further disaster occurred during WWII when a landmine landed near the church and damaged the roof and glass. It wasn't until 1967 that it was restored to its present state. Four of the windows have hood-mould faces which are in surprisingly good condition. Inside, the octagonal font is probably 14th c. but has almost certainly been reworked at some time. Above the pulpit are the Royal Arms of George III, dated 1785. The rest of the interior dates from a restoration in 1852, with the possible exception of the screen, but as it shows no sign of damage it too is probably Victorian.

STRATTON   St Michael

No of Bells:	1
19th c. Deanery:	Depwade
Hundred:	Depwade
Union house:	Pulham St Mary
21st c. Deanery:	Depwade
Benefice:	Long Stratton

10 m S of Norwich. From the A140 take the first left after the Hempnall cross-roads and before Long Stratton.

O.S. grid ref: TM 204936
Post Code: NR15 2QB

This is a strange-looking church with its stump of a tower and small bell turret and spirelet. Inside the porch is a small early stoup set into a niche in the wall. The 15th c. soft stone, goblet-shaped octagonal font has gone quite green with dampness. On the facets are depictions of saintly emblems; around the base the lions have been hacked off. An old parish chest of very plain design stands nearby. The pulpit too is virtually without decoration and the old benches likewise except for a couple of decorated ends. A small but attractive piscina with a cusped arch and a column either side can be found in the chancel. Set into a large ledger slab on the floor is a small brass, difficult to read. Beneath a window is part of a circular wall painting. Remnants only remain of what was at one time a fine rood screen. Always open!

No of Bells: 6

19th c. Deanery: Ingworth

Hundred: South Erpingham

Union house: Aylsham

21st c. Deanery: Ingworth

Benefice: Frettenham

7 m N of Norwich from where, turn right off the A140 after the B1354 junction and follow.

O.S. grid ref: TG 221208

Post Code: NR10 5LN

This is a lovely church tucked away behind trees opposite a farmyard where you can park your car. The broad 15th c. truncated tower has seated figures as pinnacles. Having suffered bomb damage during WWII much of the original has been 'recently' restored. In the nave are devilish corbels on the columns and at the west end is the octagonal font which has a gilded and painted pinnacled cover. Hanging from the arch-braced roof is a magnificent 18th c. chandelier purportedly from Russia. A little further east is the black painted effigy of Thomas Marsham (1638). The south aisle is crammed with other Marsham family memorials and monuments. Worthy of note is that of Henry Marsham (1678) accompanied by his wife Anne, son Henry and infant daughter Margaret in swaddling bands.

SUSTEAD	Sts Peter & Paul	4 m SSW of Cromer. From
No of Bells:	1	the A148 at Aylmerton
19th c. Deanery:	Repps	head south. Follow road to
Hundred:	North Erpingham	Sustead. Church is at the W
Union house:	West Beckham	end of Sustead High Street.
21st c. Deanery:	Repps	O.S. grid ref: TG 183370
Benefice:	Roughton	Post Code: NR11 8RU

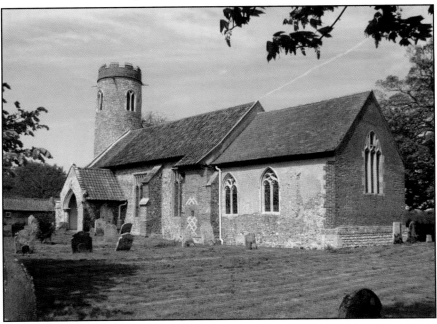

The slender tower of this ancient church dates back to the Saxon period with a mixture of building materials at its base. Its centre portion is 13th c. and the embattled parapet is 18th c. There is a good scratch dial to look for. Through the 14th c. porch in the nave is a 15th c. octagonal font with armorial shields of donative local families as crisp as the day it was carved. By the north door is an iron-bound parish chest. At one time there was a north transept and the blocked entrance is behind the pulpit. The 14th c. chancel has been 'restored' and the 13th c. double piscina and sedilia each with clustered columns have been partially plastered over. Behind a small glazed window can just be made out the old rood stairs, built from red brick. There is plenty of historical interest here and is well worth a brief visit.

SWAINSTHORPE St Peter

No of Bells: 2
19th c. Deanery: Humbleyard
Hundred: Humbleyard
Union house: Swainsthorpe
21st c. Deanery: Depwade
Benefice: Tas Valley

5½ m S of Norwich. From the A140 turn right into Swainsthorpe and follow the road. The church can be easily seen to the left.
O.S. grid ref: TG 218009
Post Code: NR14 8PH

From a drawing inside the church it is obvious that much has changed here over the last 150 years. The porch is much smaller now and the roof of the nave has been replaced. The pre-Conquest tower however remains virtually the same with its octagonal upper stage and embattled parapet. There are angels on the intersections of the roof but whether they are original or Victorian I cannot tell. The carved cornice of the simple arch-braced roof is very fine. Below, the octagonal font is a copy of a much earlier one, with eight columns around a central shaft. A lone piscina in the chancel and a stoup bowl set into the wall of the nave are probably the oldest objects to be found here. Everything else is Victorian, Judging from the drawing mentioned above, much essential restoration has taken place.

SWANNINGTON   St Margaret

No of Bells:	3
19th c. Deanery:	Sparham
Hundred:	Eynesford
Union house:	Horsham St Faiths
21st c. Deanery:	Sparham
Benefice:	Wensum

9 m NW of Norwich. From Attlebridge on the A1067 turn right. Or from the B1149 turn 4th left after Horsford to The Street.
O.S. grid ref: TG 134193
Post Code: NR9 5NP

The church has a squat tower and elongated chancel dating from around the 13th c. A plain Norman north doorway confirms the date externally. The 15th c. porch door opens into the south aisle which has tracery in the spandrils of the arch-braces of the roof, unlike the north aisle which has a quite plain roof. Hanging on the walls of the former are hatchments. On the floor of the aisle is the Norman font now standing on a more recent base. The 13th c. nave is filled with benches sporting poppy-heads on the ends, two of which are carved, one with a pelican in her piety and the other with a dragon. Most unusual is the pillar piscina which was discovered, discarded, in the stairway of the rood-loft adjacent to the pulpit during restoration. In the chancel are a small piscina and a square-headed sedilia.

SWANTON MORLEY All Saints

No of Bells:	6	
19th c. Deanery:	Brisley	
Hundred:	Launditch	
Union house:	Gressenhall	
21st c. Deanery:	Dereham & Mitford	
Benefice:	Swanton Morley	

4 m NE of East Dereham. Situated on the B1147 between E Dereham & Bawdeswell, opposite Rectory Road. Unmissable!
O.S. grid ref: TG 152812
Post Code: NR20 4PB

Dominating the scene set high above the west of the village is this imposing church and tower. Most of what the visitor sees is in the Perpendicular (14th-15th c.) style. At the east end the crypt can be seen through ventilation grills. Within the south porch is a discarded mesa or altar table, now laid as a slab on the floor. The south doorway has engaged columns and is decorated with roses and stars. The plain octagonal font is set on the base of one of the piers. The nave roof is a simple arch-braced construction whereas the chancel roof is single hammerbeam. Carved animals figure in its decoration. The Royal Arms are a mystery as they are purported to be those of Anne dated 1711 but bear the misspelt motto of Dieuit Mon Droit instead of Semper Eadem and are possibly earlier, or is it a simple artist's error?

SWANTON NOVERS St Edmund

		6 m SSW of Holt. Leave
No of Bells:	1	Holt on the B 1110 and
19th c. Deanery:	Holt	head south. After B1354
Hundred:	Holt	cross-roads take 2nd right
Union house:	Great Snoring	and continue straight on.
21st c. Deanery:	Holt	O.S. grid ref: TG 015324
Benefice:	Briningham	Post Code: NR24 2RF

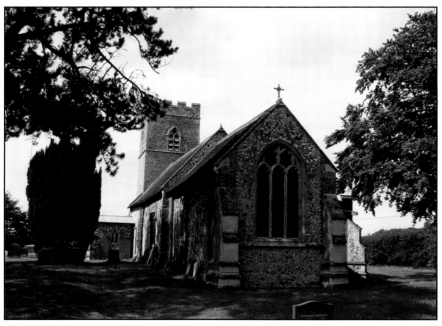

Although the church appears ancient. It was thoroughly 'restored' in 1821 and it has a disappointing Victorian interior. Despite that, there are interesting objects of historical interest. The lovely octagonal 14th c. font for instance is carved with the emblems of Matthew, Mark, Luke and John; between them is a sign of the Trinity surrounded by a crown of thorns. A similar symbol can be seen on the piscina, but with roses *(the symbol for Christ)*. The name Novers originated from the de Noers family who were great benefactors to the re-building of the church in the 14th c. There are signs that the church has its origins in the Saxon period. All the furnishings are Victorian, including the pulpit, which is a simple screen to hide the occupant's legs. Although well loved it has little to grab the attention of the enthusiast.

SWARDESTON   St Mary the Virgin
No of Bells: 4
19th c. Deanery: Humbleyard
Hundred: Humbleyard
Union house: Swainsthorpe
21st c. Deanery: Humbleyard
Benefice: Swardeston

4 m SSW of Norwich.
Leave Norwich on the
B1113. 1½ m after passing
under the flyover turn right
into Swardeston village.
O.S. grid ref: TG 199024
Post Code: NR14 8UG

According to the comprehensive guide the church was originally built in the 12th c. and dedicated to St Andrew. About 1400 it was re-dedicated to St. Mary. A plaque records that a bell fell and killed the ringer; he was buried where he died, in the tower. The roofline indicates that no chancel arch exists; the chancel door has been blocked. A plain 14th c. octagonal font stands at the west end of the lime-washed nave. Very clean and unfortunately uninteresting. (I feel the old lych-gate has more character). Large tie-beams span the long arch-braced roof. On each side of the nave are low blank arcades which seem today to have no significance or purpose but are thought-provoking nevertheless. The screen has a modern lower part but it supports the lovely restored 14th c. cusped and crocketted upper section.

TACOLNESTON   All Saints   10 m SW of Norwich. Leave
No of Bells: 6   Norwich on the B1113 and
19th c. Deanery: Depwade   head for Tacolneston. The
Hundred: Depwade   church is on a left-hand bend
Union house: Pulham St Mary   before the village proper.
21st c. Deanery: Humbleyard   O.S. grid ref: TM 149956
Benefice: Upper Tas Valley   Post Code: NR16 1EF

This 14th-15th c. church stands on the inside of a bend in the road near the Forncett junction. The tiled roof is one continuous expanse from west to east and there is no chancel arch. There are three scratch dials to find. In the south aisle is a stone coffin lid behind a Perspex screen. Nearby is what remains of the beautiful rood screen bearing depictions of the Annunciation and the Temptation of St Anthony, a horrible means of displaying such a gem. At the west end of the nave is the 15th c. octagonal font and above the ringing gallery hang the Royal Arms of James I dated 1610 later re-assigned to Charles I. Also from the same Jacobean period is the pulpit. The chancel, defined only by a shallow step, contains a simple 16th c. piscina and a dropped-sill sedilia. Hopefully you may find a keyholder somewhere.

TASBURGH St Mary

No of Bells: 5
19th c. Deanery: Depwade
Hundred: Depwade
Union house: Pulham St Mary
21st c. Deanery: Depwade
Benefice: Tas Valley

8 m S of Norwich. From the A140 turn right into Tasburgh and continue to signpost pointing left to the 'Church' before Y junction.
O.S. grid ref: TM 201958
Post Code: NR15 1ND

Tasburgh church is almost always locked. The round tower appears plain but closer inspection will reveal shallow arcading halfway up. Inside the nave a doorway can be seen, originally accessed by a ladder which was withdrawn when all were safe from the invaders. The nave and chancel are narrow and lofty, they too probably have pre-Conquest foundations. The church was largely rebuilt in the late 15th century. The later Victorian restorations despoiled the character somewhat, but it is much loved and well cared for. A modern meeting room has been added since. In the chancel are decorative paintings. A niche set into the south wall was probably an Easter sepulchre. Most of the fixtures and fittings and roofs are relatively modern and the lime-washed walls give the interior a somewhat clinical appearance.

TAVERHAM St Edmund

No of Bells:	1
19th c. Deanery:	Taverham
Hundred:	Taverham
Union house:	Horsham St Faith
21st c. Deanery:	Taverham
Benefice:	Norwich North

5½ m NW of Norwich. From the A1067 turn left into Taverham and towards Costessey. The church is at the next main intersection.
O.S. grid ref: TG 160139
Post Code: NR8 6SY

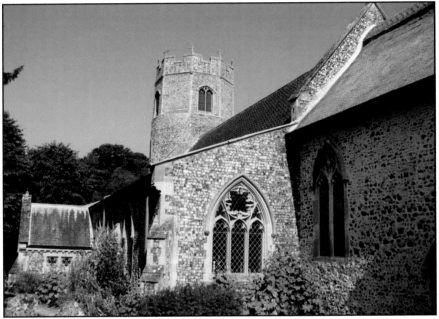

This is a difficult church to get into, always locked except between 2 and 4 pm Monday to Friday, which gives little leeway to the visitor from afar. The tower is early Norman and has had an octagonal upper stage added since. A lovely Norman doorway leads to the south aisle, and the font. It has a corona around the carved bowl and eight saintly figures depicted around the shaft. The square-headed screen is 15th c. and has been marred by brown paint at sometime in the past. However the traceried remains of a 14th c. screen (probably from elsewhere) are utilised in the altar rail. I found little of real interest in the interior here except the structure and building methods of the Normans. Although I do not condone the locking of any church, I can understand if there are real treasures inside, but here there are none.

THARSTON　St Mary

No of Bells:　5

19th c. Deanery:　Depwade

Hundred:　Depwade

Union house:　Pulham St Mary

21st c. Deanery:　Depwade

Benefice:　Tas Valley

10 m S by W of Norwich. From the A140 take the first right after the Hempnall cross-roads and before Long Stratton. Then 1st right.

O.S. grid ref:　TM 190942

Post Code:　NR15 2YG

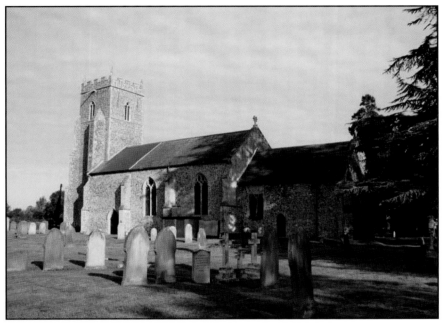

Yet another church that is permanently locked, although you are invited to become a friend of the church, I found no keyholder listed. It is similar to many other churches in appearance but interesting nevertheless. On the south side of the 15th c. tower is a stair turret leading to the belfry, on the west is a doorway with decorated spandrels. A short distance south is the mausoleum of the Harvey family, benefactors to the church and whose unusual memorials adorn the walls of the nave and chancel. The 15th c. octagonal font has angels, lions and Tudor roses around the bowl and is a delight to behold, locally carved in a style different from the norm. Although most of the furnishings are Victorian the old mediaeval bench ends have been re-used to delightful effect.

THELVETON St Andrew

No of Bells:	1	
19th c. Deanery:	Redenhall	
Hundred:	Diss	
Union house:	Pulham St Mary	
21st c. Deanery:	Redenhall	
Benefice: Dickleburgh & The Pulhams		

2 m ENE of Diss. Turn W off the A140 at roundabout S of Dickleburgh and take 1st right and follow 1 mile. In Church Road, set back. O.S. grid ref: TM 152813
Post Code: IP21 4EP

This lovely little tower-less church has a couple of treats for visitors. Above the west end of the roof of the nave is a single bell turret. Entry is via the south porch. Cautley had little to say about the church because it is heavily restored in the Victorian style of doing things. The font, he described as 'traditional' but the decoration around the shaft must have evaded his eye. Every inch is carved, whether it be re-cut or of Victorian date. I admit the seating is anything but traditional with modern pine seats and a pulpit to match. On the wall above the north door however are the Royal Arms of Charles I, probably also restored, but with so many churches without Royal Arms it is a pleasure to see them retained here, as they should be, by a law which has as yet never been repealed. (See supplement in East Norfolk)

THEMELTHORPE St Andrew

No of Bells:	1
19th c. Deanery:	Sparham
Hundred:	Eynesford
Union house:	Aylsham
21st c. Deanery:	Sparham
Benefice:	Foulsham

3 m WNW of Reepham.
Leave Reepham west on
the B1145. After 1 mile
turn right to Themelthorpe
and continue 2 miles.
O.S. grid ref: TG 057241
Post Code: NR20 5PS

A pre-Conquest church which is without dressed quoin stones at the corners and with flints laid in herringbone style, signs of Saxon work. The tower is 13th c. and without buttressing; the porch is 13th c. Although thoroughly restored in Victorian days it retains much of its charm. The roof is continuous and there is in consequence no chancel arch. An octagonal shaft supports the undecorated deep bowl of the early font. Close by are parts of the old bell-frame recently replaced. Above is a modern tie-beam and king-post roof, whitewashed between the rafters. The pulpit and benches are Victorian but the old bench-ends and poppy-heads have been incorporated in the construction of the benches. A lovely old corner piscina has access from the triple graduated sedilia. Simple but interesting!

THORNAGE   All Saints
No of Bells: 1
19th c. Deanery: Holt
Hundred: Holt
Union house: Erpingham
21st c. Deanery: Holt
Benefice: Brinton

2½ m SW of Holt. Easily found beside the main B1110 road south-west of Holt at the southern end of the village.
O.S. grid ref: TG 050363
Post Code: NR25 7AD

Saxon long and short work can be seen on the tower indicating a very early date. Unfortunately restored by a heavy hand it has lost much of its charm. An early plain octagonal font has also been badly repaired in times past. The signs of a south arcade and former aisle can be seen in the walls of the nave. Someone has seen fit to rip out all the lovely old benches and replace them with wooden chairs which detract from the dignity of the nave. Modern benches in the choir do little to compensate. Close to the altar rails is a memorial to Sir William Butt (1583). Whether it ever bore his effigy is beyond memory. It is adorned with shields relating to the family. In the floor is set a slab in memory of Elizabeth (1673), wife of Hercules Forster. A lovely corner piscina with column is adjacent to the dropped-sill sedilia.

THORPE ABBOTS   All Saints

No of Bells: 2
19th c. Deanery: Redenhall
Hundred: Earsham
Union house: Pulham St Mary
21st c. Deanery: Redenhall
Benefice: Scole

3 m E of Scole. The church
stands unmissable on the
left of the A143 behind a
lay-by 3 miles east of Scole
on the Lowestoft road.
O.S. grid ref: TM 187789
Post Code: IP21 4HS

It is difficult to gain entry to this church. A Saxon tower dominates
the smart, possibly coeval nave. On the north side the remains of an
early (possibly Saxon) doorway can be seen right of the water butt.
The 15th c. porch and 13th c. doorway are guarded by a horrible
modern glass door. Once inside it is difficult to see why so much
security is necessary. An appointment to visit has to be made via the
church's website (impossible for most). In the nave stands the font
with saintly figures and emblems. Plastered over during the
Commonwealth it was only fully revealed again when the plaster
started to deteriorate in the 1840s. Angels hang precariously from the
cornice of the modern roof. The Royal Arms are genuinely of George
III (1801-1816 style) and not Stuart as Cautley states in his volume.

THORPE PARVA　　St Mary

No of Bells:	-	
19th c. Deanery:	Redenhall	
Hundred:	Diss	
Union house:	Pulham St Mary	
21st c. Deanery:	-	
Benefice:	-	

2½ m E of Diss. From the A143 east of Diss take the narrow lane after the council houses on the brow of the hill before Billingford.
O.S. grid ref:　TM 161790
Post Code:　　NR21 4HH

As can be seen from the above photograph, little remains of this church of the now almost extinct parish of Thorpe Parva. All that remains of the parish is Hall Farm which is not far away from the remains. An outline of red bricks suggests that there might have been a west window. There are few clues and no historical records about the church but what remains indicates that high Norman arches may have been incorporated into the round tower, but little of the eastern side of the tower remains and nothing of the nave. Only an archaeological dig could reveal more details of this remote church. I was unable to ascertain when it went into disuse but I would imagine it was around the time of Queen Elizabeth I, perhaps even earlier, at the time of the Great Plague.

THURGARTON   All Saints

No of Bells: 1 (formerly 2)

19th c. Deanery: Repps

Hundred: North Erpingham

Union house: West Beckham

21st c. Deanery: -

The Churches Conservation Trust

6½ m N of Aylsham. From the A140 turn left 1 mile before Roughton and through Hanworth and take the 1st right for 1 mile.

O.S. grid ref: TG 181359

Post Code: NR11 7HT

Since the round tower fell in 1822 the bell has been housed in the upper part of the porch. The beautifully thatched church has foundations dating back to the Norman period of building but most of what is seen today is 15th and 16th c. There are two early (restored) lancet windows which were part of early 13th c. rebuilding. At the west end of the nave is the high, narrow tower arch perhaps indicative of pre-Conquest work. Remains of an early chantry chapel can be seen on the north side and an unusual flying buttress on the south. In the nave is the plain 14th c. font and nearby a 15th c. chest. Most interesting are the old poppy-head bench ends with figures carved on the armrests. Post-reformation wall paintings and early piscine and a hammerbeam roof in the chancel also feature here in this lovely interesting church.

THURNING   St Andrew   6 m S of Holt. From the
No of Bells: 1 (2 sold in 1772)   B1354 at Briston head
19th c. Deanery: Sparham   south towards Reepham.
Hundred: Eynesford   The church is 2½ miles just
Union house: Aylsham   north of Thurning
21st c. Deanery: Sparham   O.S. grid ref: TG 080294
Benefice: Reepham   Post Code: NR20 5QX

The roofline of the church is continuous; the original chancel is in ruins at the east end, only part of the north wall remains. At the west end, the 14th c. tower is without buttressing and is unusual in having only one bell window. The church is the same age as the tower with arcades and a north aisle. On the east door, now blocked, there is a scratch dial proving that it was re-sited from the south of the chancel after its collapse some time before 1720. At the west end and in the north aisle are 19th c. box pews; the ugly nave benches are from the same period. The font is plain and un-decorated. An 18th c. triple-decker pulpit, designed by Sir William Burroughs, has a commanding view over the whole congregation. There are a few memorial slabs in the aisle, one bearing an unusual name, Fountain Elwin (1735).

THUXTON   All Saints   3½ m N of Hingham.
No of Bells: 1   From the B1135 south of
19th c. Deanery: Hingham   Garveston turn left
Hundred: Mitford   towards Thuxton Station.
Union house: Gressenhall   The church is nearby.
21st c. Deanery: Dereham & Mitford   O.S. grid ref: TG 032071
Benefice: Barnham Broom & Upper Yare Post Code: NR9 4QJ

Easily recognisable by the diminutive octagonal top to the sturdy 14th
c. square tower. The nave has clerestory windows only on the south
side; at one time there was also a south aisle. The entrance porch is on
the north side and has early pillars incorporated into its design. This
would indicate the existence of a church before this one was built.
The circular Norman font has carved projections at the base of the
bowl for four columns but the columns and central shaft are
Victorian. A pulpit from the reign of James I and the Royal Arms of
Charles I are among the treasures to be found, in addition to carved
stone scattered here and there throughout the church. The carved
stone reredos is a Victorian addition. If you are fortunate enough to
gain entry it is worth a look around. Always kept locked!

THWAITE   All Saints

No of Bells: 1

19th c. Deanery: Ingworth

Hundred: South Erpingham

Union house: Aylsham

21st c. Deanery: Ingworth

Benefice: Scarrowbeck, Erpingham

4 m N of Aylsham. 1 mile
N of Erpingham on the
A140 turn left. Turn left
again at Alby church and
follow road 1 mile.
O.S. grid ref: TG 194334
Post Code: NR11 7PR

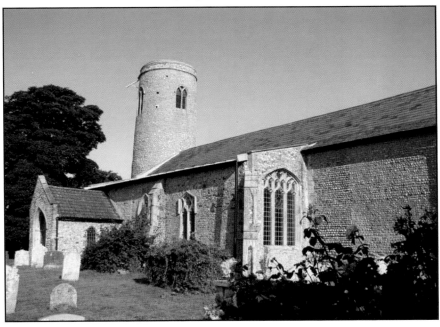

Do not confuse this church with Thwaite near Loddon although it is similarly interesting and ancient. A round Norman or slightly later tower dominates the west end. Entry to the nave is through the 15th c. south porch and aisle. A good sized iron-bound parish chest stands just inside the door. A disappointingly plain font is adjacent to the westernmost column of the 15th c. south arcade. The lovely pulpit is complete with backboard and tester and dated 1624. Behind it and partially concealed is the base of the 15th c. screen retaining its gesso decoration and original colouring. In the south aisle is a good double brass to John Puttok (1442) and his wife. Before he died he sponsored the building of the aisle in which he and his wife are buried. This is an interesting church and well worth a thorough look round.

TIBENHAM All Saints
No of Bells: 6
19th c. Deanery: Depwade
Hundred: Depwade
Union house: Pulham St Mary
21st c. Deanery: Depwade
Benefice: Pilgrim Group

6 m SE of Diss. Take the B1077 out of Diss to Winfarthing where you turn right. Right at T junc. Then left. 2nd left then 1 mile.
O.S. grid ref: TM 135898
Post Code: NR16 1QB

A splendid church that seems to have everything. Displays of its ostentation can be seen in the structure of the tower with its base course, the chequered flushwork, niche and Evangelist pinnacles. Have a walk around the church before entering by the south porch. The 15th c. font has tracery decoration around the bowl which is supported on eight columns; the adjacent arcade is early 14th c. Outstanding is the crown-like tester hanging over the splendid Jacobean pulpit. Much of the woodwork here is of a similar date. There is a unique eastern gallery constructed in 1635 for the family and servants of the Buxton family; it bears their family crest. The reading desk is also unique, having four sides and also from the Jacobean era. A lovely church and well worth an hour of your time.

TIVETSHALL St Margaret *****

No of Bells:	1
19th c. Deanery:	Redenhall
Hundred:	Diss
Union house:	Pulham St Mary
21st c. Deanery:	Redenhall
Benefice:	Winfarthing

6 m NNE of Diss. From the A140 turn west near Pulham Market towards Tivetshall. Take 2nd left and 1st right and follow ¾ mile to church.
O.S. grid ref: TM 163870
Post Code: NR15 2DB

The one remaining church of the two Tivetshalls contains the renowned Arms of Queen Elizabeth I which fills the tympanum of the chancel arch. For this alone the church has my five-star recommendation. However the 14th c. building is also impressive in many other respects. Within the leaning porch is a doorway with spandrels depicting the emblems of the Trinity and Instruments of the Passion. Flaking whitewash covers the plain octagonal font. On the west wall the filled tower arch can be seen. The screen which was originally vaulted still retains its original colouring and is complete; it is flanked on the north side by 13th c. sepulchral slab in a recess. The nave roof can only be fully appreciated with binoculars which will reveal the subtle bosses and shields at the intersections.

TIVETSHALL St Mary

No of Bells: -
19th c. Deanery: Redenhall
Hundred: Diss
Union house: Pulham St Mary
21st c. Deanery: -
Benefice: -

5½ m NNE of Diss. Turn west 4 m N of Scole near Holly Farm and take 3rd right. The church is on a 'Z' bend

O.S. grid ref: TM 166858
Post Code: NR15 2BZ

Re-thatched between the two Wars, the tower collapsed onto the nave following vibration from a passing aircraft in 1949. Just before that happened, both of the Tivetshall churches had suffered from lack of maintenance to varying degrees and it was thought necessary to close one or the other. The same dilemma had faced the parish in 1702 but at this time both churches were restored. The passing aeroplane made the decision for the PCC. In 1978 the roof was removed; the remains were eventually consolidated in 1995 by Norfolk County Council's Historic Buildings Programme. The ruins are open and interesting to look around. Basically a 15th c. building; the porch, base of the 13th c. tower and the nave and chancel walls remain sentinel over the graveyard which is still used.

TUTTINGTON Sts Peter & Paul

No of Bells:	1 (3 sold in 18th c.)
19th c. Deanery:	Ingworth
Hundred:	South Erpingham
Union house:	Aylsham
21st c. Deanery:	St Benet at Waxham
Benefice:	King's Beck

2 m E of Aylsham. From the A140 north-east of Aylsham take the road to Coldham Hall and follow to the village centre.

O.S. grid ref: TG 227272
Post Code: NR11 6AZ

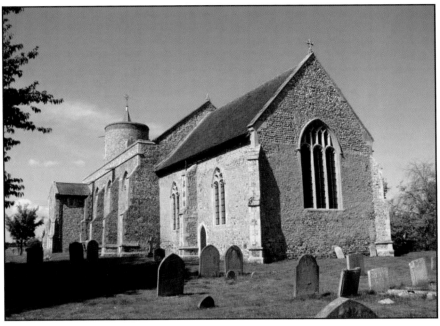

A lovely round Norman tower, it has a spirelet constructed in 1750 which replaced a larger spire. The church was probably built in the early 13th c. as the first recorded rector was endowed in 1234. The nave, however, was rebuilt in mediaeval times although the chancel remained as it was. The Victorians did some restoration in erecting a new roof and it has remained fairly intact ever since. An unusually decorated 15th c. font stands upon two steps with a Jacobean ogee cover. Beautiful 15th c. benches with a variety of interesting carvings on the ends are a treat to behold. A pulpit stands precariously on a small stem. A cusped piscina has an opening to the adjacent sedilia. The Jacobean altar is dated 1632. On the floor are many slab memorials to various 17th and 18th c. members of the Elwin family.

TWYFORD   St Nicholas
No of Bells: 1
19th c. Deanery: Sparham
Hundred: Eynesford
Union house: Gressenhall
21st c. Deanery: Sparham
Benefice: Elmham

6 m WNW of Reepham.
The church stands on the
east side the A1067
immediately north of the
few houses.
O.S. grid ref: TG 016246
Post Code: NR20 5LY

Twyford is one of the churches which is difficult to access; although there is a keyholder he is not currently listed on the notice board. A strange configuration greets the visitor with an 18th c. truncated south tower serving also as a porch. Atop the tower is a cupola with a single bell. The single roofed barn-like structure has no chancel arch but the building does have indications here and there that it has a long history dating back to the Norman period. There is a plain 12th c. square font supported on four columns. The nave roof is plaster-boarded and unappealing. Carved poppy-head benches line the nave. Behind the altar is an alabaster reredos which I believe, is mid-Victorian, is very attractive. There is, on the whole little of real interest here, so if you can't find the keyholder it won't be the end of the world.

UPPER SHERINGHAM All Saints

No of Bells:	6	
19th c. Deanery:	Repps	
Hundred:	North Erpingham	
Union house:	Sheringham	
21st c. Deanery:	Holt	
Benefice:	Weybourne	

5 m W of Cromer. From Sheringham take the B1157 south for 1 mile. The church is unmissable, just beside the road.

O.S. grid ref: TG 145418

Post Code: NR26 8AE

See also Sheringham. Here is a church that states it is here and here to stay, standing proudly on a crossroads overlooking Sheringham. A fine clerestory with alternating quatrefoil and arched windows numbering nine pairs in all. It was the parish church for both Sheringhams until 1953. The church as it stands today dates from the 14th c. although there has been a church here since before Domesday. Entry is through the 15th c. porch leading into the south aisle. The aisle has mediaeval benches with animals carved on the armrests. There are two fonts, the one in use is 14th c. with a traceried bowl supported on eight columns; the other is on the floor, broken. Behind the beautiful screen is a plain piscina and sedilia in the south-east wall of the chancel. Much more to see here than I can mention and well worth a visit.

WACTON	All Saints	11 m S by W of Norwich.
No of Bells:	1	From the A140 near Long
19th c. Deanery:	Depwade	Stratton church take the road
Hundred:	Depwade	west to Wacton and follow
Union house:	Pulham St Mary	1½ m then turn right.
21st c. Deanery:	Depwade	O.S. grid ref: TM 179917
Benefice:	Long Stratton	Post Code: NR15 2UG

The base of the tapering round tower dates from before the Conquest. The remainder of the porch-less church is 14th c. or thereabouts. Inside, through the ogee doorway, the nave roof is continuous with the chancel, divided only by the tall screen, lit from behind by the clear glass set in the gorgeous 14th c. tracery of the east window. Much of what is to be seen here is of that early date with one or two exceptions. The screen, altar rails and wine-glass pulpit for example are 17th c. Adjacent to the latter are the rood stairs ascending from a window sill and opening just above the screen. The octagonal font with lions around the base has saintly emblems and angels holding shields on the facets. The handsome matching traceried ogee piscina and graduated sedilia are beneath a square headed label. Nice one!

WELBORNE	All Saints	11 m W of Norwich. Turn
No of Bells:	1	south off the A47 at
19th c. Deanery:	Hingham	Hockering for 2½ m. to
Hundred:	Forehoe	Church Lane. Near the
Union house:	Wicklewood	Nightingale Care Home.
21st c. Deanery:	Dereham & Mitford	O.S. grid ref: TG 067102
Benefice:	Mattishall	Post Code: NR20 3LQ

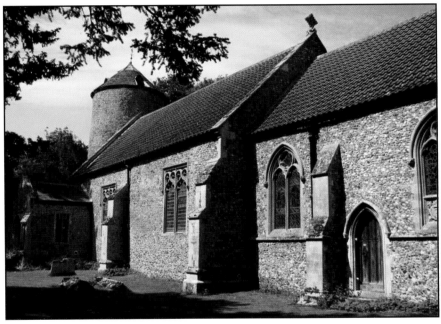

A really lovely church, this, and unexpected in a small rural community. From the outside the most distinctive thing is the Norman tower with its tiled conical cap. The south door has tracery on the upper part. A great deal of restoration has taken place. Not everything inside is ancient but a lovely mixture of the old and the new. The octagonal font has a heavy rim. A gilded and re-painted screen with the rood spans the chancel arch against which stands the well carved pulpit. Victorian benches have carved figures executed to a high degree of craftsmanship. The elaborate reredos is gilded and painted and depicts Jesus flanked by a pelican and the Agnus Dei. The small piscina and marble columned sedilia have been restored. I was fortunate to find the church open as it is usually kept locked.

WEST BECKHAM St Helen & All Saints

No of Bells: 1
19th c. Deanery: Ingworth
Hundred: South Erpingham
Union house: West Beckham
21st c. Deanery: Holt
Benefice: Weybourne

4 m E of Holt From the
A140 at Bodham head east
to W Beckham and through
the village to Church Road.
O.S. grid ref: TG 143397
Post Code: NR25 6NY

This church was built in 1891 from the demolished remains of the two churches of St Helen's E. Beckham and All Saints W. Beckham. A small bell turret with a single bell is at the west end of the nave roof. There is no tower. Inside, the walls are bare flint with modern pews. The octagonal font is coeval with the building of the church. There are a few objects pertaining to the old churches but nothing to get excited about. Virtually nothing remains of the original churches. The building stone has been utilised but that is about all. A few hundred yards to the south-east is what remains of West Beckham church. The graveyard there is still in use. All that can be seen of the old church is a line of ledger slabs and a small consolidated heap of flints which once formed the south wall.

WEST HARLING   All Saints
No of Bells: 8 tubular bells
19th c. Deanery: Rockland
Hundred: Guiltcross
Union house: Kenninghall
21st c. Deanery: -
The Churches Conservation Trust

1½ m WSW of East
Harling. North of the
A1066. Turn into lane
opposite 'The Paper House'
and follow the track.
O.S. grid ref: TL 973852
Post Code: NR16 2SF

You will find this church open at weekends and a keyholder lives nearby for weekday visits. Unlike most churches maintained by The Trust, this one has not been entirely stripped of everything. Fresh flowers still decorate the chancel which is 13th c. and the oldest part of the church. A century later the tower with a spire was rebuilt, the latter was removed in 1756 and the upper stage rebuilt. The nave is 15th c. and originally had a south chapel which was removed in 1733. In the nave is the 15th c. octagonal font with shield and quatrefoil decoration. Victorian benches fill the aisle and ancient brasses are set into the floor. The windows are full of colourful glass and the interior is illuminated with coloured sunlight. The piscina in the chancel has been removed but the two drains remain.

WEST RUNTON   Holy Trinity
No of Bells: 1
19th c. Deanery: Repps
Hundred: North Erpingham
Union house: Sheringham
21st c. Deanery: Repps
Benefice: Aylmerton

3 m W of Cromer on the coast road. The church stands on the seaward side adjacent to the road in the centre of the village.
O.S. grid ref: TG 179429
Post Code: NR27 9QT

The building of this church can be traced back to the 13th c. but little of the original still remains, just some vaulting and a sanctus bell window. Two unusual nautical themed carvings can be seen on the west gable. 14th c. arcades separate the nave from the north and south aisles and support the 19th c. scissor-frame roof. The font is a bulky 15th c. model with eight engaged columns supporting the octagonal bowl with traceried facets, the ogee cover is a 1964 memorial to a parishioner. Furnishings and fittings including the wine-glass pulpit are almost all Victorian: the lectern is no exception but it is beautifully carved. Even the double piscina and sedilia were restored during that period, both having cusped and crocketted traceried arches. Hanoverian Royal Arms hang on the wall of the north aisle.

WEST WRETHAM   St Lawrence

No of Bells: -
19th c. Deanery: Rockland
Hundred: -
Union house: -
21st c. Deanery: -
Benefice: -

6 m NNE of Thetford. Just
north of 'Thorpe Camp'
In the grounds of Hall
Farm. It is advisable to ask
permission to look round.
O.S. grid ref: TL 900914
Post Code: IP24 1RH

For many years the ruins of West Wretham church have stood neglected and covered in ivy and surrounded by brambles and nettles, creating an almost impregnable fortress. Now some clearance has taken place and it is possible to enter the ruin (with care) to examine the interior. A solid, possibly 14th c. square tower with an octagonal upper stage dominates the scene. Inside the tower a west doorway has been reduced in size by creating a smaller entrance with brickwork. A lancet window is visible in the nave wall. Decorated style windows have lost most of their tracery. There are various legends apparently surrounding this ruin, told by those who live nearby. This is an interesting ruin to have a look around but as it is on private land it is best to ask permission first.

WESTFIELD St Andrew
No of Bells: 1
19th c. Deanery: Hingham
Hundred: Mitford
Union house: Gressenhall
21st c. Deanery: Dereham & Mitford
Benefice: Reymerston

2 m S of East Dereham in Dereham Road. From Dereham on the A1075 turn off left to Westfield for 1 mile.
O.S. grid ref: TF 993099
Post Code: NR19 1QG

A quite ordinary church dating from the 14th and 15th centuries which has lost its chancel and has a heavily buttressed east wall. The clean uninterrupted roofline is quite modern in comparison. The tower has a pinnacle at each corner and shows no sign of once having a steeper pitch to the roof, and that too has been rebuilt to some degree. The flushwork on the otherwise unremarkable 15th c. porch is conspicuous. Inside the church all is austere and simple with a plain octagonal font and whitewashed walls. The pulpit is hexagonal from floor to top, and is certainly unusual and appears Jacobean. Otherwise there is little of interest here and it is sad that it is not left open to visitors. Although there is a keyholder listed it is not an easy task to find anyone at home.

WESTON LONGVILLE All Saints

No of Bells: 6
19th c Deanery: Sparham
Hundred: Eynesford
Union house: Horsham St Faith
21st c. Deanery: Sparham
Benefice: Wensum

6 m S of Reepham. From the A1067 after Attlebridge follow the road for just over 1 mile. The church is on the left at a T-junction.
O.S. grid ref: TG 113159
Post Code: NR9 5JU

This is the parish and church of Parson Woodforde. Much of the church has been restored since his days here. The 13th c. tower is the oldest part of the building. The nave and chancel are mainly 14th c. There is a plain, modern, octagonal font standing on four 13th c. columns. Set into the west step is the outline of a Saxon Calvary, the oldest object to be found here. A modern glass-faced ringing gallery has been constructed in the tower; the Royal Arms of George III hang on the wall nearby. Past the forest of poppy-headed benches mediaeval paintings can be seen on the chancel arch. The adjacent 15th c. screen is painted with twelve apostles and in very good condition, as is the lovely matching piscina and sedilia beneath a carved label with faces and floral designs. Well worth a visit.

WEYBOURNE   All Saints

No of Bells: 1
19th c Deanery: Holt
Hundred: Holt
Union house: Erpingham
21st c. Deanery: Holt
Benefice: Weybourne

4 m NE of Holt. The church stands on the seaward side of the A140 in the village centre. Best to park in the road opposite.
O.S. grid ref: TG111432
Post Code: NR25 7SE

Part of the Saxon tower of an earlier church remain north of the chancel. An Augustinian Priory in the 13th c. it now stands in ruins. The church was built around the same time as the north door implies. The tower was built about 200 years later. A small parvise used to be above the porch but was removed during restorations some considerable time ago. Inside the nave the hammerbeam roof is modern, reconstructed during Victorian restoration by Herbert Green. The chancel is off centre to the nave owing, due probably to the utilisation of the Saxon tower wall already mentioned. The simple arched piscina with a pillar drain is juxtaposed to a triple graduated sedilia. The copy of the seal of the old priory is displayed on the wall. All the poppy-heads were carved about 1900 by three sisters.

WHINBURGH   St Mary

No of Bells: 2
19th c Deanery: Holt
Hundred: Mitford
Union house: Gressenhall
21st c. Deanery: Dereham & Mitford
Benefice: Reymerston

3½ m SSE of E. Dereham just off the B1135. Take 2nd left once over the railway bridge into Church Road, Whinburgh.
O.S. grid ref: TG 007089
Post Code: NR19 1QS

The somewhat truncated and capped 14th c. tower is set to south and serves as a porch. Cautley had little to say in his 'Norfolk Churches' and seemed unimpressed. A good variety of window designs can be seen from outside especially the five-light west window. In the nave stands a plain 14th c. octagonal font on a clumsy plinth. The roof is dour as is most of the interior with the possible exception of the poppy-heads on the bench ends. A Jacobean panel let into one is nicely carved. Everything else is Victorian. A flashy banner over the chancel arch is eye-catching but quite unbefitting. A set of carved Hanoverian Royal Arms hangs high on the wall. In my own opinion the brick floor with its herring-bone design was probably the most pleasing thing to see here. The church is always kept locked.

WHITWELL   St Michael

No of Bells:	8
19th c Deanery:	Sparham
Hundred:	Eynesford
Union house:	Reepham
21st c. Deanery:	Sparham
Benefice:	Reepham

12 m NW of Norwich. From Norwich on the A1067, take the B1145 to Reepham. The church is just south of the centre of the town.
O.S. grid ref: TG 102229
Post Code: NR10 4JW

This is one of three churches which once stood in this graveyard. That of Reepham is the only one still used as such. Whitwell church is the westernmost and was made redundant in the 1970s and is now used as a church hall, which is sad because it is the finer of the two. Its 14th c. tower is pinnacled and the window tracery of the nave is quite lovely. Over the porch is a small semicircular opening. The interior has been altered in such a way that it is no longer recognisable as a church if it were not for the beautiful Jacobean pulpit, complete with back-board and canopy, which has been retained. It seems a shame that the church is no longer used but at least it still serves the community in a useful and practical way. It is possible to see inside during activities within, but otherwise it is usually kept locked.

WICKLEWOOD   All Saints

No of Bells:	1 (at one time 2)	
19th c Deanery:	Hingham	
Hundred:	Forehoe	
Union house:	Wicklewood	
21st c. Deanery:	Humbleyard	
Benefice:	High Oak & Hingham	

3 m W of Wymondham. From the B1108 south of Kimberley turn left towards Wicklewood. Continue 1 mile to destination.

O.S. grid ref: TG 070024
Post Code: NR18 9HT

An earlier church dedicated to St Andrew also once stood in the same churchyard but was ruinous by 1367. This church with its south tower also serving as an entrance porch was modified during the latter part of the 14th c. using some materials from St Andrew's. In the ringing chamber is an oven, once used to bake the wafers for Communion. The octagonal font is 15th c. with shields within geometric designs. It has a tall conical cover which is heavily crocketted. Most of the furnishings and fittings are Victorian after some heavy-handed restorations took place. It is nice to find that poppy-heads have been added to the bench ends, even though they too are 19th c. A corbel piscina can be seen in the chancel, the plain sedilia is cut into the wall and is divided by the altar rail.

WICKMERE St Andrew

No of Bells: 1
19th c Deanery: Ingworth
Hundred: South Erpingham
Union house: Aylsham
21st c. Deanery: Ingworth
Benefice: Seven churches Itteringham

5 m N of Aylsham. From the A140 at Erpingham turn left, just past Calthorpe church turn right. Bear left; turn right & over x- roads.
O.S. grid ref: TG 165338
Post Code: NR11 7JE

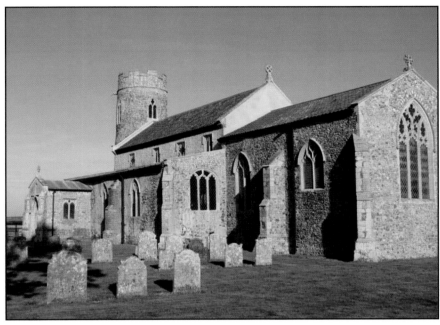

The round tapering tower which contains much carstone in its fabric is probably pre-Conquest with some later additions such as the embattled parapet. A small staircase rises up the north-west face. A large edifice for a small parish, there was obviously money here; judging by the memorials it was Walpole money that paid for the building. Attached to the south aisle is the 15th c. restored porch, the handle and iron-work on the door possibly 14th c. The 15th c. clerestory is supported on octagonal arcades. An octagonal font has Tudor roses and shields. Many interesting carvings can be seen on the bench-ends, two of which are coeval with the building. Part of the mutilated screen seems to have been incorporated in the pulpit. In the chancel the piscina and sedilia have also seen better days.

WINFARTHING St Mary

No of Bells:	6
19th c. Deanery:	Redenhall
Hundred:	Diss
Union house:	Pulham St Mary
21st c. Deanery:	Redenhall
Benefice:	Winfarthing

4 m N of Diss. Leave Diss on the B1077 to Winfarthing and turn right once in the village. The church is almost on the corner.
O.S. grid ref: TM 109857
Post Code: IP22 2EA

This is a fine church and is associated with the Sword of Winfarthing which it is said had supernatural powers. The church has Norman foundations and a splendid Norman font seemingly (although not) carved from a single lump of stone. Note the two faces on the pillars of the base. Two small quatrefoil windows form a clerestory which was created shortly after the nave in the early 15th c. The tower is even later; this is evident by the buttresses at the north-west corner of the nave built around it. Close to the font is a brass memorial to Matthew Hallyet (1586) and another to his son, Thomas (1612). The cusped piscina in the chancel is flanked by the dropped-sill sedilia. An ancient parish chest with three clasps is displayed. A Jacobean holy table bears the date 1613. The carved pulpit was made in 1906.

WIVETON	St Mary	4½ m NW of Holt.
No of Bells:	6	Between Cley & Blakeney
19th c. Deanery:	Holt	on the A149 turn south to
Hundred:	Holt	Wiveton and go through the
Union house:	Great Snoring	village to the crossroads.
21st c. Deanery:	Holt	O.S. grid ref: TG 044428
Benefice:	Glaven Valley (Blakeney)	Post Code: NR25 7TP

Within sight of the magnificent church at Cley, this is a fine church in its own right. Once of equal importance, a changing coastline has favoured Cley. The church dates from the 14th c. but there may have been an earlier edifice here. The tower indicates a 13th c. date with its Y tracery in the belfry stage. Interest is both inside and outside the church. The 14th c. font has eroded carving, particularly around the stem where there are shallow canopied niches. The panels of the bowl look to have had their occupants erased. Above is a 15th c. rood screen utilised as a gallery to the ringing chamber. The roofs of the aisles are arch-braced with tracery in the spandrels. Victorian 'restoration' has despoiled the church to a great extent but there are still plenty of interesting things to look at here.

WILBY   All Saints   3½ m S of Attleborough.
No of Bells: 5   Leave the A11 south of
19th c Deanery: Rockland   Attleborough towards Old
Hundred: Shropham   Buckenham, take 2nd right
Union house: Kenninghall   then right again.
21st c. Deanery: Thetford & Rockland   O.S. grid ref: TM 031899
Benefice: Quidenham   Post Code: NR16 2JP

Although embattled the 14th c. tower has no parapet. On the east face
the line of the old thatched roof which caught fire in 1633 can be
clearly seen. The fire resulted in the chancel arch being given a
pinkish tinge by the heat which destroyed most of the interior. It was
restored by Robert Wilton who lived at the Hall, at the cost of £790.
Today the interior remains as it was in 1635 with the three-decker
pulpit against the north wall amidst the pews. Because of its good
condition, no restoration took place during the Victorian period. The
14th c. font, which has pedimented tracery on the eight facets of the
bowl, survived the fire. This is also one of the few churches which
still has its poor-man's box three locks (many just have one). The
Royal Arms of Charles I complete the unique historical display.

WOLTERTON St Margaret

No of Bells:	-	
19th c. Deanery:	Ingworth	
Hundred:	South Erpingham	
Union house:	Aylsham	
21st c. Deanery:	-	
Benefice:	-	

4 m NNW of Aylsham.
Turn off the A140 through
Erpingham and Calthorpe
to Mannington Hall Walks.
Ruins are on private land.
O.S. grid ref: TG 164321
Post Code: NR11 7BB

[The postcode refers to the Hall in which grounds the tower stands]
This was probably part of a late 13th c. church, abandoned when the
village was moved to make way for Mannington Hall, which was
built by the Walpoles in about 1737. The tower was apparently left
intact to enhance the landscaping of the grounds. All there is to see
here is what can be seen in the photograph above, taken from the edge
of the former graveyard. All traces of headstones and monuments
have been cleared away. The church had this round tower which was
constructed with an octagonal top and not as an afterthought. The
upper bell stage is now crumbling and falling masonry is a very real
threat if any attempt is made to examine it closer. The line of the nave
roof is evident and there is no sign of an entrance half-way up.

WOOD DALLING St Andrew

No of Bells:	1 (originally 5)
19th c. Deanery:	Sparham
Hundred:	Eynesford
Union house:	Aylsham
21st c. Deanery:	Sparham
Benefice:	Reepham

3 m N of Reepham. From the A140 turn left go 3 miles towards Heydon. Turn 1st left after Crabgate. Church is in Reepham Rd.
O.S. grid ref: TG 090270
Post Code: NR11 6SN

Although this may appear to be a 15th c. church it is in fact 13th c. with some later additions. Before 1778 there were north and south transepts. A four-light 15th c. clerestory enhances the character of the building. Over the south porch is a parvise which may have been a treasury in the past. Above the doorway is a carved grotesque head. The font is Victorian. On the floor of the north aisle close to the old bier is an effigy of some past incumbent. Beyond the forest of 15th c. poppy-heads of the benches is a wineglass style pulpit, perhaps mediaeval. In the chancel the corner piscina has a cinquefoil ogee arch adjoining a dropped-sill sedilia which was possibly partially destroyed when the window was replaced. This is quite an interesting church, large for its parish and unfortunately poorly maintained.

WOOD NORTON   All Saints

		6 m E of Fakenham. From
No of Bells:	1 *(see text)*	the B1110 turn right at
19th c. Deanery:	Sparham	Holly Hill and follow to
Hundred:	Eynesford	destination in Foulsham
Union house:	Aylsham	Road.
21st c. Deanery:	Sparham	O.S. grid ref: TG 011278
Benefice:	Foulsham	Post Code: NR20 5BE

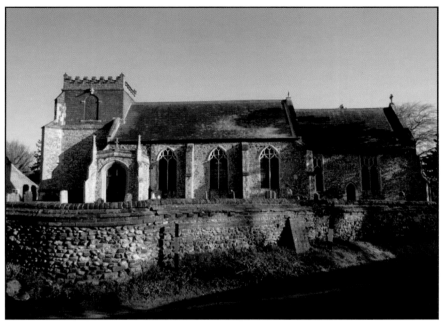

Easily identifiable by the squat, heavily buttressed half-bricked battlemented tower which was begun in the 16th c. By 1699 however the top of the tower which then contained three bells had collapsed and was rebuilt in brick. The bells were temporarily hung under a roof in the churchyard. A fine pinnacled south porch is the entrance to the Victorian nave. Restoration has left little of the character of a late mediaeval church. The 14th c. octagonally curved undecorated bowl of the font is most unusual. The Victorian pulpit stands on a stone pedestal. The chancel has been less interfered with and the corner piscina dates from about 1300. The adjacent sedilia is a dropped window sill. Most of the furnishings like the roofs are modern with a nice crown post in the chancel. Not much to enthuse about here, I fear.

WOOD NORTON   St Peter

No of Bells: -
19th c. Deanery: Sparham
Hundred: -
Union house: -
On private land, permission should be
sought before looking round.

6 m E of Fakenham. As for
All Saints *(opposite page)*
but continue to Manor
Farm. (Road opposite the
church) On private land)
O.S. grid ref: TG 016273
Post Code: NR20 5BE

Now part of a barn, this church was abandoned in 1530. There is little
to see here but whitewashed flint walls forming the back of a barn
with some blocked traceried windows. The west wall is recent and
added when the roof was raised to its present height. A knock on the
door of the farmhouse will bring forth the owner, who, if he is at
home, will be happy to explain some of the history of the lost church
and show you around. As this was an earlier church it is possible that
the piscina mentioned at All Saints *(opposite page)* was once in situ
here and was rescued along with other ecclesiastical ephemera when
the rest of this church was demolished and re-used there; possibly the
font too, which also predates the building of All Saints church, though
the two churches did exist together before 1530.

WOODRISING   St Nicholas

No of Bells: 1
19th c. Deanery: Hingham
Hundred: Mitford
Union house: Gressenhall
21st c. Deanery: Humbleyard
Benefice: High Oak & Hingham

2½ m WNW of Hingham.
Leave Hingham on the
B1108 and turn right. Follow
2½ m then turn right. Church
300 yds is on the right.
O.S. grid ref: TF 988035
Post Code: NR9 4PJ

When the tower collapsed, the bell frame was moved to a corner of the graveyard and given a thatched roof. It is still there, and currently contains one bell dated 1861. The remains of the tower have never been cleared. Inside this little church there is plenty of interest. The font is 14th c. which is perhaps indicative of the date the church was constructed. A splendid Jacobean pulpit retains its backboard but has lost its tester. The chancel arch has two corbel heads; the one near the pulpit looks horrified! Beyond in the chancel there is a double piscina and graduated sedilia, and above hangs a hatchment, one of four here. The church is probably best known for its association with the Howard and Southwell families, many members of whom are interred here and have effigies and memorials to prove the point.

WORTHING   St Margaret

No of Bells: 1
19th c. Deanery: Brisley
Hundred: Launditch
Union house: Gressenhall
21st c. Deanery: Sparham
Benefice: Elmham

4½ m N of East Dereham.
From the B1145 east of
North Elmham turn right,
once over the bridge bear
right for 400 yds.
O.S. grid ref: TF 994196
Post Code: NR20 5HR

This is an ancient church that dates from Norman times and retains a good Norman south doorway with a column either side and two orders of decoration. The north door is coeval but much simpler and has been bricked up. The top of the tower fell in the 18th c. and never rebuilt. The chancel was demolished at the beginning of the 19th c. There is no east window and from the east has the appearance of a barn. Near the porch is a scratch dial with holes to indicate the morning services. The interior is rather stark with Victorian benches either side of the nave. The Norman base of the font is supported on a pile of bricks upon which are two churchyard crosses, one of them hollowed out to create a font. Most ingenious! The church is always kept locked because of its remoteness, which is a great shame.

WRAMPLINGHAM Sts Peter & Paul
No of Bells: 3
19th c. Deanery: Hingham
Hundred: Forehoe
Union house: Wicklewood
21st c. Deanery: Dereham & Mitford
Benefice: Barnham Broom Upper Yare

3 m NNE of Wymondham.
Turn south off the B1108 at
Barford and follow the road
1½ miles winding through
the village.
O.S. grid ref: TG 113061
Post Code: NR18 0RY

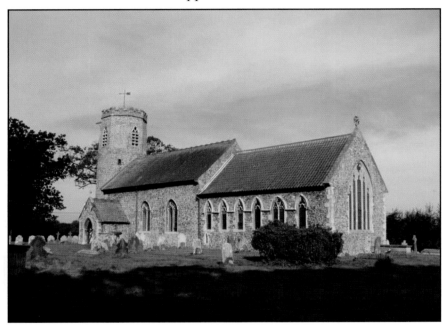

The large 13th c. chancel with its six beautiful windows is the outstanding feature of this fine church, which also has a round coeval tower and 14th c. octagonal top. Inside, the windows have beautiful arches with hood moulds and head stops and columns. The easternmost window on the south side has destroyed what was once a double piscina and arch over the graduated sedilia. On the same wall at the west end is a small low lancet window; two larger ones are in the tower. A rather disappointing plain octagonal font and cover do nothing to excite the imagination. The nave is filled with Victorian benches but in the 19th c. north aisle are some mediaeval ones with poppy-heads, mutilated animals and a face. This is an interesting church to visit with plenty of architectural features.

WRENINGHAM All Saints

No of Bells:	2	
19th c. Deanery:	Humbleyard	
Hundred:	Humbleyard	
Union house:	Swainsthorpe	
21st c. Deanery:	Humbleyard	
Benefice:	Upper Tas Valley	

8 m SW of Norwich. Just off the B1113 south of Bracon Ash turn right to Wreningham. The church is within 400 yds on the right. O.S. grid ref: TM 163989 Post Code: NR16 1BH

The parish of (Great) Wreningham has swallowed up the parishes of Little Wreningham St Mary and Nelonde St Peter and all traces of their churches have disappeared. Collapse of the 12th c. tower in 1852 initiated the Victorian restoration of the whole church, when a north transept was added and the porch rebuilt, obscuring the SW window of the nave. The 15th c. octagonal font has quatrefoil design around the bowl. There are modern roofs, and the pulpit is Jacobean in style. In the sanctuary is a small multi-foiled arch beneath which is the piscina, but the sedilia, if there ever was one, has long since gone. Most of the benches are Victorian as one might expect but they do have poppy-heads in the traditional style. The guide book, written in part by the 'church mouse' is the work of local children. Well done!

WYMONDHAM   Our Lady & St Thomas of Canterbury *****

No of Bells: 10
19th c. Deanery: Hingham
Hundred: Forehoe/ Halfhundred
Union house: Wicklewood
21st c. Deanery: Humbleyard
Benefice: Wymondham

9 m WSW of Norwich.
From Norwich follow the
A11 to Wymondham, and
Becketswell Road.
O.S. grid ref: TG 107015
Post Code: NR18 9PH

Magnificent is the one word that describes the impressive Abbey church; cathedral-like in proportions and opulence. Originally built in 1107 when twelve monks established a priory. The long history of events which followed is best told elsewhere: the church is only a part of the great Abbey. The 15th c. 142-feet-tall west tower was built by the parish but never finished. Norman arcades separate the aisles, the roofs are hammerbeam construction with magnificent carvings. In fact everything here is splendid from the golden reredos to the font, carved in 1410 and is a splendid example of the East Anglian type; it has a tall gilded cover. The Royal Arms are of King George II and are very large. The sedilia in the chancel is terracotta and of the same hand that made the wonderful Bedingfield monument at Oxborough.

YAXHAM	St Peter	2 m SE of East Dereham.
No of Bells:	6	South of the A47 at E.
19th c. Deanery:	Hingham	Dereham. Just north of the
Hundred:	Mitford	B1135 in Church Lane,
Union house:	Gressenhall	Yaxham.
21st c. Deanery:	Dereham & Mitford	O.S. grid ref: TG 007107
Benefice:	Mattishall	Post Code: NR19 1RQ

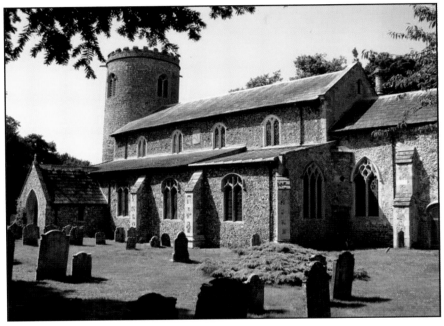

The Saxon base of the tower was originally defensive with an eastern entrance which can be seen from the nave. It was raised in the 14th c. to its full height when the church was built. A sundial is situated centrally on the south of the four light clerestory. The entrance door has tracery on its upper half. The tall octagonal 14th c. font has splendid decorative tracery and was copied by the Victorians for Cromer church. A southern 14th c. arcade runs the length of the nave alternating in octagonal and quatrefoil pillars. The roof of the south aisle still retains some original colouring. Much of the interior was furnished in the Victorian period with interesting carvings on the bench-ends. Even the piscina was remodelled but retains the original drain; the sedilia has been panelled. A lovely peaceful church to visit.

Ruined or lost churches of central Norfolk not featured elsewhere in this guide.

It must be noted that this list is not comprehensive and other sources may reveal other more obscure churches. I have attempted to list all the churches in the area covered by this volume. Hundreds of churches no longer exist. Many were demolished and rebuilt, many still exist today, some with the same dedication. I have abridged the information available for simplicity. I accept that more details may be available in other sources that I have not researched as well as from those I have. All the information was obtained from one or more of the following sources: Kings Norfolk, Arthur Mee; White's Norfolk 1864, William White; Ruined and disused churches of Norfolk, Neil Batcock for Norfolk Archaeological Unit.

Parish / dedication / age / cause / date of decline / remains / map ref.

Algarsthorpe, St Mary Magdalen. Saxon, Village deserted. Abandoned early 16th c. No visible remains TG 134086

Barnham Broome, St Michael. u/k construction date. Two churches in the same churchyard. Abandoned 14th c. Low wall north of present church. TG 082078

Bickerston or **Bixton.** St Andrew. 11th c. Consolidated with Barnham Broom. Remains of nave and chancel walls. TG 086087

Blo Norton, St Margaret. u/k construction date Decay and the close proximity of St Andrew. Abandoned 1394. Stood in the same churchyard as St Andrew. No visible remains. TM 012796

Breccles Parva, Unknown dedication. Probably Saxon. Depopulation of the parish.. Abandoned pre 1327 No visible remains. TL 967937

Cantelose or Cantley, All Saints. Possibly Saxon. After 1397 it was designated a chapel to Hethersett until about 1540, then abandoned in 16th c. No visible remains. TG 181045

Carleton Rode, Unknown dedication. Saxon. Unknown cause. Abandoned by 13th c. Only mentioned in Domesday. No visible remains. TM 11?92?

Dykebeck, Unknown dedication. Saxon. Unknown cause. Abandoned possibly 13th - 14th c. Near Wymondham. Mentioned in Domesday.

No visible remains. TG 095012

East Beckham, St Helen. u/k construction date. Remote from populated area. Abandoned 17th c. Churchyard rubble remains. TG 155398

Ermingland.　　See **Irmingland.**

Foulsham,　nothing more known.　　Domesday book stated 2 churches.

Gowthorpe, St James. u/k construction date. Abandoned and village deserted c. 1590. No visible remains. TG 210021

Guist Thorpe, All Saints. u/k construction date. Two churches in one village. All Saints salvaged to repair St Andrew in 1547. No visible remains TG 004264

Guton, St Swithin. Situated in Brandiston churchyard. No traces remain.

Hackford, All Saints. 14th - 15th c. Never rebuilt after a fire which also destroyed many houses in 1543 Consolidated with Whitwell. Finally demolished in1790. Only the west wall of the south porch remains. TG 414288

Harling Thorpe, unknown. 13th c. Close proximity of East, Middle & West Harling. 17th c. TL 945839

Helmingham, St Mary. Saxon. Two churches mentioned in Domesday. Abandoned about 13th c. Now known as Morton on the Hill No visible remains. TG 125166

Hethersett. See Cantelose

Holverston, St Mary. Late 11th or 12th c Gradual decline of a small parish, abandoned probably 14th c. Parish united with Rockland St Mary in1358. No visible remains. TG 304030

Irmingland, St Andrew. u/k construction date. Due to decline in the population, abandoned in the latter pat of the 16th c. Less than ten householders in 1428. No visible remains. TG 123294

Itteringham St Nicholas. 11th - 12 c. Reason for abandonment unknown 14th c. Became a chapel before its final demise. No visible remains. TG 154303

Kenningham, Unknown dedication. u/k construction date. Village deserted, abandoned mid 15th c. No visible remains. TM 204996

Kerdiston, St Mary. Saxon. Parish depopulated. Abandoned before 14th c.

No visible remains. TG 084239

Ketteringham, St Peter. Saxon. Stood on the site of the present 13th c. church

Langham Parva, St Mary. u/k construction date. Close proximity of Langham Magna church. Abandoned 16th c. No visible remains. TG 004413

Letton, All Saints. Possibly Saxon. Parish depopulated when Letton Hall was built. Abandoned mid 16th c. Low walls and foundations. TF 975154

Little Carbrooke, Unknown dedication u/k construction date. Consolidated with Great Carbrooke. Village deserted, probably due to the Black Death sometime before 1424 No visible remains. TF 936018

Little Hockham, St Mary u/k construction date. Village deserted, church abandoned about 15th c. No visible remains. TL 948909

Little Moulton, All Saints. u/k construction date. Village deserted. Abandoned and demolished 1570 No visible remains. TM 171888

Little Wacton, St Mary. u/k construction date. Close proximity to Great Wacton church. Abandoned c. 1520 No visible remains. TM 173916

Little Wreningham, St Mary. u/k construction date. Abandoned due to total depopulation c. 1406 Site unknown. No visible remains. In the approximate region of grid reference TM 163988

Markshall, St Edmund. Saxon. Depopulation of village. Abandoned early 16th c. No visible remains TG 228048

Middle Harling, St Andrew. u/k construction date. Close proximity of West Harling. Abandoned before 1543 No visible remains TL 979851

Nelonde, St Peter. Saxon .Village deserted. Abandoned and demolished in 1540. No visible remains. TM 148983

New Buckenham, St Mary. 12th - 13th c. New church of St Martin built in 1240s. Continued as a chapel until the Dissolution. Mid 16th c. No visible remains. TM 085903

Old Buckenham, St Andrew. u/k construction date. Two churches in the same village. Abandoned at the Dissolution 1536 Served by the monks of the priory. Used as a barn and stables. No visible remains. TM 073913

Snetterton, St Andrew. u/k construction date. Two churches in the same village. Abandoned 16th c. No visible remains. TL 994912

Stratton, St Peter . u/k construction date. Abandoned and consolidated with Stratton St Michael early 16th c. Was only 150 yds to the SE of St Michael's church No visible remains. TM 206935

North Tuddenham, unknown. 2 churches mentioned in Domesday.

Saxthorpe, St Dunston.   No visible remains..

Snetterton, St Andrew. u/k construction date. Two churches in the same village. Abandoned 16th c. No visible remains. TL 994912

Stratton, St Peter.   100yds w of Stratton St Michael's. Ruinous at the end of the 15th c.   No visible remains.

Swainsthorpe, St Mary. Construction date unknown. Shared a churchyard with St Peter's. Remains of low walls just inside gate. TG 218009

West Beckham, All Saints. u/k construction date. Abandoned and new church built 300 yards to the NW to serve both East & West Beckham in 1890. Graveyard still in use. Low walls. TG 146391

Wicklewood, St Andrew. Possibly Saxon. Two churches in the same churchyard. Abandoned soon after 1367 No visible remains. TG 069023

Index of names mentioned in the text

Daynes, John	Beeston Regis
Dewing	Gresham
Drury, Drugo	Riddlesworth
Drury, Mary	Besthorpe
Drury, Sir William	Besthorpe
Elwin, Fountain	Thurning
Elwin, Rev. Whitwell	Booton
Felbrygge, Sir Simon	Felbrigg
Fellows, Mrs	Felthorpe
Forster, Elizabeth	Thornage
Forster, Hercules	Thornage
Freston, Richard	Mendham
Godbold, Mr	Mendham
Gonville, Edmund	Rushford
Graver, George Cooper	Attlebridge
Grigson	Hardingham
Gunton	Matlask
Gurdon	Cranworth
Gurney	Keswick
Hallyet, Matthew	Winfarthing
Hallyet, Thomas	Winfarthing
Harling / Herling	East Harling
Hastyngs, Sir Hugh	Elsing
Herward, Annee	Aldeborough
Hevenyngham, Ann	Ketteringham
Hevenyngham, Thomas	Ketteringham
Heydon	Saxlingham
Hobart, Henry	Intwood
Howard	Woodrising
Hunt, Edmund	Hempstead
Hunt, Edward	Hindolveston
Hunt, Margaret	Hindolveston
Huntingfield, William de	Mendham
Jermy, Clement	Marlingford
Jermy, William	Aylsham
Jernegan	Costessey
Jodrell	Saxlingham

Jodrell, Adela	Glandford
Jodrell, Sir Alfred	Bayfield
Jodrell, Sir Alfred	Glandford
Kelling, de	Kelling
Kemp	Gissing
Kendall, John	New Buckenham
Kerdiston, Sir Roger de	Reepham
Kerridge	Gissing
Ketton-Cremers	Felbrigg
Knevett	Ashwellthorpe
Lany, Rev. Benjamin	Mulbarton
Lestrange, Roger	Hoe
Lothian, Marquess of	Blickling
Lovell, Anne	East Harling
Lovell, Sir Thomas	East Harling
Makyngs, Richard	Morston
Marcon, Canon Walter	Edgefield
Marsham, Anne	Stratton Strawless
Marsham, Harry	Stratton Strawless
Marsham, Margaret	Stratton Strawless
Marsham, Thomas	Stratton Strawless
Morley, Isabel	Hingham
Morley, Thomas	Hingham
Mott	Barningham Winter
Muskett	Intwood
Mustarder, Sir William	Sparham
Neve, Oliver de	Great Witchingham
Noers, de	Swanton Novers
Orford, Earl of	Mannington
Page	Saxthorpe
Palgrave, Dame Elizabeth	Barningham Northwood
Palgrave, John	Barningham Northwood
Palgrave, Sir Austin	Barningham Northwood
Paston	Barningham Winter
Paston	Oxnead
Pitman	Oulton
Platers, Dame Frances	Dickleburgh

Pole de la, Isabel	Hingham
Pope, Margaret	Barningham Northwood
Prince-Smith, Lady	Morton-on-the-Hill
Radcliffe, Lt Col Charles	Barningham Winter
Reve, Sir Edmund	Long Stratton
Rich, Sir Edwin	Mulbarton
Robertson, John	Guestwick
Rosey, Baldwin de	Rockland St Andrew
Rush, James	Hethel
Sadler	Colby
Southwell	Woodrising
Southwell, Robert	Morton-on-the-Hill
Spurgin	Gresham
Strutt, Dame Elizabeth	Kimberley
Swaffham, Robert de	Long Stratton
Symondes, Agnes	Cley
Symondes, John	Cley
Thornhill	Riddlesworth
Thorpe, Edmund de	Ashwellthorpe
Tomson, John	Colney
Unthank	Intwood
Waldergrave	Costessey
Walpole	Wickmere
Walpole	Wolterton
Walsh	Colby
Wickes, Boley Rice	Guist
Wiggett	Guist
Wilton, Robert	Wilby
Windham	Felbrigg
Withberga, Saint	East Dereham
Wodehouse, Lord	Hingham
Wodehouse, Sir Thomas	Kimberley
Woodforde, Parson James	Weston Longville
Wright, Ann	Kilverstone
Wright, Charles	Kilverstone
Wynter	Barningham Winter

Saints, Their Emblems and Feast Days.

Often while visiting churches we come across a screen, font or window depicting a Saint who is unnamed and, to the untaught eye, unidentifiable. Below is a list which may in some way, help to recognize who they are. There are some that have no definitive symbols, emblems or particular dress and as such will remain a mystery. A Bishop always hold a crozier; archbishops a cross; a martyr sometimes holds a sword, for example Thomas Becket. There are thousands of Saints here are those you may encounter locally:

All Saints Day	November 1st
Agatha:	Bare breasts and sword or pincers, sometimes with her severed breasts on a platter.
Agnes:	A sword, sometimes thrust into her neck or bosom. Occasionally a lamb, her emblem is 'Agnus Dei'. January 21st.
Alban:	A tall cross or sword. First martyr of Britain. June 22nd.
Ambrose:	One of the four Latin doctors. Dressed as a bishop (of Milan). Usually with a beehive. December 7th.
Andrew:	A saltire and occasionally fishing nets. November 30th.
Anne:	Seen teaching the Virgin Mary, her daughter. July 26th.
Anthony of Egypt:	Pigs and Bells or T-shaped cross.
Appollonia:	Holding a tooth or having teeth extracted.
Augustine of Canterbury:	Dressed as a bishop. May 26th.
Augustine of Hippo:	One of the four Latin Doctors. Flaming heart. Dressed as a bishop (of Hippo). August 28th.
Barbara:	Tower and Chalice.
Barnabus:	Apostle. June 11th.
Bartholomew:	A flaying knife. He was flayed alive. August 24th.
Benedict or Benet:	Seen as an abbot, devils at his feet. Occasionally seen with his finger to his lips demanding silence. (Founder of the Benedictine order) July 11th.
Blessed Virgin Mary:	With a halo holding the infant Jesus.
Blide:	Crowned with a Bible in hand. She was the mother of St Walstan of Bawburgh.
Botolph:	Sometimes portrayed as an abbot holding a

	church. No definitive symbol.
Catherine of Alexandria:	Usually standing on a wheel which is sometimes enhanced with spikes and/or knives. November 25th.
Celia:	Garland of flowers.
Cecilia:	Usually with an organ or other musical instrument. November 22nd.
Charles, King and martyr:	January 30th.
Christopher:	Child on shoulders crossing a river.
Clare of Assisi:	Book and monstrance or pyx. August 11th.
Clement:	Anchor around his neck and Crozier. Sometimes represented as a Pope. November 23rd.
Cleophe:	Usually seen with her four sons.
David:	Patron saint of Wales. March 1st
Denis or Denys:	Severed head complete with mitre, usually held in his hands. Bishop (of Paris). October 9th.
Digna:	Sister of St. Emeria, no emblem.
Dunstan:	Dressed as an Archbishop with a pair of pincers. May 19th.
Edmund king and martyr:	Arrows or a wolf guarding or carrying his severed head. King of the East Angles. November 20th.
Edward the Confessor:	Wearing a crown and holding a ring. October 13th.
Eligius or Eloy:	Leg of a horse or hammer or both.
Elizabeth:	No definitive symbol but is seen at the moment of the Visitation. Mother of John the Baptist.
Emeria:	No definitive emblem. Seen at Houghton St Giles presenting a book to a child. Her sister was St Digna.
Erasmus:	Usually depicted on or with his entrails being wound onto a windlass.
Ethelbert:	Sword and church.
Etheldreda:	Crowned and dressed as an abbess (of Ely). June 23rd.
Fabian:	Silver dove and olive branch.
Faith:	Palm branch and gridiron on which she was roasted alive.
Felix:	Dressed as a bishop. March 8th.
Fersey or Fursey:	Irish abbot, no definitive emblem.
Francis:	Stigmata on his hands.
Francis of Assisi:	Dressed as a friar holding a cross and

	surrounded by animals. October 4th.
George:	A dragon. Sometimes on horseback. April 23rd.
Germanus or Germain:	Dressed as a bishop with Cross and Crozier.
Gervaise and Protasius:	No emblem. Dedication at Little Plumstead.
Giles:	Hart (deer) at his feet, occasionally pierced in the leg by an arrow. September 1st.
Gregory the Great:	One of the Latin doctors. Depicted as a Pope with a dove and scroll of music. September 3rd.
Guthlac	An obscure saint wearing animal skins. Born in Lincolnshire. April 11th..
Helen :	Crowned and with a cross. Said to be the daughter of Old King Cole or Coel.
James the Great:	Scallop shell/s / wearing pilgrim's robes and sword or staff. May 1st and/or July 25th.
James the Less:	Fuller's club, resembling a hockey stick.
Jerome:	One of the Latin doctors. Cardinal's hat, inkhorn or book and a lion. September 30th.
John of Bridlington:	Holding a crozier, only seen at Hempstead.
John the Baptist :	Eagle (as represented on a lectern)
John the Apostle:	A chalice with serpent or the Devil emerging. Sometimes depicted carrying Agnus Dei. December 27th.
Joses:	or Joseph, brother of Jesus. A palm.
Jude:	Holding a boat or carpenter's square. October 28th.
Julian the hospitaller;	An oar. May 8th.
Juliana:	The Devil on a halter, only seen at Hempstead.
Lawrence/Laurence	A gridiron, on which he was roasted alive. August 10th.
Leonard:	Manacles / chains and fetters. Dressed as an abbot.
Lucy:	Holding a plate on which are eyes. (Uncommon.) December 13th.
Luke:	Evangelist. Ox most often seen on fonts. October 18th.
Margaret of Antioch:	Cross and dragon. She is occasionally seen in the mouth of the dragon. July 20th.
Mark:	A winged lion; usually seen on fonts. April 25th.
Martin:	Dressed as a bishop giving alms to beggars. November 11th.

Mary Magdalene:	Anointment pot or bowl. July 22nd.
Mary of Cleophas:	With her four sons. James the Less, Joses, Jude and Simon.
Mary the Virgin:	With a halo holding the Infant Jesus. August 15th or September 8th.
Matthew:	A man with angelic wings. Bible and purse or money box. September 21st.
Matthias:	Sword, axe or spear. May 14th.
Michael:	Scales for weighing the souls of the dead. Armed and feathered with wings. The Archangel. September 29th.
Nicholas:	Three golden balls or purses. Patron saint of bankers and pawnbrokers. Also as Santa Claus (*Saint Ni-Claus*).
Patrick:	Patron saint of Northern Ireland. March 17th.
Paul:	Sword usually pointing downwards and book. June 29th.
Paulinus:	Bishop (of York) October 10th.
Peter:	As an old man, with crossed keys. (of the gates to heaven). Represented also by an inverted cross. June 29th.
Petronilla:	Book and key. Daughter of St Peter. She starved herself to death rather than marry.
Philip the Apostle:	A cross or a basket of loaves and fishes. May 1st.
Remigius:	A dove. Bishop (of Rheims). October 1st.
Salome:	Usually seen with her four children. She was the wife of Zebedee, the mother of James and John, two of the apostles of Jesus, and possibly the sister of Mary, mother of Jesus. Not to be confused with Salome daughter of Herod, who demanded the head of John the Baptist.
Sebastian:	A young man with his body pierced with arrows or holding arrows.
Simon:	A fish. Occasionally a saw. October 28th.
Sir John Schorne:	A boot with Devil held prisoner therein.
Stephen:	Dressed as a deacon. Holding stones or standing beside a heap of stones. December 26th.
Swithin:	Usually just dressed as a bishop (of Winchester). July 15th.
Sylvester:	A leper at his feet.

Theobald:	No definitive emblem.
Thomas Becket	Archbishop (of Canterbury) December 29th.
Thomas the Apostle:	A spear. July 3rd.
Thomas Becket:	Dressed as an archbishop.
Uncumber:	A lady with a long beard.
Valentine:	February 14th.
Walstan:	Crowned. Scythe and oxen or agricultural tool.
Wilgefortis	Also known as Uncumber *(see above)*
William of Norwich:	Nailed to a cross or with hammer and nails.
Withburga:	Crowned as an abbess, two deer at her feet.

Symbols of the Evangelists are usually found on fonts and in windows: Matthew a winged man; Mark a lion; Luke an ox; John an eagle.

Representations of the Four Evangelists

 Matthew

 Mark

 Luke

 John

Instruments of the Passion.

Instruments of the Passion are often seen on fonts, benches, screens etc. occasionally held by angels in the roofs of naves. They were the items featured at the Crucifixion and are: a cross with a draped sheet, the letters 'INRI', the crown of thorns, scourges, a seamless robe, three dice, a ladder with a sponge on a stick, a lantern, the five wounds (represented by hands, feet and heart), the cock that crowed, thirty pieces of silver, hammer nails and pincers. Those immediately below are displayed on a font.

The Emblems of the Trinity

The Emblems are to be found almost anywhere in a church: above the west door, the porch, the roof, the font the screen the pulpit, the reredos and so on. The Emblems also come in a number of different forms: an equilateral triangle, interlocking triangles (Solomon's Seal), a trefoil, three interlocking circles, and a shield with a Y in the centre, or as a crowned Ͳ often found in the flushwork base-course around the base of the tower or porch. Here a few examples

Symbolic Animals and Plants

Carved bench-ends are only one place where the symbols of Christianity can be found. Symbolism can be found almost everywhere, often unrecognisable or thought to be something else, the rose for example, often thought to be Tudor in origin but symbolic of Christ. Other symbolic examples are: The Dove *(the Holy Spirit)*, Fish *(a secret sign of Christianity)*, Lamb *(God)*, Lily *(purity and the Blessed Virgin Mary)*, Pelican *(sacrifice on the cross)*, Phoenix *(the resurrection)*, Pomegranate *(Unity of the Church)*, Tree of Jesse *(ancestry of Christ)*, Unicorn *(the Incarnation of Christ)*.

Patronages of the Saints

Adam: gardeners
Agatha: nurses and bell founders
Albert the Great: scientists
Alexander: charcoal burners
Alexius: beggars
Alice: the blind and paralyzed
Alphonsus Liguori: theologians
Amand: vintners and hotelkeepers
Ambrose: learning
Andrew: fishermen
Andrew: Russia, fisherman and Scotland
Angela: widows
Anne: women in labour and horsewomen
Anthony: domestic animals
Anthony of Padua: gravediggers
Apollonia: dentists
Archangel Gabriel: broadcasters
Augustine: printers
Barbara: architects
Bartholomew: plasterers
Benedict: monks
Bernard: hikers, skiers, beekeepers and candle makers
Brendan: sailors, mountain climbers and skiers
Bridget: Sweden
Catherine: secretaries
Catherine of Alexandria: philosophers
Catherine of Bologna: artists and craftsmen
Cecelia: musicians
Charles: clergy
Christina: archers
Christopher: travellers
Claire: needlewomen
Clare of Assisi: television
Claude: sculptors
Cosmas and Damian: surgeons
Daniel: prisoners
David: Wales and poets
Dominic: astronomers, and the Dominican Republic
Dorothy: brides and florists

Dunstan:	jewellers and goldsmiths
Eligius:	blacksmiths
Elizabeth:	widows and young brides
Elizabeth of Hungary:	rose growers, bakers and charities
Emily:	single women
Fiacre:	taxi drivers
Flora:	the abandoned
Florian:	fire fighters
Frances Xavier Cabrini:	emigrants, missionaries
Francis:	ecologists, merchants, and Italy
Francis de Sales:	journalists, writers and authors
Francis of Assisi:	ecologists and small animals
Gabriel:	postal workers
Genesius:	actors and secretaries
George:	boy scouts, farmers, and soldiers
Gerard:	expectant mothers
Gertrude:	West Indies
Giles:	cripples
Gregory:	Teachers
Helen:	archaeologists
Henry:	the childless and handicapped
Holy Innocents:	foundlings
Isadore:	farmers and shepherds
James:	labourers and veterinarians
Jerome:	librarians and abandoned children
Joan of Arc:	soldiers, France and fighting women
Joaquin:	grandfathers
John:	booksellers and engravers
John Vianney:	priests
Jonathan:	friendship
Joseph:	carpenters
Joseph of Arimathea:	funeral directors
Joseph of Cupertino:	air travellers
Juan:	paper makers and engravers
Jude:	desperate situations
Kevin:	Dublin and nature
Lawrence:	cooks
Leo:	artists
Leonard:	childbirth and prisoners
Lidwina:	invalids
Louise:	widows

Louise de Marillac:	social workers
Lucy:	optometrists, ophthalmologists
Luke:	brewers, painters, glassworkers and physicians
Margaret:	pregnant women
Mark:	notaries
Martha:	servants and cooks
Martin:	the poor
Martin de Porres:	hairdressers
Martin of Tours:	tailors, sewing and garment workers
Martin:	veterinarians, hairdressers and love animals
Mary Magdalene:	flight crew and aviation
Mary:	mothers and all life
Matthew:	bankers, accountants, and tax collectors
Michael:	police officers, paratroopers and grocers
Monica:	married women and mothers
Nicholas:	children
Nicholas of Myra:	brides and pawnbrokers
Nicholas of Tolentine:	mariners
Patrick:	Ireland and snakebites
Paul:	public relations
Paula:	widows
Peter:	bridge builders, fisherman
Peter Celestine:	bookbinders
Phillip:	difficult marriages
Raphael:	the blind
Raymond :	obstetricians, midwives
Rita:	impossible tasks and oil wells
Roch:	invalids
Sebastian:	athletes
Stephen:	stonemasons and bricklayers
Thomas Aquinas:	scholars and students
Thomas More:	lawyers and judges and law students
Thomas the Apostle:	architects and builders
Urban:	vineyards, wine producers and sellers
Valentine:	lovers
Vincent:	charity and hospital workers
Vincent Ferrer:	builders
Vitus:	dancers and comedians
William of Norwich:	kidnapped children

Architectural Styles (Saxon - Pre-Conquest)

Round Saxon window at Howe with large internal splay (Coltishall)

Anglo-Saxon building can be identified by 'long and short' work as shown left. Quoin stones are placed vertical alternating with horizontal.

Anglo-Saxon architecture is typified by narrow or small windows and the use of pointed arches with heavy stonework and thick mullions.

Thornage

Burnham Deepdale

Saxon windows in the tower at Haddiscoe.

Saxon windows in the tower at Bessingham.

278

Architectural Styles (Norman)

Norman arcading around the octagonal tower, and windows in detail (right) at Thorpe St Mathias near Haddiscoe.

The Norman architects introduced the use of rounded, sometimes highly decorated arches with zigzag or chevron designs. Engaged columns, two, three or even four either side were not uncommon. Windows followed a similar pattern with slim mullions dividing the windows; rounded arches and columns with capitals giving an impression of strength and permanence are also indications of a Norman building.

| Norman doorway at Hales near Loddon with a good round arch and five orders of decoration and three pairs of engaged columns. | Considered one of the best Norman doorways in the county, at Heckingham. Four pairs of columns and five orders of decoration. |

Architectural Styles (Norman)

The west end of Castle Rising St Lawrence showing many of the typical Norman styles of architecture. Notice particularly the interlocking arches each side of the central window and the striations in the stonework of the wall.

Norman slit window with rounded arches; revealing the 3 ft thickness of the wall in the internal splay. (Thornham, Suffolk)

Exterior   Interior

Early English introduced in the mid-12th c.

Lancet windows with pointed arches appeared for the first time in the Early English period. Burgh St. Mary and Ashby St. Mary (left) . Arminghall (right) .

Transitional Period: second half of the 12th c.

Two lancets set side by side developed into larger windows, heralding simple Y tracery in the late Early English period. Both examples are at Carleton Rode.

281

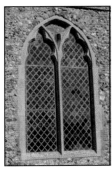

Fersfield

Flordon

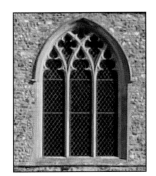

Honingham

Transitional Period before the Black Death

Decorated Gothic Geometrical early 14th c.

The east window at Snetterton.

Brettenham.

Decorated Gothic became popular after the Black Death in the 14th c. and developed into three distinct styles:
Geometrical with simple geometric Patterns;
Curvilinear with many variations on a simple theme;
Reticulated which became even more complicated and net-like within the tracery. Probably initiated by wood-carvers and copied by the stone masons.

Decorated Gothic Curvilinear and Reticulated Tracery late 14th c.

Left:
The south transept window
at Besthorpe.
Mouchettes appear for the first time around this period.

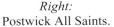

Right:
Postwick All Saints.

Below: Reticulated tracery set into a Tudor window at Brockdish.

Below: Cautley called this 'one of the loveliest windows imaginable'. It is unfortunate that it is in the 14th c. ruined south transept at Cley on the north Norfolk coast. Such a shame it isn't still glazed!

Perpendicular c. 1350 - 1490

The lovely 15th c. Perpendicular east window at North Tuddenham

Perpendicular east window in the south aisle at Bressingham.

Left:
Just one of the windows at Swanton Morley.

Right:
The west window of the tower at Blakeney St Nicholas

Tudor Period

Tudor window, Moulton St Michael.

The Tudor period saw great changes in churches and within the Church. Catholicism was outlawed and the Church of England established.

Royal Arms of the monarch appeared on the walls, usually over the chancel arch, the most prominent place to be seen, stating that the King, not the Pope, was head of the Church.

Tudor architecture can be fairly easily recognised by the low arch over the doors and windows.

Bricks became very popular at this time and were a sign of wealth and were the fashion where they could be afforded.

Stratton Strawless

Tudor chancel
doorway at
Bramerton

The Tudor porch at the Saxon church
of Feltwell St. Nicholas.
This is a very simple example. Many were much more
elaborate with crow-step gables and even brick pinnacles.

Other Architectural Features

'Sound Holes' in towers.

'Sound holes' were more likely to allow light in, rather than to let sound out. Belfry openings, some with louvers, were specifically designed for projection of sound, out and down. Most are below the level of the belfry louvers on the ringing floor.

Labels and Hood-Moulds

Labels serve the same purpose as hood-moulds: to keep the water that runs down the wall off the window as well as being decorative.

Hood-mould at Banningham.

Norman hood-mould at Gissing.

Low side windows enabled those outside the church to partake in Ter Sanctus

A low side window

...and the interior view

Left:
Low side window with seating inside.

Right:
Combination window

Windows over the chancel arch are believed primarily to allow morning light onto the rood

Large three-light chancel arch window

Quatrefoil window

Other Features to be found in and around our churches

Scratch or Mass Dials were popular before sundials to mark the times of the services.

At 9.30 a.m. a mass dial

Clock weights

Sundial.

Carillon.

Wall-post corbel

Base and shaft of a preaching cross

Woodwose, usually found on fonts.

Hour-glass and bracket.

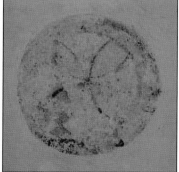

Consecration Cross where the Holy Oil was applied by the Bishop during the ceremonial consecration of the church.

15th c. parish chest

Sexton's wheel behind glass.

Pillory and stocks.

Redundant bell .... and clappers

A 13th c. iron door handle.

Organ bellows

Misericordes,
usually found in the choir

A helm

A hatchment

Poor box

Agnus Dei

Wood carvings on
bench ends

Stave locker

A Bier

Gargoyle

Knight in armour

Parish chest

Pulpits

The word pulpit derives from the Latin *pulpitum*, a stage; an elevated stand from which to preach. The ambo was the forerunner of the present pulpit. It was from about the 9th c. that two simple platforms were used, from one a preacher would read the sermon from the first four books of the New Testament, the other, a reading from the Epistles. The former, from which the sermon was read, gained in status and became more ornate and developed into a pulpit as we know it today. Eventually pulpits became properly established in England around the time of Edward VI in the 16th c. It is possible that some Norman churches had pulpits but more likely an ambo (none appear to have survived). Many sermons were preached at a cross in the street, before some churches were built or while a church was under construction. Some of these crosses still survive, usually somewhere near the church, sometimes in a market place. They are commonly marked on Ordnance Survey maps as '*cross*'.

The ambo or pulpit was placed in the centre of the nave, immediately in front of the chancel so that the priest should not find it necessary to enter the nave, the domain of the laity. However, in many churches, particularly in those with transepts, such an echo was created that the words were often inaudible. The pulpit was then moved to its present position, usually to the side of the chancel arch. Which side the pulpit should be placed depends upon the acoustics of the church. This dilemma also saw in the 17th c. the introduction of the tester from the Mediaeval Latin *testerium,* (a headpiece), also called a sounding-board or canopy. Its purpose was to reflect the sound further into the nave and preventing the sound being lost in the high roofs. The tester was often supported by a back-board and attached to the wall with brackets. The pulpit was then further adorned, usually having references to the preachings of the Gospel. Its ornamentation could be appropriate scenes from the Bible such as the Sermon on the Mount or the dove as a symbol of the Holy Ghost placed on the on the underside of the tester. At Dallinghoo in Suffolk the pulpit has the Royal Arms carved into the back-board. *(p 295)* Left of the Arms, a rose symbolising Christ, on the right a pomegranate symbolic of the unity of the Church *(many seeds in the one)*; representing overall the unity of the Church and the Crown. *(See Symbolic Plants: page 274).*

Southwold St Edmunds, Suffolk   South Burlinghan St Edmunds, Norfolk

There are a some good examples of pre-Reformation pulpits in Norfolk at Bressingham, Burnham Norton, Castle Acre, Cawston, Horsham St. Faith, North Walsham, South Burlingham, South Creake, and at Wiggenhall. In Suffolk they can be seen at, Creeting St Peter, Gazeley, Hawstead, Lakenheath, Monks Eleigh, Newton, Southwold, Stoke-by-Clare, Sudbury All Saints, Theberton, Thwaite, Tuddenham St Martin, Walberswick, Westhorpe and Wetherden to name some of the most notable. Southwold *(illustrated above)* It is particularly well decorated with traceried panels on the upper part of the stem and is painted in pastel colours of red green and gold. Another such as Southwold is the one at South Burlingham. Others with scenes from the Bible such as that at Burnham Norton, are very attractive and quite rare.

The type of pulpit with the single foot is generally known as a goblet or wine-glass pulpit and was fairly common in the 15th c. Many have since been destroyed. The Burnham Norton pulpit has depictions of the patrons John and Katherine Goldalle and Saints Ambrose, Augustine, Gregory and Jerome, (the Four Latin Doctors) and is dated 1450. Some damage was inflicted during the Civil War but is minor compared with the way some screens were treated. The church has a second, later Jacobean pulpit used for sermons, with a back-board and tester. Many other examples of goblet-style pulpits exist, a few of which are illustrated.

Of course, most pulpits stand either on four legs or on a base of wood or stone. The 16th c. pulpit was almost as elaborate, with linen-fold carving making an appearance. Many different designs decorate the panels such as those shown. On the following pages are just a few of the many examples the visitor is likely to encounter in our churches. It is not possible to judge the class of pulpit from the church's exterior; many of our small insignificant churches have beautifully carved pulpits.

As previously mentioned, during the 17th c. the tester or sound-board became popular, coupled with the decree that a pulpit was to be an obligatory item of church furniture. The style became widespread and many pulpits today still show signs of once having had a back-board and tester. Occasionally, only the brackets remain attached to the wall. At Stonham Aspal in Suffolk the tester dated 1616, (*pictured below*) has been removed and converted into a table; decorative but not very functional; better as it was, I think.

Historically some pulpits, particularly on the Continent. were made of stone. During the 19th c. the fashion for stone pulpits became widespread here in East Anglia too. Their cumbersome appearance does not always befit the backdrop of an East Anglian country church in my view. The examples that follow are just a few of the many hundreds of pulpits to be found in the churches of Norfolk and Suffolk.

Jacobean: Thwaite, Norfolk

15th c.: Westhorpe, Suffolk

Wetherden, Suffolk

15th c.: Stoke-by-Clare, Suffolk

294

Linen-fold.   Geometric.   Figures.

Detail of the Royal Arms on the backboard at Dallinghoo, Suffolk

Walberswick, Suffolk   Hawstead, Suffolk

Dallinghoo, Suffolk

Great Cressingham

Heydon

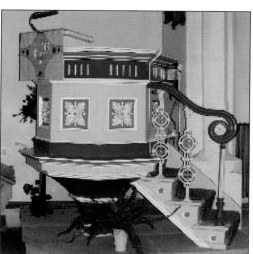

Tunstall.

Winfarthing

The pulpit at Aslacton has these 16th c. carvings of David and Goliath. (above). David with Goliath's head is shown (right).

Quidenham

Warham, All Saints

Burnham Norton

Double-and Triple-Decker Pulpits

Double-decker, Reymerston

Triple-Decker at Thompson

In the 18th c. double and triple-decker pulpits were introduced. The lower level was for community announcements by the parish clerk, the centre for reading the gospel, and the top for delivery of the sermon.

The pulpit at Trowse Newton St Andrew, near Norwich is quite plain in itself but has seats upon which are seated these three fantastic carved wooden figures playing musical instruments. The group was donated to the church by the Colman family. Their history is uncertain, but thought to be 18th c. Flemish, perhaps originally from a great organ case.

GLOSSARY of Terms, Architectural and Ecclesiastical

Achievement
The correct name for Armorial Bearings which include the shield (the Coat of Arms) supporters, lion and unicorn, the helm, crown, garter and banner etc. (see Coat of Arms)

Annunciation
Referring to the Archangel Gabriel giving Mary the news that she was to conceive the son of God.

Antiphonary
A book containing a collection of biblical songs.

Apse
A semi-circular domed projection at the east end of the church, usually forming a chancel. Also called an apsis.

Apsidal
Being or having an apse.

Arcade
A series of arches, usually one or both sides of the nave where an aisle is present. These can also be blank, blind or closed where an aisle has previously been or for decorative purposes.

Arch-braced
A braced wooden arch which carries the weight of the roof. Large spans are sometimes accompanied by tie-beams if there is a risk of the walls spreading out with the weight of the roof.

Aumbry
A small cupboard usually set into the wall of the sanctuary in which is stored the Holy Oils used at baptisms and confirmations etc. If the contents are present an eternal flame is usually burning close by.

Banner Stave Lockers
A tall narrow cupboard commonly near or beneath the tower in which mediaeval guild banner staves were stored.

Barrel roof
A roof boarded with planks giving it the appearance of the inside of a barrel.

Base course
Usually seen around the base of a tower or porch, less commonly elsewhere, to give a decorative effect. Usually flushwork.

Battering/ Battered
The leaning outwards of an inner wall as it rises to the top while the external face remains vertical.

Bier
A stand or four-wheeled trolley on which a corpse or nowadays a coffin is placed to lie in state, and to be carried or wheeled to the grave. These can even be horse drawn but are not the same as a hearse.

Billet moulding
Also known as log decoration, due to resemblance to a line or series of small logs in one or more rows.

Black Death	Refers to the period of the plague between 1348 and 1349 which in less than two years reduced the population of East Anglia by one-third.
Box Pew	Pews with sides of three feet or more which became popular in the 17th c. and in which the gentry could be separated from the rabble; occasionally fitted out with cushions and curtains.
Brasses	Memorial portraits which were popular for those that could afford them from the 14th to the 17th century.
BVM	Blessed Virgin Mary.
Canopy of Honour	An ornamental roof-like projection usually above the rood or rood screen. Occasionally over an altar.
Capital/cap	The top of a pier or column, upon which the arch rests.
Carillon	A set of bells sounded either from a keyboard or mechanically.
Carstone	Otherwise known as gingerbread stone due to its similarity to a ginger biscuit. It is in fact a soft brown sandstone sometimes found scattered in fields or quarried from Snettisham.
Chamfer	A surface made by smoothing off the angle between two stone faces.
Chevron	Zigzag moulding (Typical of 12th c. Norman).
Cinquefoil	Five-lobed.
Clerestory	The part of the nave wall above the side aisles with windows to allow more light into the nave, i.e. 'clear storey' the storey of clear glass.
Clunch	Hard chalk material.
Coat of Arms	The name given to the Heraldic shield. Originally worn as a vest over armour to identify the wearer. Often erroneously used as a term for the Achievement.
Cob	Un-burnt clay mixed with straw.
Coeval	Being of the same date; contemporary with.
Collar	A timber beam connecting rafters or wall-posts.
Conventual	Being part of or pertaining to a convent.
Corbel	A piece of carved stone or wood projecting from a wall; usually to support a wall-post or part of a roof. Almost always carved or decorated with foliage, grotesques or heads of kings or queens etc.

Cornice	Decorative projection along top of wall.
Course	Horizontal layer of stones or bricks in a wall, sometimes decorative.
Credence Shelf	A shelf or table upon which is placed the bread & wine used in the Eucharist in the belief that if it is poisoned it will somehow manifest itself.
Crenel	A gap in a battlemented parapet.
Crenellated	Embattled, having battlements.
Cresset	A reservoir for an oil or fat lamp.
Crocket	Carved decoration on the sloping side of a spire or pinnacle, usually thorn-shaped and pointing skyward.
Cupola	A small domed turret on a roof or top of a tower, usually with a door.
Cusped /cusping	A carved pointed figure created by the intersection of three or more arcs or foils, giving a foliate appearance.
Decalogue board	A board bearing the Ten Commandments. Traditionally flanked by Moses and Aaron..
Decorated	Architectural style around 13th – 14th c. 1280 - 1377.
Diapered	Decorated in a diamond pattern. Usually referred to screens or flint-work.
Doctors	Four Doctors recognised by the Western Church for their doctrine. They are St. Ambrose, St. Augustine, St. Jerome and St. Gregory.
Dog-tooth	12th - 13th c. ornamentation consisting of four leaflike projections radiating from a raised centre. (from dog-tooth violet)
Donative	A benefice that can be bestowed by its founder or patron without reference to the diocesan authorities (adj. constituting such a benefice.)
Dormer	Window placed vertically in sloping roof.
Dressing	Carved stonework around openings.
Drystone	Un-mortared masonry.
Early English	Period 1175 - 1280.
Embattled	Battlemented, with battlements. Also Crenellated.
Engaged	(column) Refers to being attached to the jamb along its length. Not free-standing. (Opposite of detached).
English Renaissance	Period 1625 - 1700.
Escutcheon	Shield or shield-shaped emblem bearing a coat of arms.
Fillet	A narrow flat band.
Finial	Decorative carving at the apex of an arch, pinnacle spire

	or end of a roof.
Fleche	A slender spire, especially on a church above an intersection of the nave and transept.
Fleuron	A carved flower.
Flushwork	Patterns made in the masonry using flint or stone, neither sunken nor raised.
Fluting	Concave mouldings in parallel.
Flying buttress	Buttress which is not attached to the wall it supports at the lower portion, to allow passage through, or to save weight, or to look more elegant.
Foils	Lobes used to embellish the head of an arch or a circular opening. Trefoil, 3; quatrefoil, 4; cinquefoil, 5; octofoil, 8 etc..
Foliated	Carved with or representing leaves.
Footings	Bottom part of wall.
Freestone	High-quality sandstone or limestone.
Fresco	Painting on wet plaster wall.
Gable/ Gablette	A wall covering the end of a roof-ridge / Smaller version.
Galilee	A small chapel or porch at the west end of some mediaeval churches. For use when the church is closed.
Gallery	A platform raised above the congregation for musicians or as an additional seating area for members of the congregation. Usually at the west end.
Gargoyle	A carved stone usually with a spout to discharge rainwater well clear of the foundations. Not to be confused with grotesques.

Georgian	Period 1700 - 1825.
Gnomon	That part of a sundial which casts the shadow.
Gothic	Architectural period 12th - 16th century.
Green man	Harking back to folklore, a green man is usually depicted with a foliate face mask, representing fertility. Seen on screens and columns.
Grisaille	A glass monochrome picture in shades of grey.
Groined	A roof with sharp edges at intersection of cross-vaults.
Grotesques	Outlandish, distorted or bizarre characterisations of people or animals, not necessarily ugly as in gargoyles.
Half-shaft	Roll-moulding on either side of opening.
Hammerbeam	Beam jutting out horizontally at right angles at the top of

	a wall to support other beams and arch-braces.
Hanoverian	Pertaining to the reign of the House of Hanover, 1714 - 1837
Hatchments	Lozenge shaped frames bearing the coat of arms or Achievement of a deceased person, made for the funeral and displayed outside the home of the deceased for one year and later retained in the church as a memorial. (Corruption of Achievement).
Headstock	The wooden beam which carries the weight of a bell.
Heartshrine	A small niche, similar in appearance to a piscina, into which an embalmed heart was placed.
Herringbone	Brick or stone laid diagonally.
Hood or Hoodmould	A moulding over an arch, window or door to deflect dripping water, or just decorative.
Hour glass	A instrument with two glass chambers and a narrow connection channel containing sand which flowed from one chamber to the other over a period of one hour by which the preacher could time his sermons.
Impost	Wall bracket to support arch.
Intramural	Within the wall. Early practice of burial for VIPs.
Ionic	Order of Greek architecture characterized by a column with scroll-shapes on either side of the capital.
Jacobean	Period 1603 - 1625. Reign of King James I.
Jamb	Side of an arch, door or window against which the door or window closes.
Joist	Timber stretched from wall-to-wall to support floor boards.
King post	A vertical roof support set between a horizontal cross beam and rafter to offer additional support for the ridge. (see also Queen post).
Knop	A decorative knob or boss.
Knopped	Having knobs or bosses usually as decoration.
Label	A square moulding over a door, window or object; a dripstone.
Lancet	(window) A long, narrow window with pointed head. (1190 - 1280 in date).
Laudian	Pertaining to Archbishop William Laud (1573 - 1645).
Linen-fold	Decorative wood, or occasionally stone, carving developed in the Tudor period giving the appearance of folded linen.

Lintel	Horizontal stone or beam bridging opening.
Long and short work	A Saxon technique of having one quoin stone lengthways and the next width-ways and so on as the corner progressed upwards.
Loop	narrow opening in a wall
Louvre / louver	(Bell) Louver – to allow the sound of bells to escape through the tower wall.
Low side window	A low window in the west of the chancel from or through which a bell could be sounded and/or the Ter Sanctus observed by those outside the church.
Lucarne	A small slit or opening to allow light into spires, turret stairs and towers.
Mass dial	see Scratch dial.
Mensa	A stone slab forming the top of an altar. Usually has five consecration crosses around the edge.
Merlon	The solid part of embattled parapet.
Misericord	Projection under a choir stall or seat, giving (when the seat is turned up) support to a person standing. Usually carved with grotesques or religious emblems under the seat.
Moulding	A form of masonry or wood decoration.
Mullion	Vertical division of window.
Mural	A wall or a painting on a wall.
Nailhead	Pyramidal moulding.
Nave	The body of the church, the central aisle.
Needle	A tie beam which passes through a wall, with an eye in the end [like a sewing needle] and through which is passed a cross-member to prevent it withdrawing or the wall/s spreading.
Newel	The centre-post of a circular staircase.
Niche	A recess usually arched, made in a wall to contain a statue or other object.
Nookshaft	A shaft set in the angle of a jamb or pier.

Norman	Period 1066 – 1190 Romanesque.
Ogee-headed	Arch moulding showing in section a double continuous curve, convex below passing into concave above, back to front S. thus:-
Open joint	A wide, un-mortared space between faces of stones.

Order	Relating to the carved sections of an arch or doorway.
Oriel	A projecting window in a wall; originally a form of
porch,	often of wood.
Pamment	Earthenware floor tile usually 1 foot square.
Parapet	A low wall on the outer side of a main wall.
Parclose screen	A screen to delineate a private chapel or to enclose part of the nave for whatever reason.
Parvise	A balcony in front of a church or an enclosed courtyard. Name also given to the chamber above a porch.
Pateræ	A circular ornament, resembling a dish, often worked in relief on friezes.
Peculiar	A church or parish under the jurisdiction of a diocese other than that in which it lies.
Pediment	A low-pitched gable over porticos, doors, windows, etc.
Perpendicular	English architectural period, circa. 1377 - 1547.
Pier	A support for arch, usually square as opposed to pillar or column which is round.
Pilaster	A shallow pier used to buttress a wall.
Pinnacle	An ornament crowning a spire, tower etc. or small spire on top of a building.
Piscina	A basin, usually set in or against a wall, with a drain running directly into the ground (supposedly to prevent sacrilegious use of Holy water) for washing vessels after the sacrament.
Pitch	The slope of a roof.
Pitching	Rough cobbling.
Plinth	Projecting base of wall.
Pointing	Mortar or cement in joints between brickwork.
Poppyheads	Ornamental carving at the end of church benches and / or pews. *[There are endless variations, very few looking like poppy heads]*
Priest's door , chancel door	A private entrance for the priest so he could avoid having to enter the nave, which was for the laity.
Principal	A main truss or rafter supporting a roof.
Purlin	A horizontal timber in a roof supporting rafters.
Quartering/s	Combination of different coats of arms on one shield. (*pl.* the Coats of Arms so displayed).

Quatrefoil	Four-lobed.
Queen posts	Similar in purpose as a king post but always in pairs width-wise.
Quoin	Dressed corner-stone at the outside angle of a building.
Reliquary	A coffer or shrine or place for keeping or displaying religious relics.
Reredos	The decorative screen behind the altar.
Respond/s	Half-piers found in the jambs of arches.
Retable	A frame enclosing carved or painted panels placed at the back of an altar (similar to a reredos).
Reveal	The thickness of the wall from the inside edge to the window or door.
Rib	Raised moulding dividing vault.
Romanesque	Prevailing architectural style, eighth to twelfth century, with rounded arches.
Roofridge	Summit line of roof.
Rowell	A circular frame with candles placed around the circumference and raised by means of a pulley, to illuminate the rood or canopy of honour.
Royal Arms	The shield shaped heraldic device, usually displayed in the Achievement, issued to the Monarch by the College of Heraldry. Common term for the Achievement.
Rubble	Un-worked stone/s not laid in courses.
Rustication	Worked ashlar stone, with faces left deliberately rough.
Sacring bell	A bell which is rung during the Sacrament to inform those outside the church.
Sacristy	A room in a church to house the sacred vessels and vestments, similar in use to a vestry, and occasionally used as such.
Saltire	A diagonal, equal-limbed diagonal cross. St Andrew's-style cross.
Sanctuary	The part of a church nearest to the altar, usually behind the altar rail.
Sarum	Old Salisbury. *(See also Antiphonary.)*
Saxon	Pre-1066.
Sciapus	A legendary Scandinavian figure with enormous feet.
Scratch dial	A crude sundial with central hole (into which is inserted a gnomon) with rays usually scratched on a buttress or quoin-stone of a church to indicate the time of the

	next service. Also called a mass-dial.
Sedilia [pl.]	Group of (usually 3) seats for clergy during parts of long mediaeval masses (usually in or on the south wall of the sanctuary, frequently a dropped window sill.) *[one seat: 'sedile']*
Septaria	A semi-hard brownish clay-like stone with calcite bonding.
Serpent	Early deep-toned wind instrument, shaped as a double S.
Seven Sacraments (The)	Baptism, Holy Communion, Confirmation, Holy Orders, Reconciliation, Matrimony & Anointing of the sick.
Seven Sacraments Font	An 15th c. font, the Seven Sacraments displayed around the facets of the octagonal bowl.
Shaft	A narrow column. i.e. supporting the font.
Shingle	A wooden tile, usually of cedar.
Soffit	The underside of arch, opening or eaves.
Sounding board	see Tester.
Spandrel	The space (roughly triangular in shape each side) between an arch and its square hood-mould. Also found in roofs in the space between the beam and arch-brace and/or rafter.
Splay	A chamfered, or sloping face. Window reveal which is wider on the inner wall than at the window.
Squint	Observation hole in wall or room.
Stool	A level base or foot, usually wedge shaped on which a figure would stand in a niche.
Stoup	A carved bowl for holding holy water to purify oneself before or upon entering the church.
Stringcourse	Continuous horizontal mouldings on a wall-face.
Stuart	Pertaining to the reign of House of Stuart, 1603 - 1714.
Sundial	Means of indicating the time by the shadow cast by a gnomon, usually on the south porch gable or the tower.
Tester	A suspended canopy over a pulpit (also called a 'sounding board').
Tie beam	A large horizontal beam at the base of a roof (or top of a wall) to prevent the walls spreading outwards with the weight of the roof. Occasionally piercing the wall and pinned-through outside. *(see Needle).*
Tracery	Intersecting rib-work in upper part of window or decoratively carved in wood.

Transept	Either of the arms of a cross-shaped church at right angles to the main body or nave of the church. Usually North or South.
Transom	Horizontal division of a window.
Trefoil	Three-lobed. *(See also Foils.)*
Tudor	Period 1547 - 1600.
Turret	A small tower, round or polygonal, tapered or straight.
Tympanic	Pertaining to the tympanum.
Tympanum	The stonework filling the space between the horizontal lintel of a doorway and the arch above it. [Pl. tympana].
Victorian	Pertaining to the reign of Queen Victoria, 1837 - 1901.
Volute	A decorative spiral scroll in stonework found on some Ionic capitals.
Voussoir	Any of the wedge-shaped stones forming part of an arch, not the keystone.
Wag(g)on roof	see Barrel roof.
Wainscote	A panel on the lower portion of a wall, in a different material from that of the upper part, usually wood.
Wall-post	Part of the roof which projects vertically down the wall on which the roof is supported.
Wall-plate	Horizontal beam upon which sits the roof.
Wall-stair	Staircase built into thickness of wall, as rood-stairs or stairs to the parvise or tower.
Weathering	The sloping surface to throw off rainwater on buttresses and battlements etc.
Weep	This term applies to the chancel being misaligned with the nave, fabled to represent the head of Jesus inclined when on the Cross. More realistically applied to miscalculation when laying the foundations or using the shadow of the sun against the tower

Wodewose or Woodwose. Wild man with beard carrying a club. Usually found on the shaft of a font accompanied by lions, occasionally as a pinnacle. *(it has been sometimes erroneously referred to as a Woodhouse)*

Pages for your notes

The shaded area is covered by this volume

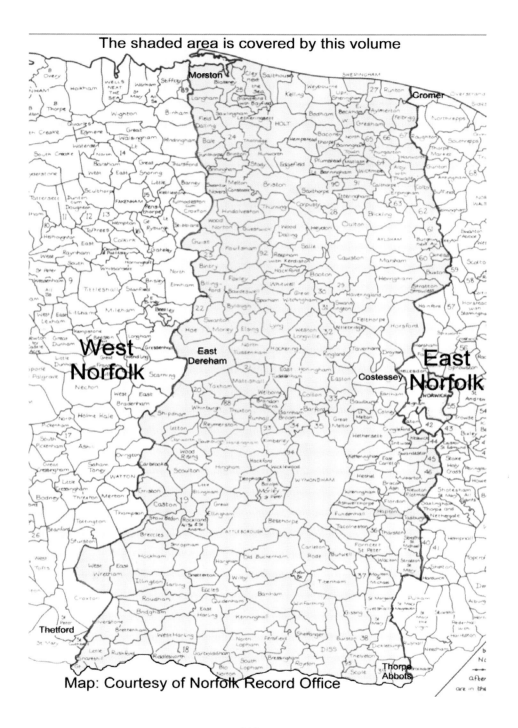

West Norfolk

East Dereham

East Norfolk

Map: Courtesy of Norfolk Record Office